On Wellington

C&C
—————————————————
CAMPAIGNS & COMMANDERS
GREGORY J. W. URWIN, SERIES EDITOR

Campaigns and Commanders

GENERAL EDITOR
Gregory J. W. Urwin, *Temple University, Philadelphia, Pennsylvania*

ADVISORY BOARD
Lawrence E. Babits, *East Carolina University, Greenville*
James C. Bradford, *Texas A&M University, College Station*
Robert M. Epstein, *U.S. Army School of Advanced Military Studies, Fort Leavenworth, Kansas*
David M. Glantz, *Carlisle, Pennsylvania*
Jerome A. Greene, *Denver, Colorado*
Victor Davis Hanson, *California State University, Fresno*
Herman Hattaway, *University of Missouri, Kansas City*
John A. Houlding, *Rückersdorf, Germany*
Eugenia C. Kiesling, *U.S. Military Academy, West Point, New York*
Timothy K. Nenninger, *National Archives, Washington, D.C.*
Bruce Vandervort, *Virginia Military Institute, Lexington*

On Wellington
A Critique of Waterloo

Carl von Clausewitz

Translated and edited by
Peter Hofschröer

University of Oklahoma Press : Norman

Library of Congress Cataloging-in-Publication Data

Clausewitz, Carl von, 1780–1831.
  [Feldzug von 1815 in Frankreich. English]
  On Wellington : a critique of Waterloo / Carl von Clausewitz ; translated and edited by Peter Hofschröer.
      p. cm. — (Campaigns and commanders ; v. 25)
  Originally published in German as Der Feldzug von 1815 in Frankreich, as v. 8 in the posthumously published work Hinterlassene Werke des Generals Carl von Clausewitz über Krieg und Kriegführung. Berlin : F. Dümmler, 1832–1837.
  Includes bibliographical references and index.
  ISBN 978-0-8061-4108-4 ISBN 978-0-8061-6904-0 (paper)

  1. Waterloo, Battle of, Waterloo, Belgium, 1815—Personal narratives, German.
  2. Napoleonic Wars, 1800–1815—Campaigns—Belgium—Waterloo.
  3. Napoleonic Wars, 1800–1815—Personal narratives, German.
  4. Wellington, Arthur Wellesley, Duke of, 1769–1852—Military leadership.
  5. Napoleon I, Emperor of the French, 1769–1821—Contemporaries.
  I. Hofschröer, Peter. II. Title.
  DC241.5.C53 2010
  940.2'742—dc22
                          2010000530

On Wellington: A Critique of Waterloo is Volume 25 in the Campaigns and Commanders series.

The paper in this book meets the guidelines for permanence and durability of the Committee on Production Guidelines for Book Longevity of the Council on Library Resources, Inc. ∞

Copyright © 2010 by the University of Oklahoma Press, Norman, Publishing Division of the University. Paperback published 2021. Manufactured in the U.S.A.

All rights reserved. No part of this publication may be reproduced, stored in a retrieval system, or transmitted, in any form or by any means, electronic, mechanical, photocopying, recording, or otherwise—except as permitted under Section 107 or 108 of the United States Copyright Act—without the prior written permission of the University of Oklahoma Press.

Contents

Introduction, by Peter Hofschröer   3

The Campaign of 1815 in France
1. The French Armed Forces—Organization of the Standing Army   31
2. Depot Troops and the *Armée Extraordinaire*   33
3. Napoleon's Exaggeration of the Available Resources   34
4. Order of Battle of the French Army   36
5. The National Guard   40
6. Allied Deployment in April   41
7. Defense   43
8. Preemptive Attack on Wellington and Blücher   46
9. The Allied Armed Forces   47
10. Order of Battle and Disposition of Forces on Both Sides   48
11. Reflections on Wellington's Deployment—Necessary Assumptions   54
12. Critique   59
13. Disposition and Concentration of the Prussian Army   60
14. Objective of the French Attack   61
15. The Point of Union of the Two Allied Armies   64
16. Calculation of the Time Necessary for the Concentration of the Prussian Army   65
17. Calculation of the Time Necessary for the Concentration of Wellington's Army   67
18. Reflections   67
19. Bonaparte Concentrates His Army   68

20.	Blücher's Concentration at Sombreffe	70
21.	Wellington's Concentration	71
22.	Bonaparte's Offensive Is Directed at Blücher	72
23.	The Engagement at Charleroi	75
24.	Situation on the Morning of June 16	79
25.	The Battle of Ligny	81
26.	Blücher's Deployment	82
27.	Dispositions on the Front at Ligny	83
28.	Dispositions on the Sombreffe Front	84
29.	The Duke of Wellington Arrives	84
30.	Bonaparte's Plan of Attack	86
31.	Critical Commentary	88
32.	Main Events of the Battle	94
33.	The Third Army Corps' Actions	99
34.	Critical Commentary on the Battle as a Whole: Blücher	102
35.	Bonaparte	106
36.	The Engagement at Quatre Bras	109
37.	Observations	112
38.	Blücher's Movements on June 17	115
39.	Wellington on June 17 and 18	120
40.	The Battle of Waterloo: Wellington's Deployment	121
41.	Bonaparte's Plan of Attack	123
42.	The Key Points of the Battle: Wellington's Defense	125
43.	The Prussian Attack	130
44.	The Battle of Wavre on June 18 and 19: Grouchy's March	133
45.	General Thielemann's Deployment	135
46.	Grouchy's Attack on June 18 and 19	138
47.	The Encounter at Namur	140
48.	Reflections on the Battle: Bonaparte	143
49.	The Allies	161
50.	The Battle of Wavre	162
51.	A Second Battle against Blücher	165
52.	Consequences of the Battle	170
53.	The March on Paris: Initial Pursuit	175
54.	The March on Paris: Critical Comments	182
55.	Table of Marches	186

56. The Situation in Paris	194
57. Advance of the Remaining Armies into France	205
58. The Capture of the Fortresses	207
Epilogue, by Peter Hofschröer	209
Appendices	
A. Order of Battle of the Prussian Army at Waterloo, June 18, 1815	211
B. Order of Battle of the Anglo-Allied Army at Waterloo, June 18, 1815	218
C. Order of Battle of the French Army of the North at Waterloo, June 18, 1815	227
Published Works of Carl von Clausewitz	239
Bibliography	241
Index	247

On Wellington

Introduction

Peter Hofschröer

The Battle of Waterloo is regarded as one of the defining events of history. It marked the end of an era of turmoil that began with the French Revolution of 1789 and continued through the Revolutionary Wars and the Napoleonic Wars, finally ending in 1815. France entered this period as the most populous and powerful nation in Europe, but when it ended, Britain was well on its way to becoming the leading nation in the world and the dominant colonial power, having the largest trading empire this planet has yet to see.

After Waterloo the balance of power was restored in a Europe devastated by decades of conflict, but it would take a generation before the continental economy could recover fully, a period that became known as the "great peace." Only in the second half of the nineteenth century did any new wars of significance occur in Europe. The balance of power established at the Congress of Vienna after Napoleon's first abdication in 1814 remained largely undisturbed for half a century.

Two great men embody the forces at work in this period and have come to be its symbols. Napoleon Bonaparte (1769–1821) gave his name to this era, while the Duke of Wellington (1769–1851), who is often considered to have been his nemesis, went on to define much of early-nineteenth-century Britain, holding a number of senior posts in the British government and army.

Bonaparte hailed from Corsica and had trained as an artillery officer in the French army. It is unlikely he would have enjoyed such a meteoric career had it not been for the opportunities the French Revolution presented. As a junior officer he played an important role in the siege of the Mediterranean post of Toulon in 1793, with his handling of the artillery forcing the British fleet to evacuate. Now that fame was his, Bonaparte's rise to power continued with the "whiff of grapeshot" that established himself as a political force while quelling a royalist uprising in Paris in 1795 with his artillery. With Paris behind him, Bonaparte set off for Italy, where he made a name of himself as an army commander. The great successes of his Italian campaigns of 1796–97 contrasted with the abject failure of his Egyptian adventure in 1798. On his return to France the following year, he seized power in Paris as First Consul. Soon afterward he returned to Italy to recapture territory the Austrians had reoccupied during his absence in Egypt. But the subsequent peace made with Britain at Amiens in 1802 did not last long. In December 1804 Bonaparte crowned himself Emperor Napoleon, and the Napoleonic Wars began the next year. In the campaigns of 1805 and 1806, Napoleon extended his power throughout Central Europe, defeating the Austrians and Russians at Austerlitz in December 1805 and the Prussians at Jena and Auerstedt the following October. Now at the zenith of his power, the slide downhill started slowly, with a stalemate at Eylau in February 1807. The following year he fought hard to maintain his grip on Central Europe, suffering a defeat at Aspern-Essling before reimposing his will over the Austrians at Wagram. The war in the Iberian Peninsula also commenced that year, ending with the ascendancy of the Duke of Wellington (who led his army into France in 1814). Napoleon lost the largest army yet assembled in Europe to the vastness of Russia in 1812. Unrest in Germany led to the outbreak of war there in the spring of 1813, culminating in the greatest battle yet fought taking place at Leipzig in Saxony that October. Severely defeated, Napoleon returned to France, attempting to stave off his inevitable fall from power the following year. In April 1814 he was exiled to the island of Elba in the Mediterranean. There he stayed, watching the Allies squabble over the spoils of victory, while the newly restored Bourbon king, Louis XVIII, grew ever more unpopular. Seizing his chance in March 1815, Napoleon and his tiny entourage sailed for France, inaugurating the Hundred Days, the highlight of which was the Battle of Waterloo, his only direct contest with his "nemesis," the Duke of Wellington.

Arthur Wesley, later the first Duke of Wellington, was born in Dublin in the same year as Napoleon Bonaparte. Their careers were to run in parallel until they finally met in the Netherlands in June 1815. Had it not been for Bonaparte, France's greatest Italian, England's greatest Irishman may not have advanced to the senior echelons of the British army. He first saw action in the Netherlands in 1794 as lieutenant colonel of the 33rd Foot but only started really making a name for himself in India, where he was posted in 1799. Returning to Britain a major general, Wellesley, as he now styled himself, served in expeditions to North Germany in 1805 and Copenhagen in 1807, the latter leading to a lieutenant general's rank. But in Spain and Portugal, where a British expedition had been sent to support the Spanish revolt against invading French troops, Wellesley made a name for himself. In 1808 he won two victories at Roliça and Vimeiro but was recalled to Britain to face a court of enquiry over signing the Convention of Sintra, which obligated the Royal Navy to transport the defeated French forces home. Cleared of responsibility for this act, Wellesley returned to Portugal in 1809, charged with restoring Britain's fortunes in this theater after Sir John Moore's defeat at Corunna in January 1809. Moving over to the offensive, Wellesley crossed the Douro River and routed the French at Oporto. Ennobled as Viscount Wellington for his defeat of the French at Talavera, near Madrid, he nevertheless was compelled to fall back to Portugal, holding the Lines of Torres Vedras before returning to the offensive in 1811. Capturing the key fortresses of Ciudad Rodrigo and Badajoz in 1812, he crushed the French at Salamanca, liberating Madrid. Wellington was rewarded with the title of earl, then marquess. Falling back to consolidate his position, he then went over to the offensive again in 1813, advancing to the French border. Crossing the Nive River, he advanced as far as Toulouse before receiving news of Napoleon's abdication in Paris. Created the Duke of Wellington, he had reached the zenith of his military career. Now a man with a reputation to lose, his bungling of the opening of the Waterloo campaign could well have proved catastrophic, but somehow Wellington managed to muddle his way through and has become regarded as the victor of Waterloo. With his reputation further enhanced, the duke returned home, sporting the victor's laurels again and resuming his earlier career in politics, jealously guarding his reputation against those who even dared to question it. One British army officer who did was Capt. William Siborne, Waterloo historian and maker of two models of the battle, whom Wellington hounded to an early grave for his impudence in challenging crucial parts of the duke's version of the events. Before (and long after) his death in 1851, Wellington's manipulations of the record went largely unchallenged by Anglophone historians. His role in suppressing the publication of the English translation of Clausewitz's account of the campaign has largely escaped British historians until recently.[1]

If there is one person who symbolizes uncompromising opposition to Napoleon more than anybody else, it was Gebhardt Leberecht von Blücher (1742–1819). He made a name for himself as a hussar officer in Frederick the Great's army during the Seven Years' War (1756–63). Passed over after the fake execution of a priest in Poland in 1772, Blücher resigned his commission, returning to the Prussian army as a major in the Red Hussars only after Frederick's death in 1786. After participating in the expedition to the Netherlands in 1787, he was promoted to lieutenant colonel, fighting in the campaigns in the Rhineland against Revolutionary France in 1793 and 1794. As a full colonel he distinguished himself at Kirrweiler in 1794, being then promoted to major general. As a lieutenant general Blücher rode at the head of the Prussian cavalry at the Battle of Auerstedt in 1806, leading it to defeat. But his spirited retreat to Lübeck more than made up for this loss, though he was forced to capitulate. Suffering a nervous breakdown when Prussia did not go to war with France again in 1809, as a full general of cavalry, Blücher was given a high command with the outbreak of the Wars of Liberation in 1813. At the head of the Army of Silesia, a force consisting of both Prussian and Russian troops, he campaigned all the way to Paris, forcing Napoleon to abdicate in 1814. He was promoted to field marshal during the Battle of Leipzig in October 1813 and made prince of Wahlstadt on his return from Paris in 1814. Political pressure

---

1. See Peter Hofschröer, *1815, the Waterloo Campaign*, vol. 2, *The German Victory: From Waterloo to the Fall of Napoleon* (London, 1999), 321ff.

led to his being placed in command of the Army of the Lower Rhine in 1815, though the position was largely nominal, and the army was effectively led by its chief of staff, Col. August Wilhelm Antonius Neidhardt von Gneisenau. Blücher died on his estate in Silesia in 1819.

One minor player in this international drama was a junior officer in the Prussian army by the name of Carl Philipp Gottfried von Clausewitz. He was born on June 1, 1780, in Burg, a town near Magdeburg in Central Germany, into a family of priests of Polish origin. Although his family were not members of the landowning classes or the Prussian military nobility, his two older brothers, Friedrich Vollmar and Wilhelm Benedikt, pursued a military career. Their father, the son of a professor of theology, had been a minor official in the revenue service, a position he was able to obtain thanks to having served as an officer under Frederick the Great in the Seven Years' War. Clausewitz later claimed that his family had descended from the Upper Silesian nobility, but it would seem that in the confusion and devastation of the Thirty Years' War (1614–48), when many official records were destroyed, his great-grandfather took the opportunity of doing some social climbing by adding a "von" to his name.

Clausewitz was just twelve years old in 1792 when he enlisted in Prince Ferdinand's Thirty-fourth Infantry Regiment in Neuruppin (northwest of Berlin), Brandenburg province. He had received a basic education at a "Latin School," a center that prepared its pupils for a university education. Like so many would-be young soldiers, Clausewitz altered his birth certificate to appear older than he was. Family connections also played a role in his decision to join the army. His brothers had received their commissions in the same regiment on the recommendation of Lt. Col. Gustav Detleff von Hundt, commander of the unit from 1787 to 1788, whose wife was a relative of the Clausewitzes.

Clausewitz first held the rank of "Gefreiterkorporal" (cadet), which at this time was the typical start to life in the army for an aspiring officer. He went to war with his regiment in 1793, marching to face the invading French army in the Rhineland, there seeing his first action as a thirteen-year-old ensign during the siege of Mainz, a major fortress on the Rhine. He also fought at Kettrich

Carl von Clausewitz. Lithograph by Franz Michelis after a lost painting by Karl Wilhelm Wach. © Bildarchiv Preussischer Kulturbesitz/Art Resource. Used by permission.

and gained promotion to second lieutenant before Prussia withdrew from the Revolutionary Wars in 1795. Afterward Clausewitz returned to garrison life in Neuruppin, where he continued his education. Army reports from this period praise the teenaged officer's knowledge and intelligence and in 1801 helped him on his way to the Military Academy in Berlin, where he spent the next few years studying. There he met the great military reformer (then lieutenant colonel) Gerhard Johann David von Scharnhorst (1755–1813), who was to become his friend, guide, and mentor. Scharnhorst considered Clausewitz one of his brightest pupils, and Clausewitz considered his time at the academy the decisive point of his life.

On Scharnhorst's recommendation, Clausewitz was appointed aide to Prince August of Prussia in the spring of 1803. Promoted to "Stabskapitain" (junior captain) in November 1805, a year later he served at the prince's side at the Battle of Auerstedt, where Marshal Louis-Nicolas Davoût (1770–1823) trounced the Prussian army. Fighting at the head of a battalion of grenadiers, Clausewitz reached Prenzlau, where the army capitulated. He went into captivity with Prince August, spending ten months in Nancy, France, as a prisoner of war. The two men are known to have discussed military matters, with Clausewitz greatly influencing the prince. The foundation of the theorist's later life and achievements had now been laid.

In April 1808 Clausewitz returned to active service and went to the royal court, which was then in Königsberg (today Kaliningrad) in East Prussia. When Prince August was appointed inspector general of the artillery, Clausewitz left his service, for he did not want to be an artilleryman. Promoted to full captain in February 1809, he was given an appointment in the administration of the War Ministry and later worked under Scharnhorst, who returned to Berlin at the end of the year. During this time in Berlin, Clausewitz attended Prof. Johann Gottfried Karl Christian Kiesewetter's lectures on philosophy, where he learned dialectical methodology. Kiesewetter (1766–1819) was a pupil of Immanuel Kant and popularized his teacher's ideas.

Clausewitz was transferred to the general staff in July 1810, obtained his majority a month later, and spent that summer visiting various historical battlefields in Silesia, the province Frederick the Great had conquered from the Austrians. He also received permission to marry Countess Marie von Brühl. From October 1810 he taught staff duties and the war of outposts at the Military Academy. His work was so highly regarded that Scharnhorst recommended him for the post of personal tutor in the science of war to the then fifteen-year-old crown prince of Prussia, and Clausewitz served in this capacity from 1810 to 1812. In 1811 he also was appointed to the commission that was drawing up a new set of drill regulations for the infantry, which were published the following year.

In 1812 Clausewitz was one of a number of Prussian officers who left the service in protest against the alliance with France that preceded Napoleon's fateful invasion of Russia. Others included Col. August Wilhelm Antonius Neidhardt von Gneisenau (1761–1831), Maj. Karl Wilhelm Georg von Grolman (1777–1843), and Col. Leopold Hermann Ludwig von Boyen (1771–1848). This was one of the most difficult decisions of his life, causing a considerable conflict of interest between his duties as a Prussian officer and his political sense as a German patriot. Clausewitz felt that he had to justify his actions, and so he wrote a memorandum criticizing the effects of this alliance and calling for the preparation of a war to overthrow Napoleon. While some officers were pleased to see this troublemaker go, others saw great wisdom in his words.

Appointed to the Russian army with the rank of lieutenant colonel, Clausewitz was initially ordered to raise a unit from German prisoners of war to serve alongside Russian troops, later known as the Russo-German Legion. But delays in its organization led to his appointment as an aide to Gen. Ernst Heinrich Adolf von Pfuel, one of many German officers now advising Tsar Alexander of Russia. Clausewitz had met Pfuel, formerly an officer in the service of the German state of Württemberg, while on the Prussian General Staff in 1806. Pfuel left the army after a dispute with the tsar, and Clausewitz was transferred to the headquarters of Maj. Gen. Count Pyotr von der Pahlen, under whose command he fought at the Battles of Vitebsk, Smolensk, and Borodino in the fall of 1812.

Clausewitz was then appointed chief of staff for the Baltic city of Riga's garrison, then under the command of Count Magnus Gustav Essen, but remained in the headquarters of Count Ludwig Adolf Wittgenstein, rejoining him in November 1812. That December he was part of the Russian vanguard under Col. Johann Karl Friedrich Anton Diebitsch. Once Napoleon's army had disintegrated during the retreat from Moscow, the Prussian contingent under Maj. Gen. Johann David Ludwig von Yorck, part of the corps under the French marshal Macdonald, became isolated. Diebitsch pursued it, maneuvering between the Prussians and the remainder of Macdonald's men. Clausewitz headed the delegation that negotiated Yorck's withdrawal from the war, the general signing the Convention of Tauroggen on December 31, 1812. This act of rebellion signaled a revolt that spread through northern Germany in the coming months, starting what later became known as the Wars of Liberation (1813–15).

Clausewitz then went to Königsberg, where he was involved in raising the local militia at the end of January 1813. He then applied to rejoin the Prussian army, but Frederick William III, the king of Prussia, rejected this, saying he would reconsider if Clausewitz served well in the coming war. The charge against him for leaving Prussian service was dropped.

Scharnhorst's death from of a wound received at the Battle of Lützen in May 1813 greatly affected Clausewitz, who recorded his thoughts in a memorandum published in 1832.

That fall Blücher and Gneisenau requested that the young officer be attached to their staff, but this too was rejected, so Clausewitz served with distinction as the chief of staff of Ludwig Georg Thedel Count von Wallmoden's corps during the campaigns on the Lower Elbe around the Hanseatic port city of Hamburg in the fall of 1813 and in France in 1814. He also remained an officer of the Russo-German Legion, now in British pay. In 1813 the legion was attached to Wallmoden's corps, part of the Army of the North under the command of the crown prince of Sweden, who had previously served Napoleon as Marshal Bernadotte. The corps consisted of a mixture of local levies, legions, and free corps, with just a smattering of regular troops. Clausewitz led the corps in driving back to Hamburg a French force under General Pécheux during the Battle on the Göhrde on September 16, 1813.

Early in 1814 Clausewitz was finally transferred to Blücher's headquarters, though only as a Russian observer. But he was allowed to rejoin Prussian service after the first Peace of Paris, concluded at the end of the 1814 campaign.

The following year Clausewitz, now a full colonel, was appointed chief of staff of the III Army Corps under Gen. Johann Adolph von Thielemann. This command formed part of Blücher's Army of the Lower Rhine and was deployed in the Netherlands. During the Waterloo campaign, Clausewitz fought at the Battles of Ligny (June 16) and Wavre (June 18–19). At Wavre his corps held up the wing of Napoleon's army under Marshal Grouchy, preventing it from intervening at Waterloo.

When Thielemann was placed in command of the Military District of the Lower Rhine, a province that had been awarded to Prussia at the Congress of Vienna, Clausewitz continued to serve him as chief of staff. Based in the fortress city of Koblenz on the Rhine, the colonel held this post from the fall of 1815 to the spring of 1818.

In May 1818 Clausewitz was transferred to Berlin, where he held the post of director of the Military Academy. As the task was too mundane for a man of his intellect, this gave him little satisfaction. In his spare time he worked on various manuscripts. The genesis of his published works came from early discussions with Scharnhorst and from his experiences in the campaign of 1806. They started to take form during the campaigns of 1813–15, with Gneisenau influencing their development. In 1823–24 Clausewitz wrote his essay on the campaign of 1806, which was to be the only manuscript he completed. He held his academy appointment until August 1830, when he returned to a more active post with the army as inspector of the Second Artillery District in Breslau, Silesia. He owed this appointment to the intervention of Prince August, who was now in command of the Prussian artillery. Clausewitz left his incomplete manuscripts in Berlin, where they remained, sealed, until his death.

In March 1831 an army of observation was mobilized along the border with the Kingdom of Poland, where an uprising against its Russian rulers was taking place. Clausewitz was appointed chief of staff and had the opportunity of serving under his old friend Gneisenau, the commander of this force. As no hostilities took place, he spent his time on administrative matters, observing the war between the Russians and the local insurgents, calculating their movements, anticipating their future direction, and speculating on possible clashes. He reported events to Gneisenau every day, and the two men had detailed discussions on the situation.

Although one of the greatest military geniuses of history, this was the closest Clausewitz was ever to come to commanding an army in the field. History was not to associate his name with a great battle.

That same year a cholera epidemic broke out, and Gneisenau succumbed to the disease on August 23. Deeply shaken by this personal loss, Clausewitz returned to Breslau early, where he too caught cholera and died on November 16. An era of Prussian history passed with him. Clausewitz left no children, other than perhaps his manuscripts, and it would be some years before they came to see the light of day. His widow now took it upon herself to see that her late husband's works were completed and published, evidently fulfilling his expressed wishes. She broke open the sealed packet just a few days after his death and saw that much work would be needed to turn these texts into publishable works. She sought the help of Maj. Franz August O'Etzel, then a teacher of military geography at the Military Academy. He not only proofread the galleys but also prepared the accompanying maps. Finding a publisher was not a problem. Marie von Clausewitz approached Berlin bookseller and publisher Ferdinand Dümmler, who had served in Lützow's Freikorps, a force of German irregulars, during the Wars of Liberation. His company has published Clausewitz's works ever since. These include studies of the campaigns of 1796 in Italy, 1799 in Italy and Switzerland, 1812 in Russia, as well as the Waterloo Campaign of 1815. This work was completed by 1834, and Marie von Clausewitz died in 1836.[2]

Although known in military circles, Carl von Clausewitz did not achieve fame in his own lifetime. It is interesting to note that while Captain Siborne corresponded with the Historical Section of the Prussian General Staff to discuss the details of the Waterloo campaign, no mention was ever made of Clausewitz's important work on the subject, even though other published Prussian accounts did come into the discussion. The first time Clausewitz's treatise was used as a reference for an English-language book was in Col. Charles Chesney, R.E., *Waterloo Lectures* (1868). Chesney

---

2. For details on O'Etzel and Marie's efforts, see Clausewitz, *Vom Kriege*, in *Hinterlassene Werke*, 1183. Clausewitz's published works are listed in the bibliography.

(1826–76) was a professor of military history at the British Royal Military Academy in Sandhurst, and his book remains one of the great classics on the 1815 campaign. Nevertheless, 130 years passed before the next English-language account of Waterloo utilizing Clausewitz was published, and more than another decade before that entire work was published in English. This is somewhat surprising given the growing interest in Clausewitz in the Anglo-Saxon world since the end of the Second World War. For an explanation, one must refer to the Wellington Papers, the full collection of documents originating from the first duke's collection (now held in the Hartley Library, University of Southampton), which have been accessible to scholars since the 1980s.[3]

Clausewitz is now a household name, even among those who know little of history, let alone of military history, many regarding him as the greatest military philosopher to have lived. His most famous work, *On War,* is considered to be the one book that distills the essence of the dynamics of warfare and as such is required reading for students of military affairs. It has been in print in its original German since the publication of the first edition in 1832; the same Berlin publisher that produced the first edition released the nineteenth in 1980. Over the years this monumental work has been published in English in four different translations as well as in various other languages.

When Clausewitz died in 1831, his widow had his teaching notes published as the *Hinterlassene Werke* (Posthumous Works). The eighth volume in the series, which covers the Waterloo campaign, appeared in 1835.

While Waterloo remains a popular subject in the Anglo-Saxon world, Clausewitz's authoritative work on this campaign has never been published in English, though a French translation was printed more than a century ago. Strange as this may seem, there are extensive records of the reason for this, though historians have not ignored this text entirely. Indeed Charles Cecil Cope Jenkinson (1754–1851), the 3rd Earl of Liverpool, translated it

---

3. Hofschröer, *1815, the Waterloo Campaign,* 2 vols. (London, 1998–99). Liverpool's translation of Clausewitz's work on Waterloo is contained in file WP 8/1/2, Wellington Papers, Hartley Library, University of Southampton.

into English in manuscript in the 1850s, shortly after it was first published in German. Surprisingly, his translation has never been published. But British Waterloo historians and Wellington's biographers have all neglected to cover the reasons for this.

The story is revealing: Wellington described Clausewitz's authoritative analysis of the campaign as a "lying work" written by "mine enemy." What was it that compelled the duke to make such extraordinary comments? On September 10, 1840, Lord Liverpool wrote to Col. John Gurwood, the editor of the 1st Duke of Wellington's *Despatches,* to notify him that he had translated Clausewitz's Waterloo analysis into English.[4] Liverpool had been a British diplomat in Vienna and, as a volunteer in the Austrian army, had fought at Austerlitz in 1805. His knowledge of the German language and of military affairs was obviously advantageous. Liverpool requested that Gurwood pass on his letter to Wellington, and the colonel duly obliged. Wellington's response was to request a copy of the manuscript. Liverpool sent one but did not get a reply for nearly two years.[5] The manuscript was not returned to him, and it has remained unexamined in Wellington's papers ever since.

In 1842 popular historian Sir Archibald Alison (1792–1867) published the volume of his *History of Europe* covering 1815. The son of a pastor, born in Shropshire, and educated in Edinburgh, Alison went on to become a successful lawyer. He started writing in his spare time and began working on his *History* in 1829, drafting the concluding volume (on Waterloo) in 1842. His work went into several editions and by 1848 had sold 100,000 copies in the United States alone.

Wellington discussed the content of this volume, which was obviously of particular interest, with his close advisors Charles Arbuthnot (1767–1850), a career diplomat and politician, and Francis

---

4. For Liverpool's file copy, see Liverpool Papers, vol. 114, fols. 82–83, Additional Manuscripts [Add. MS] 38,303, British Library, London [BL]. The fine copy received by Wellington is in WP 2/71/28, Wellington Papers, Hartley Library.

5. Gurwood to Liverpool, Aug. 1, 1842, Liverpool Papers, vol. 114, fols. 191–92, Add. MS 38,303, BL. For the details on Liverpool and of Gurwood's involvement, see WP 2/71/36/37, Wellington Papers, Hartley Library; and Liverpool Papers, vol. 7, fol. 143, Add. MS 38,196, BL.

Egerton (1800–1857), the 1st Earl of Ellesmere. Egerton was the son of George Granville Leveson-Gower, second marquis of Stafford, and was educated at Eton and Christ Church, Oxford. He served as an officer in the yeomanry and then entered politics. He was a sponsor of the arts, an author, and a translator.

Arbuthnot lived in Apsley House, Wellington's residence in London, and thus readily had the duke's ear. E. A. Smith, Arbuthnot's biographer, has remarked that he was "the eyes and ears of Castlereagh and Wellington, and in a real sense the political agent of each, protecting their interests and serving their advantage whenever he could.... He identified himself so closely with Wellington in the 1820s that he was considered to have no views of his own. Greville alleged that he 'is weak, but knows everything; his sentiments are the Duke's.'"[6]

Egerton had seen much of the world and was both well educated and highly talented. As a young man, he became acquainted with Wellington and spent a considerable amount of time in the duke's close circles in subsequent years. Egerton kept regular notes of their discussions and other events that were published by his daughter in 1903 as *Personal Reminiscences of the Duke of Wellington by Francis, the First Earl of Ellesmere*. As well as being a historian and linguist, Egerton was also a well-known poet and a politician. He understood German, had translated a number of German works into English, and had published reviews of a number of studies on recent campaigns written by various Germans, regularly briefing Wellington (who did not know German) on these publications. It is no surprise then that the duke had Egerton examine Liverpool's translation of Clausewitz's Waterloo study, which he stated was accurate.[7] Despite that, this manuscript was never published, though now that he was familiar with Clausewitz's work, just a year later Egerton translated Clausewitz's *The Campaign of 1812 in Russia*, which John Murray of London first published in 1843.

Arbuthnot and Egerton suggested that Wellington should write a "Memorandum on the Battle of Waterloo," and the duke duly

---

6. E. A. Smith, *Wellington and the Arbuthnots: A Triangular Friendship* (Stroud, 1994), 159.

7. WP 8/3/2, Wellington Papers, Hartley Library; WP 2/91/148, ibid.

obliged. Egerton was currently writing a review of Gottfried Peter Rauschnick's *Life of Blücher* for the prestigious and influential *Quarterly Review*. Wellington sent his "Memorandum" to Egerton, giving him the necessary information to respond to certain points made by Clausewitz and Alison. An examination of the correspondence shows that the duke had been very much irritated by some of Clausewitz's criticisms. He went so far as to state in a letter to Gurwood dated September 17, 1842: "I am trying to finish the memorandum on Clausewitz for Lord Francis [Egerton]. I will send it to you as soon as it will be finished. But I am really too hard worked to become an author and to review these lying works called histories."[8]

A week later Wellington completed the "Memorandum."[9] It was one of only a very few written statements Wellington ever produced on the Waterloo campaign. In it he specifically criticizes a number of comments by Clausewitz (which will be examined below).

After referencing it as intended, Egerton returned the document to Wellington. The duke evidently considered it to be strictly confidential, writing to Gurwood on October 8, 1842, to point this out: "I don't mean that this paper should be published! I have written it for Lord Francis Egerton's information, to enable him to review Clausewitz's history! I don't propose to give mine enemy the gratification of writing a book!" Had Wellington's son not published it after his father's death in the Waterloo volume of the *Supplementary Despatches*, it may never have come to light until the duke's papers were made accessible to scholars in 1987.[10]

In the "Memorandum" Wellington first discusses the political background of the campaign and then briefly examines the overall military situation and the resulting deployment of the Allied forces before considering Clausewitz's comments. The first perceived criticism deals with the duke's deployment, that is the structure,

---

8. Strafford, *Personal Reminiscences of the Duke of Wellington*, 235, 236; Gurwood to Liverpool, Aug. 1, 1842; WP 8/3/10, Wellington Papers, Hartley Library. Rauschnick's *Marshal Vorwärts!* was a popular biography that had just been published in Germany.
9. Strafford, *Personal Reminiscences of the Duke of Wellington*, 235.
10. WP 2/93/17, Wellington Papers, Hartley Library. For the complete "Memorandum," see Wellington, *Supplementary Despatches*, 10:513–31.

organization, and dispositions of his army (which appears below in the chapter "Order of Battle and Disposition of Forces on Both Sides"). Wellington regards these comments as unfounded personal criticism that set "the general temper and tone of this History." He devotes a whole paragraph to complain about the way "historians . . . [are] too ready to criticize the acts and operations not only of their own Generals and armies, but likewise of those of their best friends and allies of their nation, and even those acting in co-operation with its armies."[11] Wellington warns against accepting Clausewitz's criticisms.

Reference to the original German text, however, shows that Clausewitz was not criticizing Wellington personally or even his dispositions. His complaint was that the available records of Wellington's dispositions at the time of writing were insufficient for the historian to determine them with the required accuracy.[12] It is possible that the duke misunderstood Clausewitz here, but in any case, Wellington's retort was not necessary, for the records required were not available at the time. Indeed, the Waterloo volume of Wellington's *Dispatches* (edited by John Gurwood) was published in 1838, seven years after Clausewitz's demise and three after the posthumous publication of his work on the 1815 campaign. The duke was evidently sensitive about his dispositions.

Clausewitz then considers the deployment of Wellington's army. He outlines why the Allied forces had to cover a wide front and what their intentions were should the French invade the Netherlands along any of several possible routes. After their meeting at Tirlemont on May 3, 1815, it would seem that Blücher and Wellington planned to oppose a possible offensive through Charleroi and beyond by having the Prussians take up defensive positions around Sombreffe, with Wellington moving his entire force rapidly to support them. They intended to concentrate for the decisive battle within forty-eight hours of hostilities and to assemble sufficient troops within twenty-four hours to undertake a major delaying action to allow the remainder to concentrate at the required point.

11. Wellington, *Supplementary Despatches*, 10:517.
12. Clausewitz, *Der Feldzug von 1815 in Frankreich*, 27–33.

Clausewitz considers that "[i]t was simply impossible for Wellington to concentrate his whole army on its far left flank at Nivelles or Quatre Bras in two days, as it was spread out over twenty [German] miles." Writing in the third person, Wellington rebuffs this criticism with the claim that, "having received the intelligence of that attack [on the Prussian positions before Charleroi on the morning of June 15] only at three o'clock in the afternoon of the 15th, he [Wellington] was at Quatre Bras before the same hour on the morning of the 16th, with a sufficient force to engage the left of the French army."[13] Clausewitz evidently believed that Wellington's commitment would be difficult to keep. The duke's response was to claim that although the Prussians had not informed him of the outbreak of hostilities in good time, he had nevertheless been able to bring sufficient forces to the right place in time.

But was that really the case? Wellington's own records show that he first heard the news of hostilities at 9 A.M. on June 15, but he did not react to this. The Prince of Orange certainly arrived in Brussels that afternoon, and it is most probable he confirmed this news at 3 P.M., as Wellington later admitted in private. Yet the duke's records show that he issued his first orders at 7 P.M., fifteen hours after hearing of Napoleon's offensive. This delay made it impossible for him to have had a sufficient force at Quatre Bras on the morning of June 16. In fact Wellington had ordered the troops that were there that morning—a division of Netherlanders—to leave Quatre Bras and march on Nivelles, though fortunately the

---

13. Ibid., 32; Wellington, *Supplementary Despatches*, 10:523. Both Nivelles and Quatre Bras were points of strategic importance. Nivelles was on the Brussels to Charleroi highway, south of Brussels and roughly halfway between the two cities. The Prince of Orange's headquarters was located in Nivelles, and as such it was an important point on the lines of communication. It was also a point of concentration for Allied forces. Quatre Bras was roughly halfway between Brussels, the site of Wellington's headquarters, and Namur, where Blücher's headquarters were located, and was east of Nivelles. It was guarded by a detachment of the Netherlands army. Should Quatre Bras fall to the French, then the most direct line of communication between the principal Allied commanders would be cut. The fact that Charleroi was the site of a bridge over the Sambre River gave it strategic significance should Napoleon choose to advance on Brussels. Control of this span would allow Napoleon to move his wheeled transport with greater ease, accelerating his advance. Not surprisingly, seizing Charleroi was one of his major objectives on June 15.

commander on the ground disobeyed him. It would seem Wellington did not want to admit his error of judgment and was not pleased to see attention being drawn to it.

Clausewitz's version of events immediately preceding the outbreak of hostilities on June 15 and of the responses of the two Allied senior commanders reads:

> The news Blücher received on June 14 that led to him ordering his army to concentrate on the night of June 14–15 seems not to have caused Wellington to make a decisive move. Even on the evening of June 15, when he received the report that [Lt. Gen. Wieprecht Hans Karl Friedrich Ernst Heinrich Count von] Ziethen had been attacked at Charleroi and was being driven back by the main French army, he still did not consider it wise to begin moving his Reserve toward the left wing and even less advisable to weaken his right. Rather, he thought Bonaparte would advance up the road from Mons and so considered the battle at Charleroi a feint. All he did was to place his troops on alert. Only at midnight, when the news arrived from General [Wilhelm Caspar Ferdinand Baron von] Dörnberg, commanding the outposts at Mons, that he was not being attacked and that the enemy appeared instead to be moving to the right, did he order the Reserve to march beyond the Soignes Woods, which, according to General [Friedrich Carl Ferdinand Freiherr von] Müffling's account, was at 10 A.M. From there to the battlefield at Sombreffe was only three more [German] miles, so Wellington's Reserve could actually have made it in good time. But much time was lost while Wellington first visited his left wing at Quatre Bras and reconnoitered the enemy at Frasnes before going to meet Blücher at Sombreffe. He arrived there at 1 P.M. and could see that the enemy's main army was there, so he made the necessary arrangements with Blücher. Meanwhile, the Reserve seems to have awaited further orders at the end of the Soignes Woods, that is, at the fork in the road to Nivelles and Quatre Bras. Even then, there was still enough time. Wellington's forces were spread out, however, because it was his intention to act according to circumstances. He did not want to remove

any forces from the right wing of the Prince of Orange at Nivelles, so he was too weak to support Blücher.

This version is a fair outline of those events and is supported by the record.

Wellington's "Memorandum," however, does not concur with this sequence of events. As mentioned above, a critical question is when did Wellington really first hear of the events at the front that morning. Reports the duke had received from his outposts and informants in the preceding days indicated the buildup of French forces on the border with the Netherlands and of Napoleon's arrival there, indicating that war was about to commence. On June 9 the Allied forces at the front were placed on alert. On the thirteenth Wellington had movement orders drafted.[14] Then on the evening of June 14, Lt. Col. Sir Henry Hardinge, Wellington's representative at Prussian headquarters in Namur, wrote to Wellington, "The prevalent opinion here seems to be that Buonaparte intends to commence offensive operations." That night the numerous campfires on the French side of the border opposite the outposts of the Prussian I Army Corps indicated a substantial concentration of troops. The French attacked the Prussians at Thuin about 4 A.M. Forty-five minutes later Ziethen reported the situation to both Namur and Brussels. The message to Blücher arrived at 8:30 A.M. and that to Wellington by 9 A.M.[15]

By not reacting to the news for ten hours, Wellington had made an error of judgment, one that could have had serious consequences for the outcome of the campaign. Not only were his troops so dispersed that, as Clausewitz remarks, he would not be able to concentrate or assemble his entire army in sufficient time to support the Prussians, but also by not having reacted for so long, he had no opportunity of moving his forces that day, exacerbating an already difficult position. If Wellington had ordered

---

14. For an account from Lt-Colonel Sir George Scovell, one of Wellington's senior staff officers, of the orders being written, see WO 37/12, fol. 2, The National Archives, London.

15. Wellington, *Supplementary Despatches*, 10:476; Charras, *Histoire de la campagne de 1815*, 1:124–25; *Militärisches*, 1:252; De Bas & T'Serclaes de Wommersom, *La campagne de 1815 aux pays-bas*, 1:375.

his troops to move that morning, then at least those in Brussels could have marched part of the way to the front that day. It would then have been no problem for him to assist the Prussians on June 16, with the Battle of Ligny likely becoming the intended holding action. Wellington, it would seem, tried to explain away his error by claiming that he had heard the news later than he actually did.

Wellington's "Memorandum" then discusses the matter in more detail. He writes, "the first account received by Wellington was from the Prince of Orange, who had come in from the outposts of the army of the Netherlands to dine with Wellington at three o'clock in the afternoon." The Prince of Orange, commander of Wellington's I Corps, arrived in Brussels between 2 and 3 P.M. on June 15. Major General Baron Behr, commander of the fortress of Mons, sent him a report passing on information received from Major General von Steinmetz, whose brigade of Prussians had been the first attacked by the French. (A copy of this message can be found in Wellington's records.) Wellington's claim to have first received the news at 3 P.M. conflicts not only with his record of receiving the news by 9 A.M., as mentioned above, but also with his official report to the secretary of war, Earl Bathurst, of June 19, known as the "Waterloo Despatch," in which he states, "I did not hear of these events till the evening of the 15th."[16]

The "Memorandum" continues: "While the Prince [of Orange] was with Wellington, the staff officer employed by Prince Blücher at Wellington's headquarters, General Müffling, came to Wellington to inform him that he had just received intelligence of the movement of the French army and their attack upon the Prussian troops at Thuin." Ziethen's journal contains an entry showing that he sent a report to Müffling from Charleroi, about four hours from Brussels, at about 11 A.M. Müffling's memoirs note the receipt of a report from Ziethen at 3 P.M., corroborating Wellington's claim to have heard the news at that time.[17]

---

16. Wellington, *Supplementary Despatches*, 10:481; Wellington, *Despatches*, 12:478. For the message from Behr, see Wellington, *Supplementary Despatches*, 10:524.

17. Wellington, *Supplementary Despatches*, 10:524; *Militärisches*, 1:253; Müffling, *Aus meinem Leben*, 228.

The disparities in Wellington's versions of events are obvious, but what could explain them? Is it plausible that just four days after the events in question, Wellington forgot what had happened, particularly when he had his original records at hand, only to remember them in detail nearly thirty years later? Various accounts had been published since June 19, 1815, one of the most convincing of these coming from a British officer based in Brussels on June 15, 1815, who was part of a mess that came to hear of the outbreak of hostilities at 3 P.M. Having been published in the official forces publication, the *United Service Journal,* in 1841, informed opinion was aware that this conflicted with Wellington's "Waterloo Despatch."[18] It would seem that the duke now considered his earlier statement no longer untenable. As both the Prince of Orange and Müffling had witnessed the events at 3 P.M., did Wellington feel that he could safely plump for that time now?

Were the troops Wellington actually had available at Quatre Bras on the morning of June 16, 1815, "a sufficient force to engage the left of the French army" as stated in his "Memorandum"? When he arrived at Quatre Bras about 10 A.M. on June 15, the only Allied troops there were eight battalions and two batteries of Netherlanders, just under 8,000 men.[19] After having examined the situation and noted just a "popping of muskets," the only force Wellington appears to have ordered up to Quatre Bras was Lt. Gen. Sir Thomas Picton's division, around 7,000 men. While there is no direct evidence that it was Wellington who had this order sent, eyewitness accounts do mention its arrival between noon and 1 P.M. on the fifteenth. As the division was situated around an hour's ride from Quatre Bras, the order was probably sent between 11 A.M. and noon, when Wellington was at Quatre Bras. There is nothing to suggest that he ordered any more troops there at this time.

The next paragraph in the "Memorandum" repeats Wellington's claim to have first heard the news of the outbreak of hostilities at 3 P.M. It continues with the assertion: "Orders were forthwith sent [at 3 P.M.] for the march of the whole army to its

18. *United Service Journal, 1841,* pt. 2, 172.
19. Wellington, *Supplementary Despatches,* 10:523; De Bas & T'Serclaes de Wommersom, *La campagne de 1815 aux pays-bas,* 3:96–97.

left. The whole moved on that evening and in the night, each division and portion separately, but unmolested."[20]

Müffling's recollection was different. He states that Wellington issued his first orders at 6 P.M. and not "forthwith." The British officer mentioned earlier described this scene in some detail, noting how the orderlies were called to headquarters around this time and then were seen rushing off with their orders later. Furthermore Wellington's own records show that these orders were issued between 6 and 7 P.M. and did not instruct the army to march anywhere, let alone to its left, but rather for it to assemble. Three hours later the first movement orders were issued, and in view of the time of day as well as the distance these dispatches had to be carried, then the very earliest they could be implemented would be at daybreak on June 16. Thus "the whole" certainly did not move "that evening and in the night," as Wellington claims and as he must well have known. Wellington also issued further movement orders on the morning of the sixteenth. These documents were published on Wellington's instruction in 1838, just four years before he wrote this "Memorandum." It is interesting to note that he indeed consulted them while composing the "Memorandum." Arbuthnot pointed this out in a letter to Egerton dated July 22, 1842, and sent from Wellington's London residence Apsley House, writing, "He [Wellington] stayed with me for some time, and read to me various parts from page 375 to 476 [of volume 12 of the *Dispatches*]." (The reference given is for Wellington's outgoing correspondence from May 11 to June 17, 1815, including the orders issued on June 15.)[21]

Later on in the "Memorandum," Wellington makes certain claims about his troop positions and movements that day that warrant further examination. He states:

> In the mean time [between 1 and 3 P.M.] the reserve of the Allied army under the command of the Duke of Wellington had

---

20. Wellington, *Supplementary Despatches*, 10:524.
21. Müffling, *Aus meinem Leben*, 229; *United Service Journal, 1841*, pt. 2, 172; Wellington, *Despatches*, 12:474–75; Strafford, *Personal Reminiscences of the Duke of Wellington*, 235–37.

arrived at Quatre Bras. The historian [Clausewitz] asserts that the Duke of Wellington had ordered these troops to halt at the point at which they quitted the Forêt de Soignies [*sic*]. He can have no proof of this fact, of which there is no evidence; and in point of fact the two armies were united about mid-day of the 16th of June, on the left of the position of the Allied army under the command of the Duke of Wellington. These troops, forming the reserve, and having arrived from Bruxelles, were now joined by those of the 1st division of infantry, and the cavalry ([Wellington's] footnote: The Duke of Wellington was at Quatre Bras about 3 o'clock, on his return from Ligny).[22]

The Reserve did not arrive at Quatre Bras between 1 and 3 P.M. First to arrive at Quatre Bras was Picton's division, only a part of the Reserve, and this was from about 3 P.M. The Brunswickers arrived a little later, but it is unlikely that Wellington ordered them up, for the time at which they received their orders indicates these were sent while Wellington was with Blücher.[23] The Nassauers arrived about 8 P.M., and the 5th Hanoverian Brigade only reached Genappe by 11 P.M.[24]

Wellington's claim that Clausewitz had "no evidence" the Reserve had been ordered to halt after leaving the Soignes Woods flies not only in the face of the facts but also is contradicted by the orders he cites in the "Memorandum." These orders, issued at 10 P.M. on June 15, state, "The troops in Bruxelles (5th and 6th divisions, Duke of Brunswick's and Nassau troops) to march when assembled from Bruxelles by the road of Namur to the point where the road to Nivelles separates."[25] It leaves little doubt that Wellington was knowingly instructing Egerton to make a false statement on this matter.

Reference to accounts of members of this corps confirms the accuracy of Clausewitz's point. The unnamed officer of Picton's

---

22. Wellington, *Supplementary Despatches*, 10:525.
23. See, for instance, Edward Costello, *Adventures of a Soldier, Written by Himself* (London, 1852), 151.
24. Pflugk-Harttung, *Vorgeschichte*, 305–306, 307.
25. Wellington, *Despatches* (1847 ed.), 8:142.

division mentioned that "after two long halts, [the division] reached Quatre Bras about two o'clock." Captain Leach of the 95th Rifles recorded, "Our division and the Brunswick troops, after a halt of an hour or two near Waterloo, were directed to advance; and we arrived at Quatre Bras about two hours after midday." In fact the Brunswickers were not directed to Quatre Bras but were merely ordered up to Genappe, where a narrow bridge created a bottleneck, and were ordered to Quatre Bras later. Edward Costello, also in the 95th Rifles, wrote a more detailed account: "We halted at the verge of the wood, on the left of the road, behind the village of Waterloo, where we remained for some hours. . . . About nine o'clock the Duke of Wellington with his staff came riding from Brussels and passed us to the front." Lt. John Kincaid of the 95th added further details: "The whole of the division having . . . advanced to the village of Waterloo, where, forming in a field adjoining the road, our men were allowed to prepare their breakfasts. . . . Lord Wellington joined us about nine o'clock; and, from his very particular orders, [we were] to see that the roads were kept clear of baggage. . . . About twelve o'clock an order arrived for the troops to advance." Clausewitz was certainly correct here. Wellington clearly knew the Reserve did halt upon leaving the Soignes Woods, the orders he gave when there were not for any of these troops to advance, and the order to move to Quatre Bras arrived back there three hours after he had passed.[26]

Wellington's claim that "the two armies were united about midday" is equally questionable. The first Allied reinforcements only started arriving at Quatre Bras after 2 P.M., and as mentioned above, they did not receive their orders to do so until the time Wellington later claimed that they were already at Quatre Bras.

The Brunswickers' official report states, "It must have been two o'clock when the Corps received orders to move urgently [from Genappe] to Quatre Bras and it marched off immediately."[27]

---

26. *United Service Journal, 1841*, pt. 2, 174; Leach, *Life of an Old Soldier*, 374–75; Costello, *Adventures of a Soldier*, 150–51; John Kincaid, *Adventures in the Rifle Brigade* (London, 1830), 154–55.

27. Capt. William Siborne, Waterloo Correspondence, vol. 4, fols. 29–34, Add. MS 34,706, BL.

Genappe was about a half-hour's ride from Quatre Bras, so this order would have left the latter town around 1:30 P.M. By then Wellington had left for his meeting with Blücher, so he could not have issued the order. Instead the Prince of Orange probably did so, for he was then the senior commander on the ground.

Finally, Wellington's claim that "the 1st Division of infantry and the cavalry joined him at Quatre Bras about 3 P.M." also conflicts with the record. Lieutenant Powell of the 1st Foot Guards, First Division, wrote: "At about 3 P.M. the Division arrived within half a mile of Nivelles, and took up a position looking over the town, supposing our day's work was done. We were, however, scarcely halted, and the men disencumbered of their loads, when an Aide-de-camp brought the order to advance immediately." The division arrived at Quatre Bras about 5 P.M. Maj. Gen. Sir Hussey Vivian, commander of the Sixth Brigade of cavalry, mentioned in a letter to his wife dated June 23, 1815, "we . . . of course pressed on with all speed we possibly could, but unfortunately arrived too late at Quatre Bras." The cavalry did not see action on the sixteenth because it only arrived after dark, something Wellington surely would have noticed.[28]

Moreover, in his "after orders" of 10 P.M. on June 15, Wellington had not instructed a single unit to move to Quatre Bras. Nevertheless, at midnight, he told Müffling to inform Blücher that 20,000 men would be at Quatre Bras by 10 A.M. the next morning, this despite the fact that the only troops Wellington had ordered to move anywhere were sent to Nivelles and Enghien, not to Quatre Bras.[29]

Around midnight more news from the front arrived, a report stating that the French had advanced as far as Quatre Bras that evening. The Prince of Orange, a witness to this event, told Constant Rebecque, his chief of staff, "At first, the Duke believed that the attack on Charleroi to be a feint; only when the report of the appearance of the enemy at Frasnes arrived, did he decide to move

---

28. Herbert Taylor Siborne, ed., *Waterloo Letters* (London, 1891), 250–51; Claud Vivian, *Richard Hussey Vivian, First Baron Vivian—A Memoir* (London, 1897), 265.

29. Wellington, *Supplementary Despatches*, 10:474; Nostitz, "Das Tagebuch," 22n.

all his forces to Quatre Bras." Yet there is no record of any such order being sent or received. Dörnberg later claimed that Wellington sent him to Picton early on June 16 with orders for his division to move from Waterloo to Quatre Bras. This also conflicts with the record, and as mentioned above, Picton was still near Waterloo at 9 A.M., not receiving any orders until noon. Moreover, the general had been with Wellington at the Duchess of Richmond's ball the previous night, so it should not have been necessary for Dörnberg to ride to Waterloo with these orders. It is clear that Wellington only decided to move part of his forces to Quatre Bras, and then only a small part, after he had been there and examined the situation in person on the morning of June 16.[30]

So what does the record show?

At 10 P.M. on June 15, the First Division was ordered to Braine-le-Comte. It reached there at 9 A.M. the next day, where it awaited further orders. But none arrived, so presumably none were sent. The division then marched to Nivelles on its commander's initiative, where at 3 P.M. orders to march to Quatre Bras finally arrived. As the Third Division was directed to march only to Nivelles but marched on Quatre Bras once there, presumably these orders were only issued then.[31] Field Marshal Henry Paget, Earl of Uxbridge, the commander of Wellington's cavalry, too only appears to have been sent orders to move on Quatre Bras after 4 P.M. on June 16. Other than the Fifth Division, there is no record of Wellington directing any other unit to Quatre Bras. Additional divisions did not receive such orders until the afternoon of June 16, that is, after the fighting there had started. The Prince of Orange's statement that Wellington had decided to "move all his forces to Quatre Bras" about midnight on June 15–16 is questionable. That indeed may have been what Wellington told the prince, but this statement conflicts with Wellington's actions.

Furthermore, taking into account the times at which these orders were received and the distances they had to travel, it would appear that they were sent while Wellington was at his meeting with Blücher that afternoon. It is more likely the Prince of Orange

---

30. Journal of Constant Rebecque; Pflugk-Harttung, *Vorgeschichte*, 292.
31. Lettow-Vorbeck, *Napoleons Untergang 1815*, 522.

issued them as a response to the buildup of French forces at Quatre Bras, but this was not how the duke presented it to history.

In previous days Wellington had promised the Prussians that he would come to their aid on June 16 with 20,000 men. As mentioned above, at midnight he told Müffling that he would have the troops there by 10 A.M. Yet in the early afternoon, only the Second Netherlands Division was present at Quatre Bras, this being less than 8,000 men strong, and all that had been ordered to move there was the Fifth Division, not much more than 7,000 men. Assuming the French would not attack here, and bearing in mind the need to leave a detachment to guard this vital crossroads, Wellington unlikely would have been able to move half the promised number of men to support the Prussians at Ligny within the time specified.

The record confirms Clausewitz's point that Wellington "was too weak to support Blücher," whereas the duke's warning not to accept Clausewitz's criticisms was unfounded. It was simply not possible for Wellington to have kept the promises of support he made to his Prussian allies. He clearly resented this issue being examined, and since its revelation to English readers would have damaged his reputation, it comes as no surprise that Lord Liverpool's translation of Clausewitz's "lying" work never saw the light of day in Wellington's lifetime. But now it is here made available for the first time in nearly two hundred years, an indication of just how successful Wellington's manipulation of the record has been.

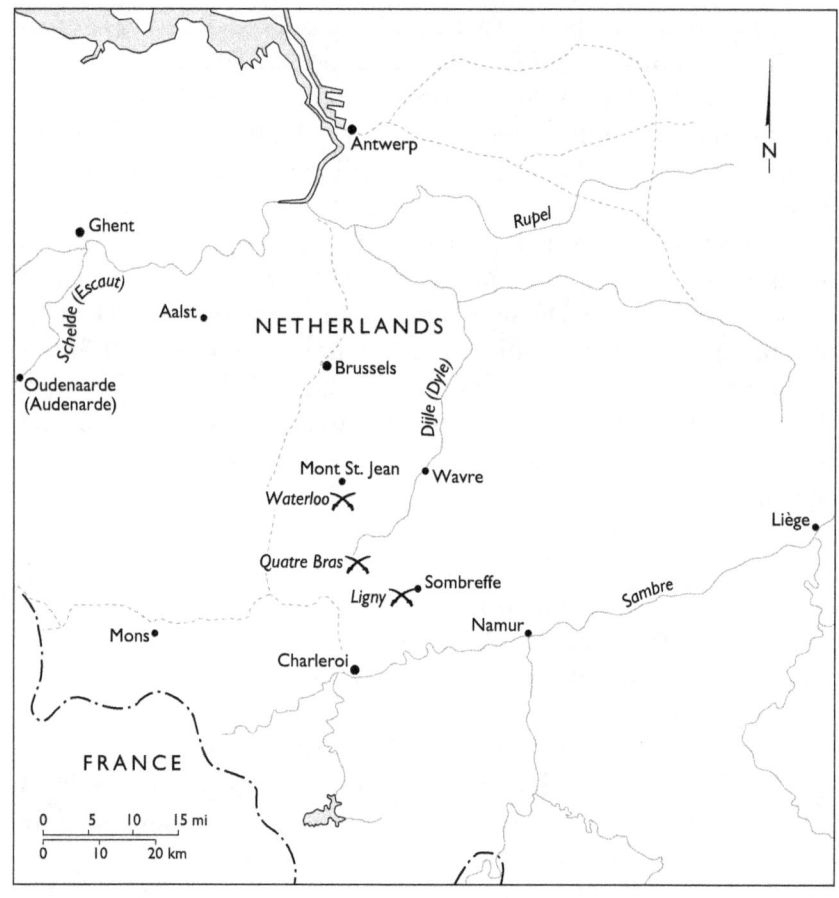

Area of operations, 1815.

The Campaign of 1815 in France

1. The French Armed Forces—Organization of the Standing Army

When Louis XVIII left France,[1] the army was 115,000 men strong. Bonaparte gave the number as only 93,000 men.[2]

Ten weeks later, on June 1, the total under arms and with the colors amounted to 217,000 men. Even if we accept the smaller figure for the Royal Army, the actual increase was by only 124,000 men.

Furthermore, Bonaparte's *Mémoires* indicate that on June 1, 150,000 men were still in the depots.[3] Obviously, they were not ready for action, as he took any forces that were even marginally useful directly onto the battlefield.

There was no shortage of men: that is, of trained troops. Adding up the forces at Napoleon's disposal when the war ended in 1814—the army in Spain and operating against Wellington,[4] the troops in Italy, the Netherlands, and the French fortresses—the

---

1. Louis XVIII (1755–1824), the Bourbon king of France after Napoleon's first abdication in 1814, left Paris for temporary exile in Ghent, the United Netherlands, after Napoleon's return from Elba.
2. Napoleon Bonaparte (1769–1821), erstwhile emperor of France, left exile on Elba on February 26, 1815, beginning the so-called Hundred Days.
3. The reference here likely is to the *Mémoires de Napoléon Bonaparte*, published in Paris in 1821.
4. Arthur Wellesley, the 1st Duke of Wellington (1769–1852). He arrived in Brussels on the night of April 4–5, 1815, and took command of the Anglo-Allied army stationed in the Kingdom of the Netherlands.

French army must still have consisted of 300,000 men.[5] In addition, 100,000 prisoners of war had returned from captivity, so in 1815, Bonaparte had over 400,000 veteran soldiers available.

As 150,000 National Guardsmen were under arms, there could not have been a lack of firearms. Bonaparte also had the number of arms being manufactured increased, so it was unlikely there were any shortages, and a scarcity of available funds at the beginning of the war was just as improbable. It would seem that, apart from the time required for training, the speed at which armed forces could be equipped was more constrained than would be apparent from an initial analysis.

Furthermore, at the end of 1813, when Bonaparte's army was destroyed at the Battle of Leipzig,[6] the replacements raised in the following three months amounted to only 150,000 men. Going back even further, to the beginning of 1813, when Bonaparte returned from Russia virtually by himself, his army having been annihilated, the number of battle-ready troops accumulated up to the ceasefire—that is, in seven months—amounted to only about 200,000 men.[7] Taking into account the size of France's population and her resources, this effort to raise a new army was rather modest. This indicates that even the most energetic government, and Bonaparte's certainly counts as one, must be careful about basing its perception of its potential reserves of manpower solely on the wealth and population of the country. It is a different matter when one is raising a *levée en masse*, or whatever one may call it, as the arming of the French nation in 1793–94 showed. The overwhelming forces the French brought to bear at that time are well documented.

The situation in Prussia was similar: At the beginning of 1813, the standing army consisted of 30,000 men and by April, at the start of the campaign in Saxony, it had grown to around 70,000

---

5. Wellington's Peninsular Army crossed the Pyrenees and started operating in southern France toward the end of 1813. The final battle in the south was fought at Toulouse on April 10, 1814, just after Napoleon's first abdication.

6. Fought October 16–18, 1813, Leipzig was the decisive battle of the Napoleonic Wars.

7. The Armistice of Pläswitz ran from June 4—a few days after the indecisive Battle of Bautzen—to August 11, 1813, when Austria entered the war on the side of the Allies.

men, an increase of 40,000 in three months.[8] In contrast, the expansion achieved by raising the Landwehr [militia] up to the end of August, roughly four months, amounted to around 150,000 men. Evidently a centralized administration, like a single standing army, had appreciably greater difficulty in mobilizing exceptionally large forces in a given period of time, compared with a provincial administration covering the whole country, when the entire provincial administration was set in motion and with the necessary energy. Furthermore, a Landwehr was subject to far fewer inherent limitations than applied to simply expanding a standing army in wartime, whatever form this may have taken.[9]

2. Depot Troops and the *Armée Extraordinaire*

As well as the 217,000 men Bonaparte had under arms on June 1, he also referred to another 150,000 men still in the depots. He did not state how many of these were eventually incorporated into the field army, but it seems likely that up to mid-June, the decisive moment, nothing significant had been undertaken.

Furthermore, he referred to an *"armée extraordinaire"* that supposedly consisted of 196,000 men: largely militia and naval forces, garrisoning France's ninety fortresses. Whether these 196,000 men were under arms is not known. He called them "effectives," but as he referred to the 150,000 men in the depots the same way, it is not certain that these 196,000 were really under arms.

Although the number of fortified places in France must have absorbed a large number of troops, there was good reason to doubt the reliability of these figures, as the weak forces encountered when

---

8. The Treaty of Tilsit (1807) ended the War of the Fourth Coalition against France. The subsequent Treaty of Paris (1808) restricted the size of the Prussian army to 42,000 men. Of these, 20,000 marched with Napoleon into Russia in 1812. Trained reservists were mobilized early in 1813, making the total forces then available around 70,000 men.

9. Founded by royal decree on March 17, 1813, the administration of each of Prussia's provinces was responsible for raising a local militia. Shortly before the recommencement of hostilities that August, regiments of local militia were allocated to the brigades of the field army.

the Prussians entered France showed. According to Bonaparte, excluding the 217,000 men at the frontier, 350,000 men were still supposed to be available in France, including those in the depots. Nevertheless, of the ninety fortresses, a considerable number were either not garrisoned or only very weakly defended, as was evident in Strasbourg, where all of Rapp's corps had to be committed to protect it.[10] Furthermore, the entire French army in Paris and later behind the Loire, consisted of no more than 80,000 men, of whom at least 40,000 had come from Bonaparte's main army, so the reinforcements cannot have been more than 40,000 men.

That being the case, when Bonaparte stated that he had 560,000 men under arms on June 1, this cannot be considered a reliable figure. If so many men were really available, it would certainly have been a poor economy of forces to have taken no more than 126,000 of them to the decisive battle on June 18. The only certainty is that he had 217,000 men available for use in the field. The numbers in reserve and in the fortresses inside the country may not have been insignificant, but as the results show, they were insufficient to offer a secure foothold in the aftermath of a total defeat.

3. Napoleon's Exaggeration of the Available Resources

Finally, Bonaparte claimed that by October 1, he would have increased his forces to 800,000 men. Yet even if the numbers given above are in question, then it is even more the case with these 800,000 men that in his *Mémoires* Bonaparte exaggerates his enormous achievements. However, here, as so often, this account does not correspond with reality. Bonaparte, like the writers who have defended him, always sought to represent the great catastrophes that befell him as the result of chance, to make the reader believe that all the pieces had been arranged with the greatest wisdom,

---

10. General of Cavalry Jean, Count Rapp (1771–1821) was a veteran of the Revolutionary Wars, having fought with Napoleon in Egypt in 1798 and 1799, at Marengo in 1800, and at Austerlitz in 1805, being wounded but recovering to serve at Jena in 1806. Wounded again in 1812 in Russia, he commanded the garrison of Danzig in 1813.

the work pressed forward with the greatest confidence and the most extraordinary energy, so that total success was but a hair's breadth away, but then treachery, accident, or indeed fate, as they say, ruined everything. Both he and they do not want to concede that great errors, great foolishness, and above all exaggeration of reality were the causes.

Judging by general impressions, Bonaparte seemed like a speculator, who pretended to have more money than he did. He had not much more than a couple of hundred thousand men at his disposal. He tried his luck with them, and had he succeeded in breaking up the coalition, or at least holding the borders of France, then the fact that he had no prospect of increasing his forces later on would have highlighted the totally pitiful performance of the opposition, as, with unsurpassed boldness, he would have achieved so much with so little. As his attempt did not succeed, and indeed now that it appears to have been completely impossible, he did not want to look like an adventurer, he instead portrayed his preparations as tremendous and the French people as having been inspired by him to make the greatest exertions. These are merely the usual expressions of his great vanity and his lack of respect for the truth. These traits of his character indicate that, as a writer of history, his work was far from having the same value for the historical researcher as that other commanders, whose memoirs are authoritative. This is not a pointless discussion, as this verdict on the strategy of this campaign would have to be entirely different if it was credible that Bonaparte was confident enough of the French people and sufficiently satisfied with his preparations to achieve the result he projected: that is, to have 800,000 men under arms and fully equipped in three months, with Paris and Lyon fortified, the former with 116,000 men and 800 guns, the latter with 25,000 men and 300 guns. Even if the Allies had actually given him three months (July, August, and September) to achieve this objective, he would have moved nearer to his goal month by month. That being the case, it is clear that if the Allies had waited until July before advancing on Paris, they would have met defensive forces that might have sufficed to bring the whole enterprise to a halt, particularly when taking into account the dilution of strength every strategic advance would have suffered from the need to secure its theater of operations. These circumstances may eventually have made the participation of the civilian population possible. This is likely to have given the French a much greater chance of success than the offensive Bonaparte actually undertook. If the numbers Bonaparte gave were little more than hot air and if actually only an army of 217,000 men was available to achieve success in his new career, then perhaps this offensive was the only likely way of offering resistance and no other way could have been considered.

4. Order of Battle of the French Army

The 217,000 men that Bonaparte had under arms at the beginning of June were divided into seven army corps, a Guard corps, four corps of observation, and an army corps for the Vendée. On completion, their numbers were roughly as follows:

1. The main army facing the Netherlands: The Imperial Guard and five corps—130,000 men
2. On the Upper Rhine
    a) At Strasbourg under Rapp—V Army Corps 20,000 men
    b) At Huningue under Lecourbe[11]—I Observation Corps 5,000 men
    Total 25,000 men
3. On the border with Italy
    a) At Chambéry under Suchet[12]—VII Army Corps 16,000 men

---

11. Claude-Jacques, Count Lecourbe (1758–1815) came from a military family. He fought in the Revolutionary Wars, being promoted to general in 1799. His career was interrupted for several years due to his association with Gen. Jean-Victor Moreau. Lecourbe returned to military service shortly after Napoleon's first abdication in 1814. Not a Bonapartist, he nevertheless continued to serve during the Hundred Days, fighting several engagements against Field Marshal Count von Colloredo-Mansfeld's Austrians.

12. Louis-Gabriel Suchet, Count of Albufera, marshal of France (1770–1826). Suchet worked his way up through the ranks during the Revolutionary Wars, becoming a general in 1799 and holding both field commands and staff positions. He served in Italy, then at Austerlitz (1805), Saalfeld (1806), and Jena before spending several years on the Iberian Peninsula, capturing Valencia in 1812.

b) In Provence under Brune 6,000 men[13]
2nd Observation Corps 22,000 men
4. On the border with Spain 8,000 men
   a) At Toulouse under Decaen 4,000 men[14]
   3rd Observation Corps
   b) At Bordeaux under Clauzel 4,000 men[15]
5. In the Vendée under Lamarque 25,000 men[16]
Total 210,000 men

This does not quite tally with 217,000 men, though the difference is insignificant.

The army on the frontier with the Netherlands was originally supposed to be 20,000 men stronger, but these men were sent to the Vendée because of the pressing danger there.

In any case, in this way, Bonaparte had concentrated the larger part of his forces against Blücher and Wellington,[17] deploying

---

13. Guillaume-Marie-Anne Brune, marshal of France (1763–1815). Promoted to general during the Revolutionary Wars, his republican sympathies did not endear him to Napoleon. Appointed marshal when Napoleon was crowned emperor in 1804, he held a command in northern Germany in 1807, only seeing action again when recalled to active service in 1815. Royalists killed Brune during the White Terror.

14. Charles-Mathieu-Isidore Decaen (1769–1832) served as a gunner in the French navy before enlisting in the infantry during the Revolutionary Wars. He served as a staff officer during the Vendée uprising in 1792. He fought in the Rhineland in 1796 and at Hohenlinden in 1800, for which he was promoted to general. After defending French dependencies in the Indian Ocean, Decaen later served on the Iberian Peninsula.

15. Bertrand, Count Clauzel, later a marshal of France (1772–1842). He fought during the Revolutionary Wars and in Italy before taking part in the Peninsular War as a loyal Bonapartist. After having unwillingly submitted to the Bourbons in 1814, he hastened to join Napoleon for the Hundred Days. After Waterloo he spent several years in America, returning to France in 1820. In 1830 Clauzel fought in Algeria, being made a marshal the following year.

16. Jean-Maximilien, Count Lamarque (1770–1832) rose to the rank of general in the Revolutionary Wars. He commanded a division in the Army of Italy in 1809 and then served on the Peninsula until the first abdication. During the Hundred Days, Lamarque was active in suppressing the royalist uprising in the Vendée. This led him to leave France after the second abdication. After his return in 1818, he entered politics.

17. Field Marshal Gebhardt Leberecht Prince Blücher von Wahlstatt (1742–1819) commanded the Prussian Army of the Lower Rhine in name only. It was

130,000 men, that is, more than two-thirds of all the forces he had on the frontiers, against the 220,000 Allied troops facing him there, although they only made up about one-third of all the opposing forces. Nevertheless, it could be said that Bonaparte, such a great master in the concentration of force at the decisive point, had fragmented his forces: the troops on the Upper Rhine and on the borders of Italy and Spain were obviously insufficient to make even a show of defending the rivers and mountains, although they may just have sufficed for merely garrisoning fortified places. Furthermore, taking into account that of the 55,000 men originally allocated to field operations, 20–30,000 could have been used to reinforce the main army, it seems to have been a great mistake not to have achieved the greatest possible concentration of forces at the decisive point, as in a position like Bonaparte's, this may well have been the only real chance of success. There is no doubt that in the battles of June 16 and 18, 20–30,000 more men could very well have been decisive, even if it is not certain the French would have won the campaign.

However, such a judgment cannot be made if this matter were to be considered from Bonaparte's perspective at the time he was raising and equipping his forces. After all, the main point of all criticisms of strategy, difficult though this may be, is to put oneself in the position of the decision-maker. If writers were to consider all eventualities, the great majority of criticisms of strategy would be totally without substance or diminish into minute distinctions of reasoning.

When Bonaparte was preparing to oppose all of Europe, he naturally had to consider the defense of all his borders, so he deployed small bodies of troops from his standing army on the borders with Southern Germany, Italy, and Spain. These were intended to be cores that newly armed forces were to join: they were cadres of the corps he was thinking of forming. When he gave these orders, he could not possibly have foreseen exactly how many weeks it would take for matters to progress to the point of one side or the other

---

not so much his advanced years but his state of mental health that incapacitated Blücher. Yet as he was the most popular senior commander in Prussia, political pressure saw that he was appointed to this command. Prussia's armed forces were in reality commanded by the chief of staff, Col. August von Gneisenau.

commencing hostilities, or how far advanced the armament of his forces would be at that point in time.

If Bonaparte could also have foreseen that his deployment on the Upper Rhine, where he had to expect the main enemy army, would never have produced a force capable of meeting it on anything like equal terms, he nevertheless had a corps strong enough at least to conduct delaying actions, to create insecurity, and to force countermeasures on the opening of hostilities that would gain time and delay the advance long enough for his victorious army from the Netherlands to rush there. His *Mémoires* indicate that this was not mere speculation, but actually what he considered doing. There is a great difference between a frontier devoid of troops capable of taking the field and one that is not, particularly when rivers and mountains such as the Vosges, the Rhine, the Jura, Alps, and the Pyrenees presented an obstacle to the attacker. Should a province not be defended, then even the most irresolute, ponderous enemy and even the hundred-headed headquarters of a coalition army would be to some extent compelled to move forward, whereas if the enemy only has a certain Daun-like caution, the smallest force would cause appreciable hesitation and indecision.[18]

Furthermore, Bonaparte could not consider denuding the eastern frontiers of his country of troops, because of the effect this would have had on the French population. Had he done so, he would have appeared to abandon half of France and betrayed the utter feebleness and insecurity of his position, which would have had serious repercussions within the political parties at home, as well as a negative influence on the results of arming his forces. It is certainly the case that Bonaparte had to place his own troops in most of these provinces to counter the possibility of a royalist uprising. Finally, it should be noted that according to the original plan, the main army was actually supposed to be 20,000 men stronger, and that only the emerging danger in the Vendée forced Bonaparte to return certain troops to the Loire.[19]

---

18. The reference here is to Leopold Joseph, Count Daun (1705–66), an Austrian field marshal whose reluctance to engage Frederick the Great at certain stages of the Seven Years' War (1753–60) is said to have cost the Austrians victory.

19. The Vendée region of France was and still is a royalist stronghold. As such, it was a major potential threat to the stability of Napoleon's regime.

In mid-June, the situation was such that in the Netherlands, Bonaparte faced 220,000 men under Blücher and Wellington, against which his 130,000 men offered no significant probability of success. At the same time, he only had 30,000 men facing Schwarzenberg's large army on the Upper Rhine, including 16 battalions of National Guard that he transferred to Rapp. Bonaparte may well have wished that he could have removed the wholly inadequate forces on the other borders to give himself a greater chance, or possibly even total certainty, of success in the Netherlands. However, at the last minute, the situation could not be changed, and so he had to try his luck with the 130,000 men he had on the northern frontier.

5. The National Guard

The supposed arming of the nation—that is, the organization of the National Guard—deserves closer examination.

In April, Bonaparte considered a general mobilization of all men between the ages of 20 and 60, organized into more than 3,000 battalions of National Guards that would have armed more than two million men.[20]

This gigantic idea was unquestionably somewhat unsound. Three main criteria were necessary for this: the unity of the nation, enthusiasm and energy from his supporters, and the necessary armaments. Only a few words are necessary to show that of these three criteria, the first had not been met, the second was not sufficiently present, and the third was far from adequate to meet such excessive demands.

However, it was not merely the extent of the mobilization that was totally illusory, but also any sort of general arming of the nation was impossible in the circumstances. Bonaparte most definitely realized this and expressly conceded as much when he spoke of the need to reduce the 44,000-man-strong Parisian National

---

20. The National Guard was France's militia. In 1815 it consisted of 300,000 men between ages twenty and forty organized into battalions of grenadiers and chasseurs. The Guard provided internal security, freeing up regular soldiers for field service, and also garrisoned a number of fortresses.

Guard to 8,000, while increasing the guerrillas in the Paris suburbs from 15,000 to 60,000. The situation in the Vendée and in the south made it absolutely clear that these departments could not be counted on to cooperate, and even in the northern departments, Bonaparte was aware that attitudes were poor and unreliable.

The result was that the entire effort to arm the nation only succeeded in raising 248 élite battalions of National Guard with a theoretical strength of 150,000 men.

Of these, 16 battalions were sent as reinforcements to General Rapp, 16 went to General Suchet in the Dauphiné, and finally around 20,000 men were sent to Bordeaux and Toulouse, leaving around 40,000 men from the National Guard to deploy with the field armies. About 110,000 National Guardsmen were left, and they, along with the naval troops, veterans, military pensioners (mainly officers and noncommissioned officers) who reenlisted voluntarily, and finally the troops in the depots and fortresses, made up the forces in the interior of the country.

6. Allied Deployment in April

Bonaparte considered if, with the troops at his disposal on April 1, he could and should have attacked the Allies in Belgium and on the Rhine. The three reasons he gave up this idea were:

1. He only had 35,000 men available in the north, and to force his way into Belgium, he would also have had to remove the troops from all the fortifications in the northern provinces. However, morale there was poor, so he could not leave them without a garrison.
2. He did not want to appear to be the aggressor.
3. The Bourbons were fermenting resistance among the people in the south and west. It seemed above all essential to first force these princes to leave French soil and nip the domestic conflict in the bud.

Although in Bonaparte's situation, the second reason appeared to be nothing but an illusion, a sort of presumption of the nature of the legal position, the other two were indeed decisive.

Even if such an untimely attack, about which much has been said, would have been a major error when seen from the point of view of the Allies, there was even less of a chance it might have succeeded.

By April 1, the Anglo-Hanoverians under the Prince of Orange were 20,000 men strong,[21] and the Prussians under General Kleist [numbered] 50,000 men.[22] Early in April, Wellington arrived from Vienna,[23] so Bonaparte had to take this possibility into consideration. Even 35,000 men under Bonaparte could have caused some problems for the 70,000 men under Wellington and Kleist, but there are no grounds whatsoever to believe he could have won the necessary victory, or even to have forced them to disperse, which would have been the least likely outcome. If all Napoleon would have achieved against these two commanders would have been to force them to evacuate part of the Netherlands, then this would not have in any way been decisive. Even if he had gained the support of the Belgians,[24] and had this really been as certain as Bonaparte believed, it would have done little to alter the balance of the overall situation.

In strategy, nothing is more important than to avoid wasting the forces that one intends to use to make an attack by striking against thin air. Even if an attack on Wellington and Kleist had really been successful, it would to an extent have to be seen as a wasteful move.

---

21. The Prince of Orange (1792–1849), future King Willem II of the Netherlands, was in command of the Anglo-Allied forces in the Netherlands until Wellington's arrival, when he was appointed commander of the I Corps. A much maligned figure, he in fact had a better grasp of the strategic situation at the outbreak of hostilities than Wellington, the source of several negative comments about the prince.

22. Gen. Friedrich Heinrich Ferdinand Emil Count Kleist von Nollendorf (1775–1823) was in charge of the Prussian forces in the Netherlands until Blücher replaced him. A political decision, Kleist was sidelined to the command of German forces allocated to besieging the fortresses in northern France.

23. Wellington was one of Britain's negotiators at the Congress of Vienna. One of Britain's goals there was to restrict Prussia's territorial claims, which almost caused a military conflict between the Allied powers.

24. In 1815 what is now Belgium was then part of Kingdom of the Netherlands. It became an independent state in the 1830s.

Indeed, if we only consider the ratio of forces of 35,000 to 70,000, there was no reason this would give Bonaparte a better chance of victory later on. Yet the issue is not merely the probability of victory, but its importance. It is obvious that a victory over a tenth of the enemy's forces cannot be as decisive as one over a third of them. Even after defeating this third (taking the Battle of Waterloo as having been won), it was nevertheless likely that Bonaparte would lose, so it is not obvious that such an insignificant success as might have been obtained against Wellington and Kleist would have produced important results.

Bonaparte was right to reject the idea of an immediate preemptive strike against the Allies. Instead, he waited for sufficient forces to be concentrated to make their defeat worthwhile.

7. Defense

Bonaparte also asked the question if he should have remained on the defensive or, by attacking part of the Allied forces before they had completed their concentration, obtained a more favorable position, from which, later on, he could wear them down.

However confident he may have been about the manufacture of arms, he foresaw that before sufficient quantities could be made available, a greatly superior force would have moved against him. He believed 600,000 men would move to oppose him, but in fact between 600,000 and 700,000 came. If we compare this to the 200,000 men he had in the field and add to them the 50,000 defending the fortresses with which the enemy came into contact, then this was a numerical superiority that even a Bonaparte had to fear.

In such circumstances, the first consideration had to be of defense, and indeed, of a defense in which he withdrew into the interior of the country, on one side toward Paris, on the other toward Lyon, as such, a defense raised to the highest level, involving a large part of the French theater of operations and a number of fortresses, specifically Paris with 116,000 men, and Lyon with 25,000.

The most important advantages of this form of defense would have been:

1. To gain time: the main battles would follow perhaps four, six, or eight weeks later, as one can never be sure how much time an irresolute army command might lose.
2. To weaken the enemy forces using the theater of operations, in which many fortresses would have to be masked, with many roads secured by garrisons.
3. The increasing participation of the French civilian population that could have become a real war of insurrection.

Bonaparte himself gives these three factors as the most favorable arguments supporting the defensive. They were the essential advantages of a national strategic defense, and their effectiveness would increase the farther he withdrew into the interior of the country. Furthermore, these reasons would have been so overpowering that there could be no question of any other type of resistance, but this depended on the unmentioned assumption being correct.

This was based on the assumption of a loyal, devoted, united, and eager country. This was inconceivable, however, for although the Bonapartist party had become much stronger in 1815, it was nevertheless just one party, opposed by the royalists and the republicans. Even if the republicans were more likely to favor the Bonapartists than to oppose them, they were still two distinct groups.

This would reduce the total support of the nation to regular and irregular cooperation, for in those parts of the country the Allies had occupied, a political party would have existed that would have provided a counterweight to resistance. At the same time, the defender, instead of being on his home territory, at the center of his strength and security, would have found himself in an uncertain position, as if half at home and half in a foreign land.

One factor that must be given special consideration, however, is the capital city. Every capital city has great strategic significance, but some more than others. This is more where all the elements of a capital city are strongly linked and most of all where there is a bundle of political factions. This was the case with Paris and that is why Bonaparte had to hold the city at any price, so his entire strategy depended on holding it. Indeed, Bonaparte had thought of fortifying and defending Paris, but this huge undertaking was actually totally illusory if he could not rely on the full cooperation of the inhabitants. His plan to disarm the Parisian National Guard and create another force composed of the lower classes in its place indicates he could not do so. As he lacked the courage to carry out this plan, this indicates how much he feared that part of the Parisian population did not fully support him. The opposition that Bonaparte encountered in the Chambers is an indication of how insecure his position was even in France. As long as he expected nothing more than the indirect exertion increasing the armament of the army would cause and as long as he conducted the war on foreign soil or on the frontiers of France with a greater or lesser degree of success, his insecure position would suffice and the force of his intellect and luck could prevail. However, as soon as substantial, direct, universal effort would have become necessary, as is the nature of a defensive war carried out in the interior of a country, then Bonaparte's doubtful position in France would no longer have been strong enough. The instrument would have shattered when it was used.

Bonaparte was well aware of this. He did not expressly say so in his *Mémoires,* as he wanted to present himself as the idol of the French people. Nevertheless, he was forced to mention the resistance in the western provinces, as well as the atmosphere of doubt in the north.

In such a situation, Bonaparte must have considered the role of a defender, an Alexander of Russia, to be unsuitable for him, preferring that of an Alexander of Macedonia, and that is why at the head of a chosen army, he preferred to trust his fate to a momentary inspiration of his talents, to a great risk and to his lucky star, rather than counting on the effect of largely drastic circumstances of which he could not be certain.

Such considerations are more important here than any mere preference for the offensive. Preference for the offensive can guide commanders in smaller, less decisive matters, but not determine the entire existence of comprehensive relationships. Nor do they deserve consideration, when the basis of a much higher, more comprehensive order is under discussion. Certainly there was no commander, who for his own and his army's sake, gave such a decisive preference to the offensive as Frederick the Great.[25] Nevertheless, he set up camp at Bunzelwitz in 1761, when the situation forced him to pin his hopes on biding his time.[26]

8. Preemptive Attack on Wellington and Blücher

There was already an Allied force to fight in the Netherlands and on the Lower Rhine before the Russians arrived and the large army on the Upper Rhine was formed. It was substantial enough for a decisive victory over it to improve the general situation, but not so large that Bonaparte did not believe he could not be successful. He wanted to open hostilities by moving against this force before the other armies reached his frontiers. He chose the last possible moment, when Schwarzenberg's force was more or less ready, and the Russians were only about fourteen days' marching away. He probably delayed the attack for so long, as most of his forces had only moved up in the last few days. Otherwise, it would have been much more advantageous to begin a little earlier, so he could have had enough time to completely destroy the forces on the Lower Rhine before the other Allied armies began to become involved.

The main idea behind Bonaparte's strategy was to separate the Allied armies in Belgium and on the Meuse with an offensive move. This was because they were the first to concentrate and be available to fight, the closest and easiest to reach, and were led by the most enterprising commanders, making them the ones to fear the most. This is why, as mentioned above, he concentrated a disproportionate number of his troops against them. This was certainly the best thing he could do; indeed, it was the only way to stabilize his position given it was both infinitely difficult and highly precarious. If he could have achieved a brilliant victory over Blücher and Wellington, the commanders in whom the Allied princes had

---

25. Frederick the Great of Prussia (1712–86) transformed his kingdom into a great power after a series of wars.

26. Frederick established a fortified camp at Bunzelwitz in Silesia (now Bolesławice in Poland), where he held off a force of Austrians and Russians under the Austrian commander Ernst Gideon von Laudon in 1761 during the Seven Years' War (1756–63).

mainly placed their trust, destroy their armies, and so deliver a blow that inspired France, dismayed the allies, and astounded Europe, then he could have hoped to gain time, climb a couple of steps up the ladder of power, and become a better match for his opponents. It would have been impossible for him to save himself from a second downfall if he did not achieve this victory or if it did not deter the Allies from immediately invading France.

9. The Allied Armed Forces

In the first half of June, the forces the Allies set in motion against Bonaparte were of the following strengths and disposition:

1. The Army in the Netherlands
   Wellington in Belgium 100,000 men, consisting of troops from Britain, Hanover, the Netherlands, Brunswick, and Nassau
   Blücher on the Meuse 115,000 men
   German Federal troops on the Moselle 20,000 men
   Subtotal 235,000 men
2. The Russian army marching toward the Middle Rhine 140,000 men
3. The Austrian army with South German Federal troops on the Upper Rhine 230,000 men
4. The Austrians and Sardinians in Italy 60,000
   Total 665,000 men

Opposing this force, the French had around:

In the standing army, 180,000 men
In the National Guard, 15,000 men
Total in the field 195,000 men

Added to this were the 80,000 fortress troops that came into action during the campaign. So the French are supposed to have held their own against or rather defeat 665,000 men with 275,000 men. Moreover, 100,000 Prussians were also marching to the front, including the Guard, V and VI Corps, and several regiments belonging to the other four corps.[27] Furthermore, Neapolitan and Danish troops, as well as the new corps continuously being raised in Germany, such as the Prussian VII Corps in Westphalia, would also have to be taken into account. To master such overwhelming forces would take half a miracle and what Bonaparte says in his *Mémoires* about possibilities similar to the campaign of 1814 to show this is pure sophistry. The successes he achieved against the Allies in February 1814 were neither tactical victories against an enemy two or three times his size, because he defeated the corps individually, either outnumbering them or having a sufficiently strong force in battle, nor did he achieve a largely strategic success against the entire enemy forces, for the campaign ended in his downfall. They were victories resulting from well-planned strategic coordination and great energy, and even with these outstanding results, he was unable to turn the whole campaign to his advantage, which showed how overwhelming the difficulties of a certain disproportion of forces can be.

That is not by any means a wish to claim that a favorable outcome was impossible for Bonaparte, but only to say that in wars between civilized societies, where the armed forces and methods they use are no longer so different, numbers are above all more decisive than one might otherwise concede and that, in all theoretical and historical probability, they determine the outcome of the war in advance.

10. Order of Battle and Disposition of Forces on Both Sides

At the beginning of June, the main French army was organized and deployed as follows:

---

27. At the outbreak of hostilities, the Prussian Army of the Lower Rhine was short of several batteries of artillery, which arrived only after the army had entered France. The Guard and the V and VI Corps were deployed in Germany and kept an eye on the Austrians, for they were opposed to Prussian expansion plans. The Guard, or rather Guard and Grenadier Corps, was actually designated VII Corps. The VII Corps to which Clausewitz refers is likely to have been the Rhineland Landwehr, which was in the process of mobilization.

DISPOSITION OF FORCES ON BOTH SIDES 49

I Corps d'Erlon at Lille 22,000 men[28]
II Corps Reille at Valenciennes 24,000 men[29]
III Corps Vandamme at Mézières 17,000 men[30]
IV Corps Gérard at Thionville 16,000 men[31]
VI Corps Lobau at Laon 14,000 men[32]
Guard Mortier in Paris 21,000 men[33]

28. Jean-Baptiste Drouet, Count d'Erlon (1765–1844), marshal of France. He joined the army as a volunteer in 1782 but only started to rise rapidly through the ranks during the Revolutionary Wars. D'Erlon fought at Hohenlinden (1800) and Austerlitz (1805) before being transferred to the Iberian Peninsula. After Waterloo he spent some years in exile in Germany after being sentenced to death in France. Charles X gave him an amnesty in 1825, and d'Erlon returned to active service, including a period in North Africa.

29. Honoré-Charles-Michel-Joseph Count Reille (1775–1860), marshal of France. Reille volunteered for the army at the beginning of the Revolutionary Wars, fought in many of its battles, and rose through the ranks, becoming a brigade general in 1803 and a division commander three years later. He fought at Wagram in 1809 before being transferred to the Iberian Peninsula, where he remained until the first abdication. Reille was not appointed marshal, however, until 1847.

30. Dominique-Joseph-René Vandamme, Count d'Unsebourg (1770–1830), marshal of France. Vandamme's military career began as a colonial soldier before the outbreak of the French Revolution. He returned to France, where he fought in the Revolutionary Wars; then at Austerlitz in 1805, in Silesia in 1806, and at Wagram in 1809; before marching to Russia in 1812. In August 1813 his command, the I Corps in Saxony, was surrounded and annihilated at Kulm, where Vandamme was captured.

31. Maurice-Étienne, Count Gérard (1773–1852), marshal of France. Son of a royal hussar, he volunteered for the army in 1791 and rose through the ranks during the Revolutionary Wars. Gérard was wounded at Austerlitz, promoted to brigade general after the Jena campaign, and commanded the Saxon cavalry at Wagram in 1809 before being transferred to Spain. Promoted to division general after fighting at Borodino in 1812, he served in the German campaigns of 1813 and in France in 1814. After Waterloo he went into politics and was made a marshal in 1830.

32. Georges Mouton, Count of Lobau (1770–1838), marshal of France. He fought during the Revolutionary Wars in France, along the Rhine, and in Italy. As a brigade general, Lobau saw action at Austerlitz, Jena, and Eylau in 1807 before being badly wounded at Friedland. After serving briefly in Spain, he fought in Austria in 1809, in Russia in 1812, and in Germany in 1813, when he was taken prisoner. After Waterloo he went into politics and was made a marshal in 1831.

33. Adolphe-Edouard-Casimir-Joseph Mortier, Duke of Treviso (1768–1835), marshal of France. The French Revolution interrupted Mortier's planned career as a businessman, sucking him into the army. He fought in the campaigns in the Netherlands and Rhineland. After accepting the surrender of the Hanoverian

4 corps of reserve cavalry 15,000 men
Total 129,000 men

The Allied armies facing the main French army were organized and deployed as follows:

Wellington
    II Corps, on the right wing (from Oudenarde to Ath, with one of Colville's brigades under General Johnstone in Nieuwpoort),[34] under General Hill:[35]
    Clinton's British Division 6,800 men[36]
    Colville's British Division 6,700 men[37]
    Prince Frederick of the Netherlands:[38]

---

army, he was made one of the first "Marshals of the Empire" in 1804. Mortier commanded the left wing of the army at Friedland in 1807 and spent the new few years on the Iberian Peninsula before commanding the Young Guard in Russia in 1812 and in Germany in 1813. He fought many engagements during the campaigns of 1813 and 1814 but fell ill days before the outbreak of hostilities in 1815.

34. Maj. Gen. George Johnstone. His military career began in the Royal Marines in North America in 1776. Johnstone spent the final years of the eighteenth century serving in Australia. He died in 1825.

35. Gen. Rowland Hill (1772–1842). Appointed ensign in the 38th Foot in 1790, he held various commands in the Mediterranean during the Revolutionary Wars before taking part in the Hanover expedition of 1805, returning to Britain after Austerlitz. Hill was then posted to the Iberian Peninsula, fighting under Wellington for several years. He was raised to the peerage after the first abdication. After Waterloo he was second in command of the army of occupation of France until 1818. Hill was appointed commander in chief of the army during Wellington's administration, a post he held for fourteen years.

36. Lt. Gen. Sir Henry Clinton (1771–1829). Appointed ensign in the 11th Foot in 1787, Clinton first served as a volunteer in the Brunswick Corps, acting with the Prussian army in the Netherlands that year. He was aide de camp to the Duke of York in the Netherlands during the Revolutionary Wars. Later Clinton saw service in India, was an observer with the Russians at Austerlitz, and accompanied Sir John Moore on the Iberian Peninsula. He then fought in Iberia again under Wellington.

37. Lt. Gen. Sir Charles Colville (1770–1843). He entered the army as an ensign in the 28th Foot in 1781, served in the West Indies from 1791 to 1797, in Ireland in 1798, and in Egypt from 1800 to 1801. He later fought on the Iberian Peninsula. After Waterloo Colville spent some years as a colonial governor.

38. Willem Frederik Karel, Prince of Orange-Nassau (1797–1881), second son of King William I of the Netherlands. Born in exile in Berlin, he grew up in the Prussian court and first saw action at age sixteen at the Battle of Leipzig in 1813.

DISPOSITION OF FORCES ON BOTH SIDES 51

Anthing's Netherlands Brigade 3,700 men[39]
Stedman's Netherlands Division 6,600 men[40]
II Corps total 23,800 men
I Corps, on the left wing from Ath to Nivelles under the Prince of Orange:
Cooke's British Division 4,100 men[41]
Alten's British Division 6,700 men[42]
Perponcher's Second Netherlands Division 8,000 men[43]
Chassé's First Netherlands Division 6,900 men[44]

The prince renounced his claim for the Grand Duchy of Luxembourg in 1816 and later held senior posts in the army, which he endeavored to modernize.

39. Lt. Gen. Carl Heinrich Wilhelm Anthing (1766–1823). Born in the German principality of Saxe-Gotha, Anthing entered Saxon service as a cadet and ensign in 1783. He fought in the Dutch army during the Revolutionary Wars but entered Prussian service in 1809. After the first abdication, he was made a lieutenant general in the French army but rejoined the Netherlands service in 1814. After Waterloo Anthing spent several years in the Dutch East Indies.

40. Lt. Gen. Jena-André Stedman (1778–1833). He joined a Dutch cavalry regiment in 1793 and fought against the French during the Revolutionary Wars, then transferred to the Batavian army once France conquered the Netherlands. Stedman received a staff post in the Dutch army in 1806, and when it was absorbed by the French in 1810, he served as a brigade general. He was taken prisoner at the capitulation of Dresden on November 11, 1813, and on his release joined the Netherlands service.

41. Maj. Gen. Sir George Cooke (1768–1837). Appointed ensign in the Foot Guards in 1784, Cooke saw action as a captain in 1794 in the Netherlands, where he fought again in 1799. He also took part in the ill-fated expedition to the Scheldt in 1809.

42. Maj. Gen. Sir Charles Count von Alten, G.C.B. (1764–1840). In 1781 he joined the Hanoverian army as a cadet, served as a captain in the campaigns of 1793–95, and was one of the first to join what later became the King's German Legion. His command of the British Light Division during the Peninsular War became legendary. After Waterloo Alten played a leading role in the reorganization of the Hanoverian army.

43. Lt. Gen. Hendrik George de Perponcher-Sedlnitsky (1771–1856). He joined the Dutch army in 1788 as an ensign in a regiment of dragoons and later became an aide de camp to Prince Willem George Frederik of Orange-Nassau (d. 1799), serving in both the Dutch and Austrian armies. In 1800 he entered British service and for a time commanded the Lusitanian Legion in Portugal. At the end of 1813, he became an aide to the Prince of Orange. In 1814 Perponcher joined the Netherlands army as a major general and was promoted to lieutenant general in April 1815.

44. Lt. Gen. David Hendrik Chassé (1765–1849). He joined the Dutch army as a cadet at the tender age of ten; his republican sympathies and opposition to

Collaert's Netherlands Cavalry Division 3,700 men[45]
I Corps total 34,400 men
Reserve in and around Brussels under Wellington's direct command:
Picton's British Division 7,000 men[46]
Lambert's British Brigade,[47] plus a Hanoverian Landwehr brigade 4,800 men[48]
General Decken's Hanoverian Landwehr Division (garrisoning Ostend, Ypres, Antwerp, and Mechelen) 9,300 men[49]

---

the Orange faction led him to enter French service in 1788. Chassé fought with the revolutionary army in the Netherlands from 1792 to 1795, then joined the forces of the Batavian Republic, which later became the army of the Kingdom of Holland, ruled by Louis Bonaparte. When Holland was incorporated into the French Empire in 1810, he became a brigade general in French service, in which he remained until the first abdication. He then joined the army of the newly founded Kingdom of the Netherlands. Chassé last saw action in 1832, fighting Belgian forces.

45. Jean-Marie-Antoine-Philippe, Baron de Collaert (1761–1816). Beginning his military career in 1778 in Austrian service, he transferred to the Dutch army in 1785, remaining there until 1811 while rising to the rank of major general. When Holland was incorporated by the French Empire, Collaert served in the French army as a brigade general, fighting in the German campaigns of 1813. He rejoined the Netherlands army in 1815, being promoted to lieutenant general.

46. Lt. Gen. Sir Thomas Picton (1758–1815). Picton joined the 12th Foot as an ensign in 1771 and was promoted to lieutenant in 1777. The following year he participated in the siege of Gibraltar. After the army reduction of 1783, he spent twelve years on half-pay. At the end of 1794, he was appointed to the 17th Foot in the West Indies, working his way up the ranks in various campaigns in the region. Returning to Britain in 1803, Picton next saw action during the expedition to Flushing in 1809. The next year he was transferred to the Iberian Peninsula, where he fought under Wellington for several years. Picton was mortally wounded during the Battle of Waterloo.

47. Maj. Gen. Sir John Lambert (1772–1847). He was commissioned as an ensign in the 1st Foot Guards in 1791 and first saw action two years later in the Netherlands as a lieutenant. After fighting in Ireland in 1798 and Holland in 1799, Lambert next saw action on the Iberian Peninsula. He fought at New Orleans on January 6, 1815, before returning to Europe in time for Waterloo. He held a command in the army of occupation after the end of the campaign.

48. The Fourth Hanoverian Landwehr Brigade was commanded by Col. Carl Best (1765–1836), a Peninsula veteran.

49. Lt. Gen. Friedrich von der Decken (1769–1840). Decken joined the Hanoverian army as a cadet in 1784. In 1803 he was one of the founders of what became the King's German Legion, originally formed from Hanoverian exiles

Duke of Brunswick's corps (in Brussels) 6,800 men[50]
Nassau troops (in Brussels) 2,900 men[51]
Cavalry Reserve under Lord Uxbridge (deployed from Gent via Ninove to Mons) 9,800 men[52]
Reserves total 40,700 men
Total of Wellington's Army 99,000 men
2. The Prussian Army under Blücher
I Corps General Ziethen at Charleroi 27,000 men[53]
II Corps General Pirch I at Namur 29,000 men[54]

---

after the French partitioned their homeland. As such, he saw action during the Peninsular War. After Waterloo, Decken was commander in chief of the Hanoverian artillery and engineers.

50. The Brunswick Corps was recruited from the territories of this North German state. Exhausted after a generation of warfare, the command had to recruit mere youths to refill its ranks. The corps commander, Duke Friedrich Wilhelm von Braunschweig-Lüneburg-Oels (1771–1815), first served in the Prussian army, before Brunswick was added to the Kingdom of Westphalia in 1807. In 1809 he fled to Britain after leading an abortive uprising in his homeland. The corps was largely wiped out in the battles of the Peninsula War. The duke was mortally wounded at Quatre Bras on June 16, 1815.

51. The Nassau contingent was commanded by Major General von Kruse. The troops in Brussels were the three battalions of the 1st Nassau Regiment under Colonel von Steuben.

52. Field Marshal Henry William Paget, 2nd Earl of Uxbridge, later marquess of Anglesey (1768–1854). At the outbreak of the French Revolutionary wars, Lord Paget (as he was then styled) raised a regiment of Staffordshire volunteers and was given the temporary rank of lieutenant colonel in 1793. As the 80th Foot, the unit took part in the Flanders campaign of 1794 under Paget's command. By 1801 he had become colonel of the 7th Light Dragoons. Now going by Uxbridge, he commanded the cavalry in 1815, skillfully covering the withdrawal from Quatre Bras on June 16 but mishandling the great cavalry charge two days later.

53. Lt. Gen. Wieprecht Hans Karl Friedrich Ernst Heinrich, Count von Ziethen (1770–1848). In 1785 Ziethen joined his father's famous regiment of hussars, gaining his first combat experience during the Revolutionary Wars. He fought at Auerstedt in 1806 and was appointed commander of a brigade in 1809. Ziethen fought throughout the campaigns of 1813 and 1814. His corps was severely mauled at Ligny, but it nevertheless played an important role at Waterloo two days later.

54. Maj. Gen. Georg Dubislav Ludwig von Pirch (I) (1763–1838). The Roman numeral after Pirch indicates that he was the senior general with that name; his younger brother, Otto von Pirch (II), though the same rank, commanded a brigade in 1815. The elder brother first saw action during the War of the Bavarian Succession (1778–79) and was part of the force that occupied Holland in 1787.

III Corps General Thielemann at Ciney 24,000 men[55]
IV Corps General Bülow at Liège 35,000 men[56]
Total for Blücher's Army 115,000 men
North German Federal troops[57] under General Hake at Trier 20,000 men[58]
Grand Total 234,000 men

11. Reflections on Wellington's Deployment— Necessary Assumptions

To draw a clear and instructive conclusion from this interconnected set of facts would require far more information than is

---

He was involved in the siege of Mainz in 1793, then fought at Jena in 1806. Pirch I fought throughout the campaigns of 1813–14. He only became commander of the II Army Corps after his predecessor was removed for complaining about the treatment of the rebellious Saxon contingent.

55. Lt. Gen. Johann Adolf Freiherr von Thielemann (1765–1824). His military career began as a cadet in the Saxon army. Thielemann fought against the French in the campaigns of 1806–1807, then with them in 1809 and 1812, commanding a cavalry brigade at Borodino. After the Russian campaign, he was appointed commander of the strategic fortress of Torgau but left Saxon service when he was ordered to hand it over to the French. Thielemann spent the campaigns of 1813–14 in Russian service before joining the Prussian army in March 1815.

56. Infantry Gen. Friedrich Wilhelm, Count Bülow von Dennewitz (1755–1816). He enlisted in the Prussian army in 1768 as a cadet in an infantry regiment and first saw action during the War of the Bavarian Succession. He held a staff post during the Revolutionary Wars before being appointed to command a brigade in 1808. Bülow commanded a corps during the campaigns of 1813–14 and was made a count for his victory at Dennewitz on September 6, 1813.

57. This corps was one of the contingents raised by the lesser German states. It consisted of troops from Hesse-Kassel, the Saxon duchies, Nassau (those not part of Wellington's army), Oldenburg, Lippe, Waldeck, Mecklenburg, and Anhalt. The Prussian general von Kleist replaced Hake as the commander.

58. Lt. Gen. Albrecht Georg Ernst Karl von Hake (1768–1835). A page of Frederick the Great, Hake became an ensign in the Royal Guard in 1785. As a young lieutenant he first saw action against the French in the campaigns of 1792–95, being awarded the Pour le Mérite for his role at Pirmasens. From 1793, he went on to hold staff and administrative posts in the army before seeing action again at Leipzig in 1813. After commanding a brigade in Bülow's corps, Hake was placed in command of the North German troops in France.

available. No historian of this campaign has to date researched the facts relating to the actual strategic conditions of the campaign, that is, a precise description of the essential circumstances prior to the two battles. What is available is just as fragmentary and inadequate as for any campaign of the seventeenth century.

The crucial points were:

First, an authentic and complete order of battle of Wellington's army, from the identity of the units and the relevant chain of command, could be derived.

In the one above, Decken's Hanoverian Landwehr Reserve was for instance included in the main reserves, but all of it stood on the right flank, took no part in the battle, and seemed to have been used for garrisoning towns such as Antwerp, Ostend, and Ypres.[59]

Lyon's Brigade,[60] part of Colville's Division, was in Nieuwpoort, also did not reach the battlefield, and also was apparently a garrisoning force.

I Corps, under the Prince of Orange, which was supposed to be on the right wing, was deployed partially on the left. Divisional organizations, for instance those of Perponcher and Chassé, were also the other way around. It is not certain what role Collaert's Netherlands Cavalry Division was given before June 18. In short, what is known about this army's order of battle is so riddled with confusion that whatever basis for strategic analysis [that] can be taken from just the order of battle, or that refer back to it—many indeed—are either missing or confusing here.[61]

Second, the defensive provisions and intentions of the Duke of Wellington.

Whatever plans Blücher and Wellington had made to invade France were irrelevant, as Bonaparte's attack preempted them.

---

59. Clausewitz's assumption here is correct. Decken's troops were used to garrison various places.

60. Maj. Gen. Sir James Lyon, KCB (d. 1844). Lyon served as an officer of marines under Lord Howe on the Glorious First, the naval victory of June 1, 1794. He was with the Reserve at Hal on June 18 and so did not see action at Waterloo.

61. Later research has clarified this issue, and a full order of battle of Wellington's army has subsequently been published.

But until they moved over to the offensive, the forces that assembled for an offensive were on the defensive, and there had to have been a plan for this situation. Yet nothing is known about such a plan for the Anglo-Allied army.[62]

Equally, there remains doubt about this for the Prussian army. Two corps took up positions in the Meuse valley, where many troops were billeted in Liège, Huy, and Namur. Another corps was on the Sambre near Charleroi, and the final one on the right bank of the Meuse near Ciney, pushed out like a pair of antennae. The headquarters were in Namur, the midpoint, thirteen to eighteen [German] miles from the forward corps, linked to Brussels by the paved highway.[63] The army was spread out eight [German] miles in breadth and eight in depth and required two days to concentrate at its center. Once concentrated, it could either have accepted battle, if it believed it was strong enough, or avoided such through movement in any direction, for there was nothing in the area that tied it down or limited its freedom of action.

This does not appear to have been the case with Wellington's army. Its deployment from Mons to the sea covered more than twenty [German] miles, and its depth from Tournai to Antwerp was about fifteen. The headquarters in Brussels was about ten [German] miles from the front line of bivouacs. An army so deployed required at least four to five days to concentrate at its center. The line of French fortifications was much too close for there to be any certainty of having four or five days for concentration, with the great city of Lille, for instance, being only a day's march from Tournai.

But was it really Wellington's intention to concentrate his army at one point? In such an event, would merely concentrating it suffice, or would this have to occur at one or another selected place to cover a particular point or for combined operations with Blücher?

And if it was not or could not be Wellington's intention to concentrate his army at a single point, was it rather for a defense in

---

62. Certainly there seems to have been no clear agreement on what action to take until the meeting at Tirlemont on May 3, 1815 (see below).

63. A German mile consisted of 7.5 kilometers, or 4.7 miles.

a more or less separate deployment of his forces? The question must therefore be asked what would the purpose of the separate positions be and how would this relate to the whole?

There is no record of this. It is likely Wellington considered Brussels particularly important, but even accepting that, and considering it to a degree to be the only place to be covered, then much still depended on how important it was considered.

Third, the base of Wellington's army, particularly its final point of retreat, or, alternatively, the degree of freedom it had in choosing this point, was a highly important consideration for its options.

Finally, what effective fortresses were available, that is, places that could be left to hold out for a length of time? The information available mentioned places where work was underway, but not of how far the work—still less arming—had progressed.

Wellington was no doubt aware of all this, but nothing is known about how far, and so it is not possible to judge if his understanding of the situation was entirely appropriate. Taking matters as they appeared superficially and without specific information, it would seem likely that Wellington believed that if Bonaparte were to take the offensive, he would advance in several columns on a wide front against him and Blücher, so Wellington would need to take appropriate measures to ensure Bonaparte would encounter the appropriate resistance everywhere while keeping a significant reserve to hand to rush to the point where the main enemy army might be found, yet still be in a position to defeat it in a battle before it reached Brussels. If the main French force were to push forward from its left, that is, from around Lille, then the Reserve in Brussels, if they joined with Hill between the Scheldt and Brussels, roughly on the Dender near Ath, would be able to fight a battle with half, or even three-quarters, of the army if time and circumstances allowed the Allied left to be drawn in as well. If the main enemy force were to advance in the center, that is, from around Maubeuge or Valenciennes, then the Reserve would unite with the Prince of Orange's corps and, circumstances permitting, part of Hill's, to offer battle on the road from Mons to Brussels. If the main enemy force were to advance from the right, toward Charleroi or Namur, then the Reserve and perhaps part of the left wing could rush to the aid of the Prussians. Clearly, only a couple of days would be required in all these eventualities, for it would only be a matter of uniting Hill's corps with that of the Prince of Orange. Linking up with the Reserve could then be achieved by withdrawing a day's march toward Brussels. Wellington's preparations appear to have been sufficient, for it was probable he would have a couple of days to accomplish this.

This was likely to have been agreed in the discussion Wellington had with Blücher at Tirlemont[64] at the beginning of May and, with regard to Blücher's selected position at Sombreffe,[65] promised to concentrate his army at Quatre Bras[66] and come to Blücher's aid should the main enemy force move against him. In this case, the expression "army" meant the greater part of it that Wellington himself may have considered his main force: the Reserve combined with the corps on the left wing. It was simply impossible for Wellington to concentrate his whole army on its far left flank at Nivelles or Quatre Bras in two days, as it was spread out over twenty [German] miles. At most, only the 6,000-strong division of Hill's corps on the left, Clinton's, based at Ath and Leuze, could get there. As Wellington's troops were deployed over such a large area, then this is the only conclusion that can be drawn and that justified him leaving Prince Frederick of Orange behind at Hal, as this was the point at which the roads from Brussels to Lille and Valenciennes diverged. These 19,000 men could certainly still have joined the battle on June 18, and there can be no other explanation of why they were left there, other than to cover Brussels from this side.

---

64. The records of this important meeting at Tirlemont—the first discussion on strategy held by the two Allied commanders—are sparse. Wellington's comments were published in 1838 in volume 12 of his *Despatches*. Here he indicates that Blücher had promised to support him if Napoleon attacked him first. It seems reasonable to assume that Wellington made a similar promise to Blücher.

65. The Sombreffe position is where the Battle of Ligny was fought on June 16, 1815.

66. Quatre Bras was an important crossroads on the Brussels to Charleroi highway. The road crossing it ran toward Nivelles to the west and Namur to the southeast. Possession of this intersection was vital to ensure that communications between Wellington and Blücher were not interrupted.

12. Critique

Taking these conjectures as historical facts and subjecting them to criticism, it is apparent that Bonaparte's method of operation and the circumstances of the moment have not been properly understood. The entire necessity of an advance in several columns on a broad front originated from other times, other commanders, and other circumstances. Bonaparte was the first to risk everything on a single great battle. This use of the word "risk" does not imply that more would be risked than if the forces and actions were divided, for there can be situations in which dividing them might have been a thousand times more hazardous than risking them in a single battle. Rather, it is a gamble because, forgetting all rational calculation, the human mind is reluctant to concentrate a decision of enormous consequence in a single moment, as a battle requires. It is as if the mind felt restricted by such a limited amount of time. A vague feeling arises that if only given time, additional strength from within would be found, all of which, if it is not based on objective facts but instead only on feelings, is just natural human weakness. Strong personalities will easily master this weakness, and in this regard, Bonaparte was one of the strongest, and so he first gambled the entire outcome on a single great battle. Furthermore, he always preferred making such decisions whenever circumstances favored it. A decisive battle can only be the aim:

1) If we know our opponent desires it and we cannot avoid it; or
2) insofar as we initiate it and then only if we have the strength to carry it out. Only if use can be made of its entire effects, should it be sought, as a great victory and great danger stand side by side.

Great danger was the case in all of Bonaparte's offensive wars, while a great victory was the case here.

If Bonaparte did not hesitate to always seek a fully effective decision in the past, when he was fighting wars mainly to satisfy his desire for glory and power, then surely nothing else could be expected here, when a modest success was of no use whatsoever and only an absolute and completely unprecedented triumph offered him a better future.

The most compelling assumption was therefore that Bonaparte would move with all his strength against a single point.

Wellington himself had never fought against Bonaparte, and this perhaps may be the reason why this assumption did not impress itself as forcibly on him as it would have on someone who had already been struck by the lightning bolt of Bonaparte's great battles.

Had Wellington made this assumption, however, he would have made entirely different arrangements for quartering his troops. As it was, whatever battlefield might be chosen anywhere in Belgium, it would in every case have been impossible for him to arrive there with a unified force and in cooperation with Blücher. Whatever assumption he came to, it could never have been his intention to leave a substantial part of his forces out of the action.

13. Disposition and Concentration of the Prussian Army

It is difficult to be certain of Wellington's intentions for his army in general and his right wing in particular, as his original report on the battle did not offer the slightest hint about them,[67] and also as no other writer has examined them thoroughly, so it would be better to instead concentrate on the results of the real facts, that is, in the event of the enemy attacking Blücher, Wellington intended to come to his aid with his Reserve and his left wing and perhaps also part of the right wing. For both this purpose and for the concentration of Blücher's army, certain observations are necessary.

As mentioned earlier, the Prussian army was deployed over an area of eight [German] miles and could be concentrated at

---

67. Here Clausewitz is referring to Wellington's "Waterloo Despatch," written on June 19, the day after the battle. It was the only statement the duke made on the affair that was published in his lifetime.

Namur in two days. This, of course, was excluding the North German Federal troops at Trier. They were indeed under Blücher's command, but they were ordered to stay on the Moselle. If this mission was no better thought through than the deployment of Wellington's right wing, it nevertheless made no difference to Blücher, for this force was not part of his army. As far as the army itself was concerned, there was, as mentioned above, no other thought than to concentrate against any enemy advance and then to move this united force against him wherever the situation demanded. Against a commander like Bonaparte and in the circumstances given, that was absolutely the correct basis for all further decisions.

14. Objective of the French Attack

So that it is clear what mission the Prussian army would have once it had concentrated, we must consider what the objective of the enemy's strategic attack could be. As mentioned previously, the aim of Bonaparte's attack could be nothing other than a brilliant victory over both of the Allied armies. If he inflicted a defeat on one or both of them, forcing Blücher to fall back over the Rhine and Wellington back to Zeeland, his trophies would have included hundreds of captured cannons and thousands of prisoners. If he had broken the morale of both armies, shaken the courage of their commanders, and weakened their spirit of enterprise, then with part of his victorious army, even only 50,000 men, he could have rushed to the Upper Rhine and joined Rapp, making a main army of 80,000 men, which, with reinforcements from the interior, could have been brought up to 100,000 men in just a few weeks. A devastating blow on the Lower Rhine would inevitably have caused delays and indecision on the Upper Rhine, while Napoleon's arrival would have turned the hesitation into fear for one's own safety. Furthermore, every Allied corps still on the left bank of the Rhine as a consequence would have immediately withdrawn rapidly, or else risked being defeated.

If the resulting ratio of forces was not now a rational basis for beginning an invasion of France, at least until the Russians arrived and Blücher and Wellington had to an extent recovered, then considering the effect this would have, it was most improbable that they would have recovered from the moral effect of the victory so quickly. Shaken by the effect of such a victory and with their judgment now impaired, facing the possibility of the armament of the nation and believing that numerous armies could be created out of thin air, the two most outstanding commanders, Wellington and Blücher, would not be at the scene, and indeed the latter over one hundred [German] miles from Allied headquarters, it might have taken an intolerable amount of time before the Allies would have been able to recommence their advance.

And how the power of such a victory would have electrified France! For the most part the vain, self-satisfied French would have abandoned both royalism and republicanism in the intoxication of victory, while the Vendeans would have laid down their arms, making Bonaparte's position in the interior of France totally different.

This is not to suggest, however, as is often done, that after such a victory, Bonaparte's position would have become as favorable, strong, and unassailable as it had once been precarious. These sorts of contrasts are mostly contrary to the nature of the matter and are an unworthy means of historical discussion. It is more likely that even after the most brilliant victory, Bonaparte's task would have remained insolubly difficult and that such a victory would only have given him just the possibility of resisting the collective might of the enemy. Even if he imagined the most important direct result of such a victory would be the fall of the British government and peace with that power, then this can only further strengthen the impression of how weak and uncertain he considered his situation, for he needed to hide it with such illusions.

What Bonaparte needed to achieve above all was a brilliant victory over the united Anglo-Netherlands army. If that was the case, however, then his undertaking had only one objective, and that was indeed the Netherlands army and not any sort of geographic object, like Brussels, or the right bank of the Meuse, or even the Rhine, et cetera.

Where a great, all-encompassing decision is at stake, geographic points and the relations of armies to them cannot be operational objectives in themselves, for the immediate advantages they offer are much too insignificant and the remote, long-term influence they could exert on military events requires too much time to be effective. A great event like a battle would sweep away all before it. Bonaparte's actions would only have been directed at such an objective insofar as it offered him a more advantageous prelude to the battle, above all by giving him the opportunity to make the battle greater and more decisive. This was what he really needed. Outflanking the enemy to attack him with reversed fronts and forcing him away from his natural line of retreat is in most cases an infallible means of intensifying the entire military action, but this is not always the case, and particularly not here.

The Prussians examined the necessity of holding the right bank of the Meuse in detail, and Blücher's deployment on both banks of the river arose from this. Wellington too considered it important to cover Brussels. Yet what would have happened if, before fighting the decisive battle, Bonaparte had taken the right bank of the Meuse, or even Brussels. The baggage trains and other elements of the army supply vehicles would have suffered insignificant losses and perhaps some food supplies too. Furthermore, if he had taken the right bank of the Meuse, the Prussian army would have been driven away from its natural line of retreat; in the case of Brussels, the British from theirs. It is apparent, however, that this would not have been a particular problem for these two commanders, as Blücher could have joined forces with Wellington for a short while and withdrawn toward Mechelen and Antwerp, while Wellington could have joined forces with Blücher and moved toward the Meuse. The damage both commanders would have suffered by losing a battle would not have been significantly worse, for their line of retreat was not long, and they did not need to worry about being cut off.

So it was predictable that Bonaparte would not consider important any flanking maneuver that would have cost him the far greater advantage of a rapid, forceful blow, and which, if he were unlucky, would have placed him in great danger. It is credible therefore that the two commanders could have united their forces at a single point and been certain that, wherever that point was, Bonaparte would find it. Their respective forces could not join up earlier due to difficulties in provisioning them. But the choice of the point of union was entirely up to them and in no way dependent on the direction Bonaparte chose.

15. The Point of Union of the Two Allied Armies

The most obvious point for the two Allied armies to link up was on the Brussels–Namur road, where they could join with least delay. Blücher's headquarters considered the area around Sombreffe to be particularly suitable as a battlefield against an enemy approaching from the Sambre. It was 2 1/2 [German] miles from Namur along this highway and only one from the highway running between Brussels and Charleroi. Wellington intended to assemble his left wing here. The Ligny Brook and one of its small tributaries that runs parallel to the highway between Sombreffe and Balâtre cut into the terrain, though not very deeply or steeply but enough to ensure the effective deployment of all arms on the left slope of the valley, which has the advantage of greater height. The deployment was of moderate width (half a [German] mile), so that just one or two corps could hold out for a long time. That left Blücher with two further corps for offensive action, with which he could decide the battle either on his own or together with Wellington.

Of course, this tactical feature was effective only against an enemy advancing from Charleroi. But as this strategic position met the needs of all possibilities, then it also suited this tactical requirement.

Were the two armies to link up here at the right time, either in one position or in two sufficiently close to each other that they could cooperate, then they would have done everything required, leaving the outcome to the result of a battle, from which, with their great superiority of numbers, they had nothing to fear. In whatever direction Bonaparte would march, either toward Brussels or toward anywhere else, he would have to find his opponent himself. Yet, as has already been mentioned, Wellington's considerations appeared not to have included such a concentration of forces and simplification of actions. If the French army showed any sign of movement, his extended deployment made concentration at a single point entirely impossible. Even had it been possible, he did not want to do so. He did not want to abandon Brussels even for a short time, and as the city lacked any protection, he did not consider that even a garrison would secure it from any raiding parties. What is certain is that if Bonaparte had advanced on Brussels via Lille or Valenciennes, Wellington would have rushed to meet him, blocking either the road from Tournai or the road from Mons. So as not to remain idle, Blücher also would have had to march there from Sombreffe, getting to the Tournai road in about thirty-six hours. At around Enghien, or at worst Hal, they would have been able to link up and face the enemy. As Sombreffe was situated on this route, it was a perfectly good choice as a concentration point in this respect as well.

But were the enemy to advance along the right bank of the Meuse, it would have been quite unsuitable for its defense. Blücher would never have thought of concentrating his army in time on the right bank of the Meuse, however, knowing how much less help the British commander could have given him there. Blücher knew better than Wellington how to discount whatever circumstances did not make urgently necessary. On the left bank of the Meuse, he was certain of Wellington's support, and if Bonaparte wanted to attack him, then he would have to cross the Meuse.

16. Calculation of the Time Necessary for the Concentration of the Prussian Army

It was apparent that Wellington was uncertain of where to expect the enemy and to be ready to move against him anywhere with most of his troops. As mentioned, Blücher had resolved to concentrate at Sombreffe on the outbreak of hostilities, where he would have been close enough to Wellington's army to support or be supported by it.

Yet considering the time both armies needed to concentrate and comparing it with what would happen in the worst case, due the extended deployment of their corps, it is impossible to come to a satisfactory conclusion.

Charleroi is the nearest point of concentration to Sombreffe, being only about 3 1/2 [German] miles away. It would take at least sixteen hours for reports of the enemy's advance to go from Charleroi to Namur and from there for the orders to concentrate to reach the quarters at Liège, the farthest away. Taking eight hours more to notify the troops and for them to have marched off, then it would be twenty-four hours before IV Corps could begin its march. The route from Liège to Sombreffe is ten [German] miles, which requires two days forced marching, that is, a total of three days before this corps could arrive. III Corps at Ciney could have arrived there in thirty-six hours, and even II Corps in Namur, twelve hours. General Ziethen's defense of the Sambre and his retreat to the area around Fleurus, if it were to hold up the enemy from morning to evening, could not gain more than one day, with the coming of night gaining the remaining time. Added to that is the probability that the first few cannon shots would not necessarily indicate that the enemy was approaching, but rather the final deployment of his troops before commencing his offensive, supported most probably from incoming reports in the days leading up to it. If such reports were received, then there was enough time available for a concentration. If one was restricted only to line of sight, however, then only II and III Corps would have been able to link up with I Corps at Sombreffe—III Corps at a push and IV Corps not at all. Blücher's headquarters were well aware of this danger, but there were some difficulties in bringing up Bülow's IV Corps. Nevertheless, on June 14, once the first movements of the French army were noticed, his corps was ordered to move to the vicinity of Hannut, only 5 [German] miles from the point of concentration, even before III Corps, 6 1/2 [German] miles from Sombreffe, could get there. As mentioned below, a chance event made it impossible to carry out this concentration immediately, so it did not happen.

Blücher believed that he could concentrate his army at Sombreffe in thirty-six hours. Even given that it was a hundred-to-one chance that the enemy's movement would be detected more than thirty-six hours before he reached the vicinity of the battlefield, it was still very risky to remain so dispersed so close to the enemy's front line. The continuous problems with provisioning caused by the Netherlands authorities prevented Blücher from closing his ranks further, so he waited for more definite news about the enemy's movements. Nevertheless, this does not absolve him of all blame.

17. Calculation of the Time Necessary for the Concentration of Wellington's Army

It is difficult to reach a judgment on the concentration of Wellington's army, for information on its disposition and the precise intentions of the right wing is not available. It is clear, however, that at the point where the least amount of time was available, that is, if the enemy advanced via Charleroi, the effect on the concentration of Wellington's army would be less favorable. Assuming that only Clinton's division, on the left wing of the corps on the right wing, could be moved to the concentration at Quatre Bras, then the divisions at Ath and Leuze would have had to march between eight and ten [German] miles, the same distance the news had to travel to reach Brussels and for orders from Brussels to reach them. Obviously, this division would have reached the battlefield even later than the Prussian IV Corps. But the left-wing corps, whose farthest division was in Le Roeulx, five [German] miles from Quatre Bras, as well as the Reserve in and around Brussels, would need thirty-six hours to reach the battlefield. If they did not, it was the result of circumstances considered in more detail below.

18. Reflections

As long as it was certain that the French had a corps in the vicinity of Lille and another at Metz, there was no danger of the entire enemy force staging a surprise attack. But in early June, these French corps left Lille and Metz, and if exactly what was happening was not known, toward the middle of the month, the Allies did receive a definite report that IV Corps was moving from the Moselle to the Meuse. From this moment on, they could no longer rely on a second report arriving prior to the outbreak of hostilities. Now was the time to concentrate more closely so that all corps would be in a position at least to reach the battlefield within twenty-four hours. There is no need to describe the changes in disposition this would have entailed, but it would have been an important advantage if Wellington's headquarters and corps had closed up on Blücher, say at Nivelles.[68] That alone would have gained at least twelve hours and avoided a number of problems. Yet none of this was done. Only the Prussian IV Corps was ordered to assemble in close quarters at Hannut, and even this order arrived too late, as is discussed below.

One reason for this was that further reports were expected to arrive before the outbreak of hostilities. Another was that Wellington in particular believed that he should concentrate his own forces only in response to moves by the main enemy army, about which nothing definite was known. War had yet to be declared and the departure of the Guard from Paris (which occurred on June 8) was not yet known, so until June 14, everyone was in a reprehensible state of indecision, one in which they had good reason to expect would become critical, one from which they had also decided to extricate themselves, but one in which they would nevertheless be taken by surprise.[69]

19. Bonaparte Concentrates His Army

Bonaparte had decided to begin the campaign on June 15. On June 6, IV Corps left Metz, and a few days later, I Corps left Lille, with the fortresses sending out additional patrols to mask their departure. On June 8, the Guard left Paris; VI Corps, Laon; and II

---

68. It is interested to note that British Waterloo historian Charles Chesney made the same observation on pages 96–98 of *Waterloo Lectures*.

69. It is a commonly held view that Napoleon's offensive on June 15 took the Allied commanders by surprise. Subsequent research has shown this not to be the case, and a detailed examination of this issue can be found in Hofschröer, *1815*, vol. 1, *Wellington, His German Allies, and the Battles of Ligny and Quatre Bras*, esp. chap. 8, "Intelligence and Communications." The reasons for Wellington's delays cannot be explained by "surprise."

Corps, Valenciennes. On June 13, all these units had arrived in the area between Philippeville and Avesnes. Bonaparte, having left Paris June 12, also arrived in Avesnes on the evening of June 13.

From Metz to Philippeville is about twenty-five [German] miles, for which IV Corps needed a week. From Paris to Avesnes is thirty [German] miles, for which the Guard needed only six days, though the direct route was not along a highway. One can never properly judge a march without precise knowledge of specific circumstances, so it is safe to assume here that Bonaparte, whose main object was to achieve surprise, moved his forces as rapidly as possible. On June 14, the French corps closed on each other and took up the following dispositions in three columns:

The right wing at Philippeville: 16,000 men, consisting of IV Corps and some cavalry.
The center at Beaumont: 64,000 men, consisting of V and VI Corps, the Guard, and the greater part of the cavalry.
The left wing at Solre-sur-Sambre: 44,000 men, consisting of I and II Corps.

These positions were four [German] miles from Charleroi.

As departing from Metz and Lille was actually not a provisional consolidation of quarters but rather a proper march to concentrate, then the Allies, if they had had a good intelligence system, might well have received reports of this before June 13, let alone June 14, and not eight or nine days after their departure, which would have put an end to their indecision. Yet this was not the case. They only heard on June 14 that the French forces were moving to concentrate and that Bonaparte was with the army, but it was still uncertain where the concentration would take place. It was Ziethen's report of the night of June 14–15 that made it clear that the enemy opposite him was growing in strength and that he expected an attack the next morning. This was certainly only thirty-six hours before the Battle of Ligny began.[70]

---

70. Clausewitz is wrong here. The Allies certainly did have a good intelligence system and were well aware of the concentration of the Army of the North on the border with the Netherlands and of Napoleon's arrival. A full account of this is

20. Blücher's Concentration at Sombreffe

On receipt of the news that the enemy was in motion and Bonaparte had arrived, orders were sent to General von Bülow on the evening of June 14 to assemble his troops so that he was one day's march from Hannut. Bülow received these orders at 5 A.M. on June 15 and duly carried them out.

During the night of June 14–15, when General Ziethen had reported the enemy's approach, a second order was sent to Bülow to concentrate at Hannut immediately and to move his headquarters there. Bülow received this order at 11 A.M. on June 15. If he had then ordered his men to begin the second march to Hannut after a short rest, which was certainly feasible as Hannut is only five [German] miles from Liège and most of the troops were between Hannut and Liège, then his corps could have assembled in Hannut on the night of June 15–16. Bülow believed that he could leave the execution of this second order to the following day, firstly because he was convinced the entire Prussian army would concentrate only at Hannut, so enough time would remain from him to get there, and secondly because he believed that as long as there was no declaration of war, then it was certain there would be no hostilities.

Bülow reported to headquarters that he would be in Hannut at noon on June 16, but this report did not reach Blücher. A third and a fourth order were sent to Bülow from Namur on June 15 instructing him to continue his march to Sombreffe on June 16. As Sombreffe is five [German] miles from Hannut and Bülow's troops would only arrive there during the night of June 15, with great effort his vanguard might have reached Sombreffe on the afternoon of June 16, but the rest of his troops only that evening. Clearly there was insufficient time.

Both of these orders were sent to Hannut, where General Bülow was supposed to be and was expected to arrive, so they were not forwarded. But on June 15, Bülow stayed in Liège and only received the orders at 10 A.M. on June 16. So much time had now

---

given in Hofschröer, *1815*, vol. 1, *Wellington, His German Allies, and the Battles of Ligny and Quatre Bras*, 136–60.

been lost that at 3 A.M. on June 17 he was only at Haute and Basse-Bodecée, an hour's march north of Gembloux and three from the battlefield. Had he arrived twelve hours earlier, he could still have decided the Battle of Ligny.

By chance, III Corps also received its marching orders, issued on the night of June 14–15, only at 10 A.M. on June 15. Nevertheless, it was on the battlefield at 10 A.M. on June 16, having left behind only a few troops in outposts. II Corps arrived a little earlier.

21. Wellington's Concentration

The news Blücher received on June 14 that led to him ordering his army to concentrate on the night of June 14–15 seems not to have caused Wellington to make a decisive move. Even on the evening of June 15, when he received the report that Ziethen had been attacked at Charleroi and was being driven back by the main French army, he still did not consider it wise to begin moving his Reserve toward the left wing and even less advisable to weaken his right. Rather, he thought Bonaparte would advance up the road from Mons and so considered the battle at Charleroi a feint. All he did was to place his troops on alert. Only at midnight, when the news arrived from General Dörnberg,[71] commanding the outposts at Mons, that he was not being attacked and that the enemy appeared instead to be moving to the right, did he order the Reserve to march beyond the Soignes Woods, which,

---

71. Maj. Gen. Wilhelm Caspar Ferdinand Freiherr von Dörnberg (1768–1850). His military career began in 1783 when he enlisted in the 1st Guards Battalion of the army of Hesse-Kassel. He saw action in France in 1792. In 1794 he transferred to the Dutch army and participated in the siege of Cyprus. In 1806 Dörnberg fought alongside Blücher as a captain in a Prussian fusilier (light infantry) battalion and was taken prisoner at Lübeck, the Baltic port city reached by part of the retreating Prussians after Jena and Auerstedt. He returned to his homeland in 1808 after it had been absorbed into the Kingdom of Westphalia, ruled by Napoleon's brother Jérôme, and was appointed colonel of the Guard Jäger (rifles). A German patriot, Dörnberg participated in the insurrection in northern Germany in 1809, fleeing to Britain when it failed. In 1812 he fought in the Russian army as a British officer. After Waterloo Dörnberg joined the Hanoverian army.

according to General Müffling's account,[72] was at 10 A.M. From there to the battlefield at Sombreffe was only three more [German] miles, so Wellington's Reserve could actually have made it in good time. But much time was lost while Wellington first visited his left wing at Quatre Bras and reconnoitered the enemy at Frasnes before going to meet Blücher at Sombreffe. He arrived there at 1 P.M. and could see that the enemy's main army was there, so he made the necessary arrangements with Blücher. Meanwhile, the Reserve seems to have awaited further orders at the end of the Soignes Woods, that is, at the fork in the road to Nivelles and Quatre Bras.[73] Even then, there was still enough time. Wellington's forces were spread out, however, because it was his intention to act according to circumstances. He did not want to remove any forces from the right wing of the Prince of Orange at Nivelles, so he was too weak to support Blücher, which will be discussed below.

22. Bonaparte's Offensive Is Directed at Blücher

Now that our discussion of the concentration of the Allied armies has brought us to the moment when Bonaparte intended to attack Ziethen, it would be advisable to consider Bonaparte's plan more carefully, particularly as to how he decided to direct his offensive in this direction and what his objectives were.

72. Maj. Gen. Friedrich Carl Ferdinand Freiherr von Müffling (1775–1851). Müffling enlisted in the Prussian fusiliers in 1787 and fought against France from 1792 to 1794. Showing an aptitude for cartography, he participated in the survey of Westphalia from 1797 to 1802. In 1805 he became a captain in the General Staff. The next year Müffling fought under the Duke of Weimar, joining Blücher at Lübeck. In 1813 he was in Blücher's staff and was chief of staff of the Prussian forces in the Netherlands until Gneisenau replaced him. Seven years later Müffling was appointed chief of staff of the Prussian army. Subsequently, the method he used for surveying the Rhineland in the 1830s was named after him. Müffling was promoted to field marshal in 1847.

73. Wellington's orders were first published in volume 12 of his *Despatches* in 1838. There Wellington's "After Orders" of 10 P.M. on June 15 are given, and these show the Reserve being ordered to the position Clausewitz gave, though this account conflicts with Wellington's claim made in the "Waterloo Despatch" of June 19, 1815, that he immediately ordered his entire army to Quatre Bras on receipt of the news of the outbreak of hostilities.

In Paris, Bonaparte would appear to have had largely accurate knowledge of the dispositions of the two Allied armies. Yet his plan of attack could still be based only on general considerations and not, for instance, on the location of individual corps, such as Ziethen's at Charleroi, as these positions could easily be changed. As his information must have been at least a week old, it cannot be assumed that his offensive against Charleroi was specifically intended for the Prussian I Corps. He knew of Blücher's plan to concentrate and deploy behind Fleurus, but he obviously could not make plans in Paris based on something as uncertain as the Prussian point of concentration that could have been moved long before without his having heard of it.

Bonaparte could only be sure that Wellington and his army would be based in and around Brussels, with Blücher and his [army] in and around Namur. It would seem he had a reasonably accurate estimate of their strength, though it is highly probable he considered this exaggerated. General Sarrazin, in his book *La Seconde Restoration*,[74] said that Bonaparte shrugged his shoulders when told he faced more than 200,000 men and repeated that he knew for certain the English had 50,000 men and that there were an equal number of Prussians on the Meuse under Blücher. Even if Bonaparte only wanted to give his people courage with such pronouncements, it is still entirely credible that he did not think Wellington had more than 60–70,000 men, and Blücher 80–90,000—around 150,000 in total—a large part of which he did not anticipate would reach the battlefield. The more-or-less exact strengths for both armies he gave in his *Mémoires* should not confuse us. These figures are clearly based on later information, and Bonaparte habitually underestimated his opponent, as is most likely to be the case here.

If Bonaparte had concentrated on his center, that is, between Maubeuge and Givet, and if he wanted to achieve maximum surprise, as this was the shortest distance, it would have been the best

---

74. Gen. Jean Sarrazin (1770–1848), a veteran of the Revolutionary and Napoleonic Wars, wrote a number of books. The one to which Clausewitz appears to refer is his *Histoire de la guerre de la Restauration, depuis le passage de la Bidassoa par les Alliés, 7 Octobre 1813, jusqu'à la loi d'amnistie du 12 Janvier 1816, etc.* published in Paris in 1816.

option. Here he would find himself facing Blücher more than Wellington, with the main body of Wellington's troops being a day's march from Blücher. If he had now moved via Charleroi, then he could hardly avoid striking Blücher. As it was obvious the two commanders would want to stay in contact, Blücher would have assembled his army on the left of the Meuse, not on the right. The route via Charleroi would have brought Bonaparte into contact either with Blücher's main body or his right wing. Bonaparte's preferred option was to strike Blücher and fight him first. This was partly because he clearly felt a greater animosity toward Blücher and the Prussians than toward Wellington and the British, partly because the Prussians were the stronger of the two armies, and finally because they were more agitated and lusting for battle. Bonaparte's *Mémoires* also confirm this view of his plans, as he says that Blücher, being an old hussar and a more audacious person, would certainly come to Wellington's aid more quickly than the cautious Wellington would to his.

If Bonaparte made contact with Blücher's main body, then he hoped to defeat it by attacking swiftly before Wellington could arrive. Making contact with the right wing offered less opportunity, but there was a good chance he would run up against Blücher himself during the pursuit and bring him to battle a little later. In doing so, however, he would force Blücher away from Wellington. In either case, it was likely he would locate Blücher during his march toward Wellington, and not properly concentrated, as that march, being a strategic flank march from dispersed quarters, was not well suited to total concentration.

This, it seems, is how Bonaparte's specific operational plan should be considered and explained. The accounts of all historians of this campaign have begun by saying that he moved between the two armies to separate them. There is, however, no clear idea behind what has become a technical term in military jargon. The gap between two armies cannot be an operational objective. For a commander like Bonaparte, facing an opponent twice his strength, it would have been unfortunate indeed if, instead of striking one half of the enemy's forces with all of his own, he would instead have struck the empty space between them, launching a blow into thin air. He would have lost time, just at a point when it was only through its most economical use that he could have doubled the effectiveness of his own strength.⁷⁵

Even if it took place rapidly, defeating one army in one direction, thereby forcing the other away, there was still the great risk the other army would attack from the rear. Unless the distance between them was sufficient to ensure there was no danger of this, a commander would find it difficult to decide to carry out an attack to push one army aside.

Bonaparte thus chose the operational line between the two armies not to separate them by forcing his way between them, but because he expected to meet Blücher's army, either concentrated or one corps at a time.

23. The Engagement at Charleroi

On the evening of June 14, the French army was drawn up in three columns at Philippeville, Beaumont, and Solre-sur-Sambre, four [German] miles from Charleroi. It is not certain if Ziethen noticed the bivouac fires or if he drew his brigades together to defend the approaches.⁷⁶ At 4 A.M. on June 15, his outposts were driven back.⁷⁷ The three French columns pushed toward the three crossings of the Sambre River at Marchienne-au-Pont, Charleroi, and Châtelet. Elements of the Second Brigade defended all three. Ziethen's outposts withdrew, but the battalion that had held out for a long time at Thuin was lost to a cavalry attack while retreating toward Marchienne.⁷⁸

---

75. One example of what Clausewitz considers a misconception is how David Chandler describes Napoleon's "strategy of a central position," in which Napoleon was supposed to have intended to have driven a wedge between the two Allied armies. David G. Chandler, *The Campaigns of Napoleon* (London: Weidenfeld and Nicolson, 1967), 173–75.

76. Clausewitz is wrong here, for Ziethen was certainly aware of the French campfires and reported his sightings. Details that morning's events at the Prussian outposts were first published in 1845, after Clausewitz's death, in the weekly journal of the Prussian army, the *Militair-Wochenblatt*.

77. The first Prussian unit engaged was a battalion of the 1st Westphalian Landwehr Regiment under Captain von Gillhausen.

78. This happened shortly after 9 A.M.

Ziethen's outposts withdrew from the area around Binche through Thuin and Ham toward the Sambre, two-and-a-half hours from Charleroi. That was necessary to cover the corps, but it would have been better to have withdrawn the exposed units in advance, given the warning that the main enemy force was advancing and was expected, making it unnecessary to put the outposts at risk.

On the morning of June 15, the brigades of Ziethen's corps were centered on:

1st	Fontaine l'Evêque
2nd	Charleroi
3rd	Fleurus
4th	Moustier-sur-Sambre
Reserve Cavalry	Gosselies, Charleroi, Fleurus, etc.

The Third Brigade can be considered the reserve, [while] the Second defended the Sambre, with the First and Fourth covering its flanks.

This deployment indicates that Ziethen did not intended to accept a decisive battle on the Sambre, for he had selected the Second Brigade's actual position behind the river at Gilly and intended defending the three crossings at Charleroi, Marchienne, and Châtelet only as long as it could be done without endangering the troops there. A second defense was planned at Gilly to gain time for the flanking brigades to reach the area to the rear of Fleurus, so the whole corps would be united, and there its combined resistance would then gain enough time for the army to concentrate.

On the whole this plan was implemented with relatively good results.

The First Brigade in fact was already at Gosselies and intended to continue to Heppignies when it encountered the vanguard of the enemy column marching through Marchienne and engaged it. But as it was supported by a regiment detached from the Third Brigade at Fleurus to link up with it, the First Brigade continued its withdrawal to the vicinity of St. Amand without great disadvantage.

The enemy did not attack the left-wing brigade. This seems to be the reason it pulled back its outposts much later and only reached Fleurus that evening, suffering no losses at all.

The situation of the Second Brigade was as follows:

The outposts were attacked at 4 A.M. At 8 A.M. the attack on Charleroi commenced, lasting until 11 A.M. Meanwhile, the French also took Marchienne, but their right column did not reach Châtelet. The Second Brigade now retreated toward Gilly. The French now awaited the arrival of their delayed III Corps under Vandamme, which only arrived at 3 P.M.[79] The time from 3 to 5 P.M. was wasted on reconnaissance and getting through Charleroi. Between 5 and 6 P.M. the attack finally started just as General Pirch II was beginning his withdrawal to Fleurus.[80] Pirch fought a rearguard action, in which he lost several men, with enemy cavalry taking one battalion before it could reach the Lambusart Woods.[81] At nightfall, Ziethen's brigades had reached the vicinity of Fleurus, with the enemy taking up a position in the Lambusart Woods.

As the enemy's offensive had begun at 4 A.M., and he had spent the previous night and the whole day on the move and in action, it was reasonably certain he would attempt nothing further that night and indeed that he would not resume his attack very early the next morning. It was clear that if a battle was going to take place at Sombreffe on June 16, it would start only in the afternoon, so the armies would have until midday to concentrate.

Ziethen's losses on June 15 are given as 1,200 men but can be estimated at a good 2,000 men. With this sacrifice, I Corps delayed the enemy army for thirty-six hours, which was a favorable result.

79. Vandamme led the center column of the Army of the North. His orders arrived late, for the officer carrying them fell from his horse and broke a leg.

80. Maj. Gen. Otto Karl Lorenz von Pirch (II) (1765–1824). The younger brother of Georg von Pirch (I), his military career began in 1775 as a cadet in the Prussian infantry. He first saw action in the War of the Bavarian Succession (1778–79), then participated in the campaign in the Netherlands in 1787 and fought against France in 1794. In 1806 he was on the Duke of Brunswick's staff at Auerstedt. Pirch II fought in several major battles in 1813, winning the newly established Iron Cross 2nd Class on the Katzbach and Iron Cross 1st Class at Leipzig. He was pensioned off at the end of 1815.

81. The battalion in question was the fusiliers (light infantry) of the 28th Infantry Regiment. At this time a Prussian infantry regiment consisted of three battalions: two of musketeers, one of fusiliers.

Only the French center and right wing pursued Ziethen. Bonaparte gave command of his left wing to Marshal Ney,[82] who arrived in Charleroi at 4 P.M. He was instructed to advance along the highway from Frasnes to Quatre Bras, pushing back all the Allied forces in his path and posting guards at every road junction.

Ney had found Reille's II Corps at Gosselies, with one of its divisions, Girard's, detached against Fleurus. D'Erlon's I Corps, however, was still between Marchienne and Gosselies. At Frasnes he encountered the First Brigade of Perponcher's Netherlands Division,[83] and having received a report from Girard that a great mass of enemy troops was present at Fleurus, he did not have the nerve to press on to Quatre Bras, partly because he did not have all his troops with him and partly because he may have been concerned about getting too far away from the main battle. He considered it sufficient to expel Prince Bernard of Weimar's Netherlands brigade from Frasnes, and his vanguard set up outposts there.[84]

---

82. Michel Ney, duke of Elchingen, prince of Moscow (1769-1815). Born in Saarlouis, Ney volunteered for a French hussar regiment in 1791, quickly rising through the ranks during the Revolutionary Wars after fighting in battles such as Neerwinden in 1793, then campaigning in Germany for several years. A division general by 1800, he then commanded VI Corps of the Grand Army during the Austerlitz campaign before leading it at Jena in 1806. His attack at Friedland in 1807 was decisive. In 1808 Ney was transferred to the Iberian Peninsula, where he campaigned until called to serve in Russia in 1812. He held a senior command in the German campaigns of 1813, fighting at Lützen in the spring before being defeated at Dennewitz in August. Wounded at Leipzig in October 1813, Ney played a major role during the campaign of France in 1814 before turning against his master. Recalled to service by Napoleon in 1815, he led the left column at the beginning of the campaign. The marshal's advance was held up by Wellington at Quatre Bras on June 16. Two days later he commanded the French troops at Waterloo. After Waterloo Ney was taken prisoner by the royalists and executed.

83. About 3,500 men strong, the First Brigade consisted of one line regiment, one light regiment, three battalions of militia, and one horse battery.

84. Maj. Gen. Prince Bernhard of Saxe-Weimar-Eisenach (1792–1862). He received his military training in the Saxon grenadier guards and first saw action in 1809, fighting in the Saxon contingent of Napoleon's Grand Army against the Austrians. He took a leave of absence in 1812, returning home in March 1813, but only returned to active service after the Battle of Leipzig. As the Saxon army was reduced in size that fall, Bernhard sought employment elsewhere, becoming colonel of the Nassau-Orange Regiment in the service of the King of the Netherlands.

On the evening of June 15, the positions of the French army were:

Left Wing
    Vanguard on the left wing in Frasnes
    II Corps between Mellet and Gosselies
    I Corps between Marchienne and Gosselies
    II Corps and the cavalry in the woods before Fleurus
Center
    Imperial Guard between Charleroi and Gilly
    VI Corps behind Charleroi
Right Wing
    IV Corps at Châtelet

Bonaparte's headquarters were in Charleroi, Ney's in Gosselies.

24. Situation on the Morning of June 16

As mentioned above, Blücher had already given orders for the concentration of his army on the night of June 14–15. Wellington only gave his on the night of June 15–16, twenty-four hours later.[85] Blücher's II and III Corps marched off on June 15. Thirty-six hours later, at midday on June 16, they were on the battlefield ready to link up with I Corps. As discussed above, however, at most the vanguard of IV Corps could get there by midday and the remaining brigades in the evening. Yet it did not actually arrive due to a chain of events, the orders that Bülow might have received at 2 P.M. on June 15 were only received at 10 A.M. on June 16, twenty hours later. That is why IV Corps was still three hours away at 6

---

85. In the "Waterloo Despatch" Wellington claims he first heard the news of the outbreak of hostilities on the evening of June 15, when he immediately ordered his entire army to Quatre Bras. Both claims are at variance with the record—he actually received the news at 9 A.M. and did not order his entire army anywhere, let alone to Quatre Bras—but as the only information Clausewitz had available was the "Despatch," then it would appear he accepted this statement at face value. Wellington's actual orders were first published in 1838 in volume 12 of his *Despatches*, so Clausewitz was not in a position to examine the discrepancies between Wellington's statements and the record.

A.M. on June 17 instead of being at Sombreffe at 6 P.M. on June 16, a difference of about fifteen hours.

What was Wellington doing?

It was midnight on June 15 when Wellington gave the order for a march to the left. To what extent he could have concentrated his troops earlier, particularly his right wing, has not been discussed. This was necessary, however, if, as was claimed, the right wing was already concentrated at Hal by midday on June 17, for it is reasonable that between the night of June 15 and midday on June 17, the order could not go to Nieuwpoort and the troops march from there to Hal.

This must be left unresolved. All that is certain is that on the morning of June 16, the positions of Wellington's army were as follows:

1. Perponcher's division and one brigade of Netherlands cavalry, of eight squadrons, at Quatre Bras.
2. Chassé's Netherlands division at Nivelles, probably with the other two brigades of Netherlands cavalry, a total of twenty squadrons.
3. Picton's division, the brigades of Lambert and Pack, and the Nassau and Brunswick contingents on the march from Brussels to Quatre Bras.
4. Cooke's and Alten's divisions, part of the left wing, on the march from the area of Enghien to Quatre Bras.
5. Lord Uxbridge's cavalry on the march from its quarters to Quatre Bras.
6. Clinton's division (part of the right wing) on the march from the area of Ath and Leuze to Quatre Bras.
7. Mitchell's brigade, of Colville's division, also part of the right wing, on the march from Renaix to Quatre Bras.
8. Stedman's and Anthing's divisions, two brigades from Colville's division, and Estorff's Hanoverian cavalry brigade on the march from their quarters to Hal, where they arrived only on June 17.

So at midday, when the Battle of Ligny began and that of Quatre Bras could also have begun, Wellington had around 8,000 men at

Quatre Bras. During the course of the battle, right up to nightfall, the remaining units arrived one after the other: the Reserve from Brussels, Cooke's and Alten's divisions, perhaps also some cavalry, bringing Wellington's strength up to maybe 40,000 men. Wellington could not decide to leave the Nivelles road, which was rather a problem for the columns of troops of the right wing rushing by along this road. Even toward evening, Wellington still had 40,000 men on the march out of 90,000 and of the 50,000 who were in place, 10,000, namely Chassé's division and twenty squadrons of cavalry, were at Nivelles, which was not attacked.

25. The Battle of Ligny

On the morning of June 16, Napoleon's forces were not quite fully concentrated for an attack. The left wing under Ney was en echelon, as the French say, between Frasnes and Marchienne, a distance of about two [German] miles, as were the center and the right wing, and VI Corps was behind Charleroi. Furthermore, the troops that attacked the Prussian outposts at 4 A.M. on June 15, probably after having marched the larger part of the night, then had to spend all day on June 15 either in action or under arms on the march. This made it impossible for an attack to take place against Blücher at Sombreffe or against the Netherlanders at Quatre Bras in the early hours of June 16. Bonaparte was aware of the situation at Sombreffe, so it did not even occur to him to begin the battle before midday. As the situation at Quatre Bras was identical, his criticism of Ney for not having seized Quatre Bras with all his forces on the evening of June 15 or the morning of June 16 is both foolish and unjustified.

Had it been possible for a real tactical blow with the main force against the [Prussian] main force to occur on the morning of June 16, it would have been a huge error to have delayed, for Bonaparte knew Blücher was concentrating his forces and that the entire Prussian army was so much larger than the 75,000 men he could bring against it, then there was nothing more important than to offer battle before the concentration was completed. For instance, III Army Corps only arrived at 10 A.M. But the French troops needed time to rest, get food, cook, and then concentrate, all of which could not occur in a short summer night, so it is no surprise that this continued into the morning of June 16. Between 11 A.M. and noon, French troops once more advanced toward General Ziethen. He had already sent his brigades back to their assigned positions and was still on the plain at Fleurus with the cavalry. The maneuvers that drove back his cavalry lasted until about 1 P.M. Bonaparte then reconnoitered the Prussian position, and the real attack could only begin around 3 P.M.

26. Blücher's Deployment

As already mentioned, the original idea had been to deploy along the Brussels highway at Sombreffe and, while Bonaparte was undertaking his attack against that position, for the larger part of the Allied forces to assault his flank. Unfortunately, when the army concentrated on the morning of June 16, it became apparent that there was no naturally strong position covering the direction from which Wellington was supposed to be approaching with part of his forces. I and II Corps were deployed between St. Amand and Sombreffe, but the area from Sombreffe to Balâtre also had to be covered, for Bülow was coming up from Gembloux. III Corps was thus ordered to take up positions there, creating two front lines, which formed an inward-pointing right angle. Apparently it was thought that the right flank, which was at the enemy's mercy, would not be the target of his main attack, because Wellington was expected to come from that direction with a substantial force. Against a secondary attack, however, this flank was considered fairly strong because of the line of villages running from St. Amand to Wagnelée.

The main error was that the Prussians thought they were facing the entire enemy force and so believed with certainty that they could count on significant support (40–50,000 men) from Wellington. An exposed flank is not a problem if 40–50,000 men are en echelon behind it. Bonaparte was expected to attack both Prussian front lines, which would not have given him a favorable position, though. This assumption proved to be mistaken, and there would be time in the course of the battle to correct it.

27. Dispositions on the Front at Ligny

The front from St. Amand to Sombreffe was covered as follows:

I Army Corps formed the actual front line, with II Army Corps remaining in reserve behind the heights.

I Army Corps had deployed its troops in a rather jumbled way, which coincidental circumstances may well have caused to happen.

While three battalions of the First Brigade were in Brye, the other six stood behind St. Amand.

Three battalions of the Third Brigade were in St. Amand, while the other six formed the last line of reserves.

The deployment was largely as follows:

Brye was held by three battalions of the First Brigade.

St. Amand by three battalions of the Third.

Ligny by four battalions of the Fourth.

The six remaining battalions of the First Brigade were deployed in the front line behind St. Amand in two lines ([position] B).[86]

All eight battalions of the Second Brigade (one having been lost) and the two remaining battalions of the Fourth were in a second line between Brye and Ligny ([positions] C and D).

Finally, the six remaining battalions of the Third Brigade were in a third line right behind the Second and Fourth Brigades ([position] E).

The Reserve Cavalry of I Army Corps first deployed in front of the villages to observe the enemy and then stood immediately in front of the Third Brigade as a reserve ([position] W).

II Army Corps drew up along the Brussels highway as the main reserve, its brigades next to each other in the regulation battle order of three lines of battalion columns ([positions] H, I, K, L), with the reserve cavalry in the rear ([position] M). Most of the artillery remained with the brigades, with only the three heavy batteries of I Corps deploying between Ligny and St. Amand ([position] F).[87]

---

86. Clausewitz here refers to a position marker on a map from the atlas published by the Prussian General Staff. See the maps for Ligny, Wavre, and Waterloo in Wagner, *Plane der Schlachten und Treffen*.

87. Prussian heavy batteries normally consisted of eight pieces, six 12-pound cannon and two 10-pound howitzers.

The objective was to accept only a preliminary engagement in the villages of St. Amand and Ligny to disrupt the enemy force and then attack when it advanced beyond the villages.

28. Dispositions on the Sombreffe Front

III Army Corps assigned the Ninth Brigade to defend the sprawling villages of Sombreffe and Mont Potriaux, as well as the area to their rear areas; the Eleventh to defend the highway at the Point du Jour; the Tenth to defend the rear behind Tongrinne and Tongrenelle, with the Twelfth Brigade and the cavalry in reserve. One battalion of the Ninth Brigade provisionally occupied Mont Potriaux, with the other eight remaining in reserve behind the village ([position] P). The Eleventh Brigade held its assigned area with one battalion ([position] R), while the other four (one had remained at the outposts on the Meuse) stood behind it ([position] Q).

Two battalions of the Tenth Brigade covered its front, with the other four in the rear.

The objective was to hold at all points for a long as possible with the skirmish line, and when this could not hold out any longer, to move against the enemy rear with closed battalions.

The artillery was deployed mainly on the heights in front of Mont Potriaux, on the highway in front of Point du Jour, and on the heights at Tongrenelle.

29. The Duke of Wellington Arrives

These dispositions were unhurriedly completed by around noon because, as mentioned above, the enemy could not commence his attack any earlier, and Ziethen's withdrawal from Fleurus did not disturb these arrangements in any way.

Around 1 P.M., Wellington arrived at the windmill at Brye to see Blücher. Wellington told him that his army was at that moment concentrating at Quatre Bras and it would rush to Blücher's aid in a few hours. "I will be here at 4 o'clock" are said to have been his words as he spurred on his horse.[88]

It would have been unreasonable to expect that Wellington and his entire army could have arrived in a few hours. Wellington no doubt meant nothing more than his left wing combined with his Reserve, which were still 40–50,000 men. Both commanders believed they had the entire French army, estimated at 130,000 men, opposite them. Blücher had 80,000 men available, so if Wellington brought up 40–50,000 men, there would be roughly the same number on both sides. Furthermore, Bülow's arrival was still expected, even if it was not certain. If Bülow's 35,000 men had arrived, victory would appear to be virtually certain. Even if, given the Allies' great numerical superiority, the situation was not as favorable as it could have been, it nevertheless seemed satisfactory, while, due to the two armies' diverging lines of retreat, a withdrawal to delay the battle for a day seemed fraught with difficulty. Each of them could have given up their natural lines of communication for a little while to turn toward the other's base, provided they were operating in unison. But they had yet to link up, and a common withdrawal would only have made their concentration more difficult. Besides, it would have made a bad impression on the troops and public opinion. All of this was probably sufficient to confirm Blücher's resolve to fight. Battle was accepted in the belief that they [the Allies] were dealing with a greatly superior force, but that by the end of the day, the superiority would be theirs, so it was only a matter of fighting a delaying action until then.

---

88. Wellington made a number of promises of support to the Prussians that he demonstrably knew he could not keep. This issue is examined in some depth in Hofschröer, *1815*, vol. 1, *Wellington, His German Allies, and the Battles of Ligny and Quatre Bras*. While the details of the various accounts of the meeting in question differ to a certain extent, what is certain is that Wellington indicated that he would have 20,000 men available that afternoon and that he would move against the French. This would not be possible on the basis of the orders the duke had issued during the previous hours.

30. Bonaparte's Plan of Attack

As discussed earlier, on June 15, Bonaparte sent I and II Corps, the Light Cavalry of the Guard, and a division of cuirassiers, in all 48,000 men under Ney, down the road to Quatre Bras. While Ney's wing advanced from Marchienne, where it had crossed the Sambre, Girard's division from II Corps was fighting General Steinmetz at Gosselies, pushing him back to Heppignies. As it had moved close to the French center, Bonaparte kept this division there. So the main army that advanced to attack Blücher consisted of about 75,000 men. Bonaparte organized and deployed it as follows:

III Corps (Vandamme), along with Girard's division and supported by a brigade of light cavalry from the Guard, 24,000 men in all, advanced through Wagnelée to attack St. Amand.

IV Corps (Gérard), 15,000 men, wheeled to the left and moved forward to attack Ligny.

Grouchy, with two corps of cavalry and some infantry (nobody says from which corps, but it was presumably the IV), advanced against Point du Jour and Tongrenelle.[89]

The Guard was deployed to the left of Fleurus, VI Corps, which arrived a little late, and Milhaud's cavalry corps to the right, in reserve.

These reserves and Grouchy's cavalry that were in sight amounted to around 36,000 men.

Bonaparte was not aware of the position of the Prussian III Corps. He believed all three Prussian corps were deployed between St. Amand and Sombreffe and was all the more sure that what he saw there was the whole force because he saw bodies of reserves at [positions] H, I, K, L, and P,[90] which, if the villages were strongly

---

89. Clausewitz's presumption here is correct. The French infantry in question was Hulot's division, part of IV Corps.

90. These refer to positions on the relevant Prussian General Staff map in Wagner, *Plane der Schlachten und Treffen*.

held, could easily amount to 80,000 men in front of him. It is not certain if he knew that IV Corps had not yet arrived. Afterward he claimed as much and so gave his battle plan a certain veneer, but it is hardly possible that he could have been entirely certain of this since any prisoners taken at the start of the battle could not have known. Leaving this to one side and following his own account, he saw the Prussian army deployed on a line in front of the Brussels highway, in doing so, giving up its original line of retreat and at the same time offering him its right flank.

Except for Thielemann's corps, this was not the main axis of the Prussian position. Rather, the Brussels highway ran more parallel than perpendicular to it. Bonaparte did not see it this way, however, and his mistake is very understandable, for the many individual blocks of Prussian brigades must have made it very difficult to get an idea of the main alignment of the whole, so it was entirely justified to see the line as running from St. Amand to Ligny, including Ligny itself, which was the most advanced point occupied, as the actual front of the whole army. The Prussian army's disposition astonished Bonaparte, leading him to conclude that Blücher was not expecting a battle on this day but had taken up this rather surprising position in the hope of gaining another day for Wellington's army to move into line next to him. Bonaparte attributed Blücher's standing face to face with the French army partly to an old Blücher wanting to present an impressive countenance and partly to his defensive deployment at Fleurus, where part of his force was entirely hidden.[91]

Bonaparte was now virtually certain that Wellington could not arrive, and his information on that was likely to be better than that about Bülow. In any case, he believed he had taken care of that problem with the mission he had given Ney. So it all came down to this: that Ney, having failed on June 15, should push on

---

91. Clausewitz's comment on the Prussian deployment coincides with the facts but conflicts with certain myths originating from Wellington, who claimed that the entire Prussian army was exposed to cannon fire and so its defeat at Ligny inevitable. The duke is recorded as having made such claims in conversations with Earl Stanhope and Baron de Ros. This myth is cherished by many Anglophone historians, but reference to any decent map shows Wellington's claim to be a fallacy.

to Quatre Bras as fast as possible on June 16 to hold back whatever could come from Wellington, then send 10,000 men back down the highway from Quatre Bras to Namur and into the rear of the Prussian army. In his enthusiasm for this plan, Bonaparte told General Gérard as he was receiving his orders: "it is possible that the outcome of the war may be decided in three hours. If Ney executes his orders properly, not one cannon from the Prussian army will get away; it is caught en flagrant delicti."[92]

31. Critical Commentary

There are good reasons to doubt if this was really Bonaparte's intention when he issued his battle orders. In his accounts, he so often has made false and untrustworthy statements, which could well have been his intention here as well, so as to appear less of a gambler, not that his attack against Blücher could be seen as such, but rather his entire second entrance onto the stage of politics. The united forces of Blücher and Wellington destroyed him, but his vanity required that this appeared to result from the mistakes of individuals and not the force of circumstances. So this line of defense, as a lawyer would say, also required Bonaparte to demonstrate that the Prussian army would have been defeated on June 16 had his plan been carried out.

No investigation has yet succeeded in determining to what extent Ney actually acted contrary to Bonaparte's orders on June 16, as Gamot's defense of the marshal, *Refutation, etc.* is not completely enlightening.[93] It does however contribute to a more exact idea of the matter, if the four orders that, according to Gamot, Ney received during June 16 are quoted here one after the other.

---

92. Napoleon, *Mémoires de Napoleon Bonaparte* (Paris, 1821), 93–94.

93. Charles-Guillaume Gamot (1766–1820), prefect (district administrator) of Auxerre. He was the first prefect to recognize Napoleon upon his return from Elba. Brother-in-law of Ney, he was present at the meeting of reconciliation between the marshal and Napoleon. In 1818 he published a refutation of Gourgaud's work on the Waterloo campaign *(La campagne de dix-huit cent quinz)*, taking Ney's side.

First Order

Charleroi, June 16, 1815
My dear Marshal,

The Emperor has just ordered the Count Valmy [Kellermann],[94] commanding the 3rd corps of reserve cavalry, to assemble and proceed to Gosselies, where he will be at your disposal.

His Majesty's intention is that the Guard Cavalry that has been marching to Brussels, remains behind and rejoins the rest of the Imperial Guard; but, so it does not have to make a retrograde move, you can, after replacing it in the line [with Kellerman's corps], leave it somewhat to the rear, where he will have sent it movement orders for the day. To this end, Lieutenant General Lefèbvre-Desnouëttes will send an officer to carry the orders.[95]

Kindly let me know if the corps has carried out its movement, and what the exact positions of the I and II Corps and the two cavalry divisions attached to them are this morning, do let me know what enemy are opposite you, and what we have learned of them.

Signed Chief of Staff,
Duke of Dalmatia

94. François-Etienne, Count Valmy (1770-1815). Son of the famous commander of the Revolutionary Wars, Kellermann junior joined the royal army in 1785. He first saw action during the Revolutionary Wars, later fighting in Italy, including at Lodi in 1796. His charge at Marengo in 1800 decided that battle. In 1805 Kellermann was wounded at Austerlitz. He campaign in the Iberian Peninsula from 1807, then in Germany in 1813, before fighting in France under Grouchy in 1814. Kellermann was wounded at Waterloo.

95. Cavalry Gen. Charles Count Lefèbvre-Desnouëttes (1773–1822). Running away from school to join the military, Lefèbvre-Desnouëttes joined the Paris National Guard in 1789. He fought in the army during the Revolutionary Wars before becoming an aide de camp to Napoleon in 1800, fighting alongside him at Marengo that year and at Austerlitz in 1805. Lefèbvre-Desnouëttes was aide de camp to Jérôme Bonaparte in Silesia in 1806–1807, then joined the Westphalian army and served in Spain, where in 1808 he was taken prisoner. Escaping in 1812, he served in Russia, then in Saxony in 1813, and finally in France in 1814. After Waterloo he sought refuge in the United States and was sentenced to death in France in 1816. In 1822 the ship carrying Lefèbvre-Desnouëttes to the Netherlands sank, and the general drowned.

Second Order

Charleroi, June 16, 1815
My dear Marshal,

An officer of the lancers has just come from telling the Emperor that the enemy is present en masse around Quatre Bras. Assemble the Corps of Counts Reille and d'Erlon, and that of the Count de Valmy, which is on its way to join you at this moment. With these, you are to attack and destroy all enemy forces that may appear. Blücher is here at Namur, and it is not to be expected that he will send troops toward Quatre Bras, so you have no concerns except for those forces coming from Brussels.

Marshal Grouchy is moving to Sombreffe, as I have told you, and the Emperor is going to Fleurus. It is to there that you should send further reports to His Majesty.

Signed
Marshal of the Empire, Chief of Staff,
Duke of Dalmatia

Third Order

Before Fleurus, June 16, 2 P.M.
My dear Marshal,

The Emperor orders me to inform you that the enemy has concentrated one corps of troops between Sombreffe and Brye, and that at half past two, Marshal Grouchy will attack it with III and IV Corps. It is His Majesty's intention that you also attack whatever is in front of you, and that, after having pressed it vigorously, you pull back toward us to combine in enveloping the corps just mentioned. If this corps should be crushed prior to this, His Majesty would then maneuver in your direction, to speed your operations as well.

Inform the Emperor of your dispositions and of whatever takes place to your fore.

Signed Marshal of the Empire, Chief of Staff,
Duke of Dalmatia

Fourth Order

Before Fleurus, June 16, 3:30 P.M.
My dear Marshal,

I wrote to you an hour ago that the Emperor was going to attack the enemy between St. Amand and Brye at half past two. At this moment, the engagement is very intense. His Majesty orders me to say that you should maneuver so as to envelope the enemy right, and throw yourself forcibly on his rear. This army is lost if you act vigorously. The fate of France is in your hands. So do not hesitate an instant to carry out the movement the Emperor commands and make your way to the heights of Brye and St. Amand to assist in a victory that could be decisive.

The enemy is caught en flagrant delit, in the act of trying to unite with the English.

Signed Chief of Staff,
Duke of Dalmatia[96]

In contrast, on page 90 Bonaparte's *Mémoires* states:

> A staff officer from the left wing reported that Marshal Ney, just as he was preparing to march to the position in front of Quatre Bras, had been held up by the cannonade he heard on the right flank and by reports he received that the Anglo-Dutch and Prussian-Saxon armies had already joined up in the area around Fleurus; that if he continued his movement under these circumstances he would be outflanked; and finally that he was prepared to execute the orders the Emperor sent him, once the Emperor was aware of this new incident. The Emperor rebuked him for having already lost eight hours; that he was pretending a new incident had happened that already existed; he reiterated his order [for Ney] to move to Quatre Bras and that as soon as he was in position, he should detach a column of 8,000 infantry,

---

96. See Charles-Guillaume Gamot, *Refutation, en ce qui concern le m[aréch]al Ney, de l'ouvrage ayant pour titre: Campagne de 1815, ou relation des operations militaires qui ont lieu pendant les cent fours, par le general Gourgaud, ecru a Sainte-Helene, par M Gamont, Officier de la légion d'honneur, et ancien Prefet-Paris* (Paris, 1818).

along with Lefèbvre-Desnouëttes's cavalry and twenty-eight cannon, on the highway from Quatre Bras to Namur; that this force should leave the road at the village of Marbais and attack the rear of the enemy army on the heights of Brye; and that, apart from this detachment, he would still have 32,000 men and 80 cannon in position at Quatre Bras, which would suffice to hold in check the elements of the English army that might arrive on June 16. Marshal Ney received this order at half-past eleven; he was near Frasnes with his vanguard; he ought to have taken up his position in front of Quatre Bras at midday. Now, from Quatre Bras to the heights of Brye is eight thousand toises [yards]; the column that he detached against Marshal Blücher's rear should therefore have reached Marbais by two o'clock. The line occupying the [French] army near Fleurus was not aggressive. Part of it was masked; the Prussian army was no cause for concern.

This account does not conflict with the four orders, but the following is evident:

1. Such a specific mission as described here does not seem to have been found among Ney's orders. Perhaps it was oral and has been lost.
2. The third order does not seem in any way to point to an earlier order of the same kind but rather interpreted the situation somewhat differently. Moreover, Soult would probably also have written about the mission that Bonaparte discussed, or he at least would have had precise knowledge of it.
3. Anyone with a little experience in these matters will find that the four orders Gamot presents have more of the ring of truth about them then the dispositions Bonaparte describes in his account.
4. Finally, in Bonaparte's account, the Guard Cavalry Division is included in the troops assigned to Marshal Ney, while the first order definitely states that it was to remain behind. Bonaparte could have forgotten this fact on St. Helena, but not two hours after he had given the order.

CRITICAL COMMENTARY   93

And now for the internal composition of this deployment:

1. Ney, with some 40,000 men, was supposed to move two [German] miles toward Brussels, where he might easily run into 50–60,000 British and Netherlands troops. He was supposed to defeat them and have no doubt as to the certainty of his success, even though British troops led by Wellington had more often given French marshals a thrashing.
2. At noon the main body of Ney's force was still at Gosselies. From there to Quatre Bras is [a] three hours' march he must first undertake, for there was little that he alone with just the vanguard could achieve at Frasnes. Then he had to begin and end a battle and immediately march back three hours to St. Amand to help end another battle being fought at roughly the same time. Although all of this was not absolutely impossible, it was still scarcely feasible.
3. Why should 10,000 men in the rear of a Prussian army 80,000 strong, in open terrain with full visibility prepare the way for complete destruction? By their mere appearance such a force could decide a doubtful battle, forcing Blücher to retire earlier, but it was still a long way from there to a total defeat like that at Jena.

It seems likely that Bonaparte's account, written in the solitude of St. Helena, was bombastic, while at the moment of action, his whole train of thought was simpler and more natural.

He saw a large part of Blücher's army in front of him, considered it weaker than it actually was (he thought III Corps only arrived during the battle), and hoped in any case to beat Blücher quickly, while Ney, with some 40,000 men, might be in a position to hold off any assistance coming his way from Wellington and to move any forces remaining against Blücher's rear. That was more or less his plan. In Bonaparte's position, it was impossible to say in advance how great this victory over Blücher could be. He had to be satisfied with whatever a very forceful blow could accomplish. Time, forces, and circumstances were insufficient for his overwhelming plan of annihilation to be realized, and if a modest victory did not help him, if it did not pull him back from the abyss toward which he staggered like a great daredevil, it only proved how insecure his position was, how dangerous his game, and it was precisely about this that he had nothing to say.

32. Main Events of the Battle

The battle consisted of three simultaneous acts: The fight around the villages of St. Amand; the fight around the village of Ligny; and the demonstration against III Army Corps.

The first of these three acts was the bloodiest, the second the most decisive, the third as such not important, though it may nevertheless be regarded as an effective feint by the French.

The events in the fight around St. Amand can be grouped together roughly as follows:

At 3 P.M. Lefol's division of the French III Corps attacked the southern village, that is, St. Amand proper. The six battalions of the Prussian First Brigade were drawn up behind the village in support of the three battalions of the Third Brigade occupying it. The battle went to and fro for an hour, drawing in and consuming the three battalions stationed at Brye. Around 4 P.M. the village fell, and the First Brigade, now hors de combat, withdrew and rallied behind Brye ([position] G).[97] The advance of Girard's division on St. Amand la Haye may possibly have contributed to this.

Blücher decided to send in two strong columns to storm and retake St. Amand la Haye.

The first column, consisting of the Second Brigade, whose eight battalions were held in reserve near Brye, was supposed to attack the village frontally, while General Jürgass,[98] with the Fifth Brigade

---

97. Clausewitz is again referring to a position on a map in Wagner, *Plane der Schlachten und Treffen.*

98. Maj. Gen. Alexander Georg Ludwig Moritz Konstantin Maximilian von Wahlen-Jürgass (1758–1833). He entered the Military Academy in 1772 before becoming an ensign in the élite cavalry regiment, the Gens d'armes. He first saw action in the War of the Bavarian Succession and then fought in Poland in 1794. In 1806 he fought at Auerstedt, where he was wounded and was taken prisoner during the retreat. Three years later Jürgass was appointed commander

and seventeen squadrons of cavalry, ten of his own and seven from III Army Corps (Marwitz's brigade),[99] was to advance through and parallel to the village of Wagnelée, taking Girard's division, defending St. Amand la Haye, in the left flank. They hoped to master this village once more, then St. Amand itself.

Pirch II made two attacks. The first failed completely, the second, under Blücher's personal leadership, reached the village and gained possession of the churchyard.

Jürgass also made two attacks that do not seem to have been coordinated precisely with those of Pirch II. In the first assault, order in the 25th Regiment, leading the march from Wagnelée, soon broke down, so the attack as a whole must be considered a complete failure. Jürgass staged a second assault with the same troops that he had rallied to the rear and was more fortunate this time, pushing forward close to St. Amand le Hameau, and here the battle came to a halt for quite a while.

Bonaparte then reinforced his left wing with a division of the Young Guard, and the French renewed their attacks. As this combat had exhausted the Second Brigade and it was out of ammunition, four battalions of the Sixth Brigade were brought up from behind Brye, while Pirch II withdrew the Second to the rear of Brye. The Seventh Brigade also moved up to reinforce the Fifth. Existing accounts do not describe the results either side achieved here precisely, but it was likely that fighting was confined to a relatively small area, within which both sides advanced and withdrew. They may have been in roughly the same situation, each having taken possession of part of the village of St. Amand la Haye. The

---

of a regiment of dragoons, then in March 1813 received his first brigade. He was wounded at Lützen and awarded the Iron Cross 2nd Class for his role in the battle. At Haynau, where his cavalry mauled the pursuing French, he was again wounded, had a horse shot from under him, and was awarded the Iron Cross 1st Class. Jürgass fought at Leipzig and in several major engagements during the 1814 campaign in France.

99. Col. Friedrich August Ludwig von der Marwitz (1777–1837). His military career began as an ensign in the Gens d'armes. He first saw action in Poland in 1794. In 1806 Marwitz fought at Jena, and his account of the campaign is one of the standard works on the subject. The next year he raised his own free corps. In May 1813 Marwitz was appointed a brigade commander in the militia, commanding these troops in a number of sieges and actions.

most that can be gathered from the various accounts, however, is that the fighting as a whole did not cross over to the near side of the small stream running past the villages of St. Amand.

As the accounts of the use and effect of the cavalry and artillery are far from clear, it is difficult to say anything definite about their role here. Perhaps this confusion reflects the confused nature of the fighting. Indeed, several units of these arms are not mentioned at all in any account. Adding together the Reserve Artillery of I Army Corps and the batteries of the First, Second, Fifth, and Seventh Brigades, which were undoubtedly present, that makes ten batteries, or eighty guns. Probably some reserve batteries of II Corps were also in action here, a total of around one hundred guns in all, engaged on a front about 3,000 paces wide.

The artillery of the French III Corps consisted of thirty-eight guns, that of Girard's division of eight. Adding to them some thirty guns from the Guard and the Reserve Cavalry would have made the total number of French guns only seventy-six. In any case, the French certainly had fewer guns than the Prussians. Despite that, it was likely that the Prussians lost more dead and wounded, which was surely due partly to the fact that they held too much artillery in reserve, replacing these guns as soon as a battery had used up its ammunition, which led to some trying to fire off all their rounds quickly.

Little use appeared to have been made of the cavalry, which seemed mainly to have been used for observation. Three French regiments attempted to outflank the Prussian right, but eight squadrons under Marwitz moved up and held them in check.

Finally, the third act of the fighting around St. Amand has to be when Blücher mistook a movement by the French Guard as indicating the French army was falling back and led the last available Prussian battalions, three from the Eighth Brigade, to St. Amand in an attempt to break through and pursue at that point. This decision sheds additional light on the fighting at St. Amand, which must have been considered static and evenly balanced, for otherwise the thought of using fresh troops to attempt a breakthrough and pursuit could never have arisen.

To sum up the results of the entire action: it consisted of the Prussians committing about forty battalions, perhaps 28,000 men, one after the other, while the French committed their III Corps, Girard's division of II Corps, and Duhesme's division of the Guard, about 24,000 infantry in all, sustaining a battle for six hours, with the Prussians contesting the villages until around 9 P.M. As a whole, the Prussians were at a disadvantage, losing all of St. Amand and half of La Haye and also suffering more dead and wounded, as well as being more weakened. Furthermore, they had more fatigued and fewer serviceable units left than the French, particularly as it is likely that not all of the French battalions took part in the actual firefights. So it was a real setback for them that we had sacrificed significantly more than the enemy in this action. Yet their success was in no way decisive, it only tipped the scales slightly.

In Ligny the fighting was more straightforward than in St. Amand, for it consisted largely of a firefight lasting five hours that took place within the village. In it the French mostly held the half of the village on the right bank of the brook, the Prussians the other half.

The French IV Corps under Gérard undertook the attack on Ligny, while the Imperial Guard, led by Bonaparte in person, decided it. It began somewhat later than that at St. Amand. The main events were as follows:

First, four battalions of the Fourth Brigade held Ligny. Three columns, one each of the three divisions of IV Corps undertook the attack. One should bear in mind, however, that the larger part of the divisions were held in reserve. The two remaining battalions of the Fourth Brigade also moved up, and the first attack was beaten off.

Second, the French renewed the attack, the Fourth Brigade's resistance began to weaken, and four battalions of the Third Brigade moved into the village in support, with two battalions staying behind to cover the batteries. General von Jagow intended to press on beyond the village with these troops and go over to the offensive,[100] but the fire from the enemy batteries made it impossible

---

100. Maj. Gen. Friedrich Wilhelm Christian Ludwig von Jagow (1771–1857). He joined the Prussian army in 1785 as a cadet in an infantry regiment. Jagow first saw action at Auerstedt in 1806 and was taken prisoner at the capitulation

to break out of the town. Meanwhile, the disorder in the village probably led to the loss of half of them [the men].

Third, so that the other half was not lost as well, the remaining four battalions of the Sixth Brigade were ordered to Ligny. One was already there and the other four were used in Pirch I's [*sic*] attack on St. Amand. Five battalions of the Eighth Brigade later followed up, having already advanced from Sombreffe to the mill of Bussy. Of the remaining four battalions of this brigade, one remained at the mill and the other three were in fact those Blücher led against St. Amand. As for the use of cavalry and artillery here, there is even less information available than on St. Amand. Given that the artillery used at St. Amand amounted to one hundred guns, then there can have been no more than sixty available at Ligny, as the artillery of both corps totaled only 160 guns.

The French IV Corps had forty cannon, but it is likely that part of the Guard Artillery was also used here, along with that of the Reserve Cavalry, so at this point on the battlefield the Prussians probably did not have any superiority in artillery.

Most of the Prussian cavalry had been moved to the right wing, for when the French broke through later on, there were only three regiments here.

The fighting at Ligny took place in a very confined space and with the bloodiest exertions. The mass of Prussian infantry committed there comprised twenty battalions, that is, about 14,000 men. The French III Corps may have been equally strong in infantry.

Around 3 P.M. Blücher ordered Thielemann to send up a brigade of his Reserve Cavalry. This was done, and Marwitz, as mentioned in the account of the fighting at St. Amand, was placed under Jürgass's command. Around 4 P.M. General Thielemann received an order to send up a brigade of infantry, and so the Twelfth Brigade marched off to Ligny. This unit was deployed

---

of Prenzlau. In 1807 he became a major and was appointed commander of a battalion of foot guards. Two years later he took over command of the Guard Jäger (rifle) Battalion. In March 1813 he received his first brigade command and fought in several major battles during the campaigns of 1813–15. Jagow was awarded the Iron Cross 2nd Class for his role at the Battle of Lützen, where he was wounded, and the Iron Cross 1st Class for Leipzig.

between Sombreffe and Ligny as a reserve, replacing the Eighth. It had sent out its skirmishers to the Ligny Brook, and, in a relatively hard fight, had covered the left flank of the troops in Ligny. Yet its losses were not significant, so it was still available as a reserve. Bonaparte had decided to break through at Ligny with the main body of his Guard, and so to decide the battle. This thrust took place around 8 P.M., marking the end of the fighting at Ligny.

Fourth, eight battalions of the Imperial Guard and 3–4,000 cavalry made the decisive attack at Ligny, driving all the Prussians out of the village. The cavalry broke through the Prussian center, now largely devoid of infantry. The Reserve Cavalry of I Army Corps rushed forward by brigades to attack the enemy cavalry and infantry but was driven back everywhere. Blücher was at the head of one of these attacks, in which his horse was wounded, and he was lucky to avoid being taken prisoner.

33. The Third Army Corps' Actions[101]

Two cavalry corps and some infantry, probably from Grouchy's IV Corps, were sent to stage a demonstration against the Prussian positions between Sombreffe and St. Balâtre, so keeping them occupied. This objective was achieved, insofar as the Tenth and Eleventh Brigades, with eleven battalions, and the Second Brigade of the Reserve Cavalry, with six squadrons, were pinned down. But the Twelfth Brigade and one brigade of the Reserve Cavalry moved off to join the other two army corps, with the Ninth Brigade being held in reserve behind Sombreffe. The main part of the infantry combat took place only between Tongrenelle and Boignée on the terrain taken by the Tenth Brigade and was insignificant. Between 7 and 8 P.M., when the skirmishers of the Twelfth Brigade were advancing across the brook between Sombreffe and Ligny, Thielemann saw the cavalry opposite him withdraw, save for some small bodies, and he believed the enemy was pulling back and wanted to

---

101. There is a printing error in the original of this text in which this section is incorrectly numbered "3." This error led to some of the subsequent sections being numbered out of sequence. These errors have been corrected here.

advance across the defile with his remaining cavalry brigade. Two squadrons were sent forward, with a battery of horse artillery following imprudently and too soon. These units had hardly reached the ridge in front of them when a few enemy regiments charged the two squadrons, taking five guns from the horse battery, which was trying to unlimber instead of immediately turning back. The three remaining guns had time to escape.

Summarizing the outline of the battle as a whole, like all recent battles, the opposing forces in the front lines were used up piecemeal in a firefight lasting many hours and involving little movement until one side finally achieved a distinct superiority of reserves when fresh masses of troops moved up. These were then used to deliver the decisive blow against the opponent's forces that were already wavering.

Bonaparte advanced with about 75,000 men against Blücher, whose three corps together amounted to a force of 78,000 men, a comparable strength.[102]

Between 3 and 8 P.M., Bonaparte contested Blücher's two main positions at St. Amand and Ligny with about 30,000 men. He used about 6,000 to pin down the Prussian III Army Corps while keeping 33,000 in reserve, far behind the front line. Of these, he sent about another 6,000 to fight at St. Amand.

As early as around 6 P.M., he decided to use the Guard to deliver the decisive blow at Ligny. Then he received news that a substantial body of troops was visible at the distance of an hour from his left flank. As it may have been an enemy force coming from Brussels, Bonaparte stopped this maneuver. Actually, it was d'Erlon marching from Frasnes to St. Amand, and it is still not known on whose authority. Scouts were immediately sent off to reconnoiter, but almost two hours were lost before the news came back that it was the French I Corps. That is why the assault on Ligny did not take place until 8 P.M.

Even then, Bonaparte sent in only part of his reserves, about half of them, just the remainder of the Guard, still leaving VI Corps in reserve.

---

102. While Clausewitz's figure for the size of the French forces at Ligny is largely correct, the Prussian forces may have numbered as much as 80,000.

At the beginning of the battle, Blücher's I Army Corps, 27,000 men, was in position between Ligny and St. Amand, while III Army Corps, 22,000 men, was deployed between Sombreffe and St. Balâtre, leaving only II Army Corps, 29,000 men, in reserve. Indeed, as the enemy did not seriously attack III Army Corps, it might have been closed up and considered a reserve. Of course Blücher also was counting on Bülow's arrival. As neither happened, the number of the Prussian reserves was always unfavorable. As mentioned above, II Army Corps, the true reserve, was used in bits and pieces to sustain the battle, leaving nothing to make the decisive attack, even if the situation on the battlefield had remained entirely static or perhaps turned in the Prussians' favor.

As the day came to an end, the strength and positions of the opposing forces were roughly as follows:

Blücher had committed 38,000 infantry to the two villages. They had suffered significant losses, had partly used up all their ammunition, and could only be regarded as exhausted remnants. Behind the villages were 6,000 infantry, consisting of individual battalions that, however, had yet to do any fighting. The remainder of the 56,000 men of I and II Army Corps were cavalry and artillery, of which only a few were still fresh.

Had III Army Corps fought alongside the others or had it been used appropriately, then it would have constituted a reserve of some 18,000 men, so one could say that when the battle was decided, Blücher still had a reserve of 24,000 men.

Although at first Bonaparte was a few thousand men weaker than Blücher, he now had several thousand more fresh men available. The reason for this was that he held back more men and used his forces more economically in the firefights.

This small superiority in numbers of reserves would not be particularly decisive, of course, but it should nevertheless be regarded as the first reason for victory.

The second was the unequal results of the firefights up to then. Although when Bonaparte advanced against Ligny, the Prussians still held part of the village but had lost the rest. Indeed, they still held on between Wagnelée and St. Amand but had lost villages and terrain. Everywhere, then, the battle had already gone against them to an extent, and the decisive assault was about to happen.

The third and most important reason is unquestionably that Blücher did not have troops that were still fresh, that is, the III Corps, at hand. The Twelfth Brigade, of course, was close by but was too little. The Ninth was also not far away, but no proper thought had been given to it or to the whole of Thielemann's corps, so it was not available to make a decisive attack and could only be used to cover a retreat. Yet perhaps and most likely, Thielemann's dispersed deployment should have been seen as an advantage in the long run. Had the III Corps been available, it might have been used up along with the others without achieving a favorable result, something that, given the course of the entire battle, only a decisive superiority of force could have achieved, as would have occurred had Bülow's corps arrived. Had the III Corps been used as well, losses in the battle would probably have been 10,000 men more.

34. Critical Commentary on the Battle as a Whole: Blücher

First, Blücher's main error would seem to be a certain lack of clarity in his plan that led to his deployment on a dual front, along with the neutralization of 20,000 men. The position from Sombreffe to St. Balâtre was good, if the objective was to protect a line of retreat to the Meuse. In such an event, however, this front would have to be held while Wellington operated independently and not jointly against the common enemy. As, in such open terrain, it would not be possible to conceal Wellington's march along the road from Quatre Bras, then joining forces in this way would have been of such little use and actually would have been a disadvantage. In this way Wellington would have taken the entirely natural direction for a force sent against the enemy flank, a form of attack that always requires the greatest care. Indeed, when you are the stronger side with the broader base of operations, [a flank attack] is more likely to be decisive.

If in the worst case, however, the intention was to abandon the line of communication with the Meuse, then undertaking a holding action at Sombreffe would be entirely unnecessary, with one brigade at the most being used to delay the enemy. Securing this position was clearly not needed to cover Bülow's arrival, since 35,000 men, if they were supposed to operate as a flanking force (like Wellington in the first case), would have been able to cross Ligny Brook anyway were the enemy actually to have covered it, which is not at all likely.

When starting as great an action as a battle, nothing seems more essential than to be absolutely sure about the most likely conditions. Of these none is as important and influential as the lines of retreat, for they determine the position of the fronts as well as all the main lines of possible movement in the battle. Here Blücher had only half a solution, that is, he was caught between two fronts facing different directions.

Second, even while the battle was underway, say around 4 or 5 P.M., Thielemann could still have been ordered to form up his corps and advance from Mont Potriaux and Point du Jour against the enemy's right flank. Gérard's corps would then either have to give way or the Guard would have to be committed sooner. Even if Grouchy and the Guard had attacked Thielemann, forcing him back over the Ligny Brook, the French reserves would still have been absorbed sooner, and the blow against the center at Ligny probably would not have taken place. The battle probably would not have been decided on the evening of June 16, or in any case, it would have weakened the French army much more.

Third, the defense of the village of St. Amand proper seems to have been a costly sideshow. If it was supposed to be a forward outpost, then the defense of such outposts can only be justified for two reasons:

> a. If they had been inherently very strong, so that they had forced the attacker to commit disproportionate forces against this strength, because he could not have ignored them. Furthermore, apart from their inherent strength, the front line of the army more or less supported them. If these advantages were not present, for instance if an outpost had been vulnerable to an enveloping attack by the enemy and had soon been lost; to retake it, a chaotic and disadvantageous fight would most likely have resulted.

b. It was sometimes necessary to occupy a forward position because it would give the attacker too much cover during his approach. In this case it is a necessary evil.

St. Amand proper was not a particularly strong position. The army's front line could hardly support it, and it did not even cover the front line sufficiently to prevent an attack on Ligny, for instance. From the first point of view, there was clearly no reason to occupy it. The second point certainly did apply to St. Amand la Haye, whose defense it made more difficult by being connected to St. Amand, even if that was only at the narrow end near the castle, where the line of defense could be cut. With regard to the front line between Ligny and La Haye, the village of St. Amand proper was nothing less than awkward for the Prussians. It strengthened the front rather because any French attack coming from it would have to move through 800 paces of Prussian canister fire. In fact, the French do not seem to have ever advanced from there toward the ridge. An entire brigade was used up defending this village, probably without causing the French comparable losses, giving the adverse impression of losing ground.

Fourth, the premature offensive against St. Amand le Hameau and the attempt at another from Ligny also did not correspond with the battle as a whole. The defender should have included a certain offensive principle in his defense, combining resistance with a counterattack, but this counterattack should only have occurred when and where it could have been carried out with advantage: if the French advance had left them situated between the Prussian forces, when he had suffered substantial losses and could have only just held his ground—generally, only when the Prussians' resistance had exhausted their forces. Jürgass's attack through Wagnelée toward Le Hameau obviously came much too soon to be decisive there. Had Jürgass's attack actually pushed on to behind La Haye, he surely would have had to come to a halt there, in a defensive position without the slightest advantage. But the defense is not supposed to be for fighting at a disadvantage. Had Wagnelée been occupied from the outset and had, in particular, a strong contingent of artillery covered it, the French could certainly never have occupied La Haye. Holding Wagnelée would have been decisive, and being to the rear, it would have been very inconvenient for the French commander. But even after the French had occupied La Haye, it would probably have been better just to occupy Wagnelée, holding the garrison of La Haye in check. As long as Wagnelée, Brye, and Ligny were in Prussian hands, the French could not possibly have broken out from the two villages of St. Amand. Rather, the whole position would seem better suited to gaining time and inflicting fearful losses on the French. Only when it became possible to decide the entire battle would it have been the time to push forward from Wagnelée, but then this attack would have to have been sustained. If, however, the situation was such that a counterattack would not turn the battle around, then it had to be avoided, for these forces could be better employed in the defense.

Jagow's attempt to break out of Ligny was even less justifiable. If it had been successful, all he would have achieved would have been to be in the open, surrounded by the French divisions, and unable to defend himself, thus suffering tremendous casualties.

Prussian generals were too much of the opinion that attacking was better than standing and firing. Each has its place.

Fifth, Prussian troops were used up too quickly in static fighting. Their officers called for reinforcements too soon and were given them too easily. Consequently, they committed more men than the French without gaining any ground, suffered more dead and wounded, and exhausted fresh bodies of troops more quickly. It hardly needs mentioning that having maps and plans of every description available, it is now easy, with hindsight, to determine the actual causes of the failure and, having thought through the whole sequence of events, to establish the errors. Yet doing so in the heat of action would not be so easy. In war, action is like swimming against the tide, when normal attributes are insufficient to achieve even mediocre results. That is the case particularly when examining the subject of war: the object of criticism is to establish the facts and not to sit in judgment.

When examining the mistakes identified here, one needs to take into account that the Prussian troops consisted for the most part of Landwehr participating in only their second campaign; that among them were many entirely new formations from provinces that had either never, or not until recently, belonged to the Prussian state; that the French army, while also only recently raised, nevertheless contained elements that had belonged to the best army in the world; and that Bonaparte was the greatest commander of the time—then there is nothing particularly exceptional in the success at Ligny. It was a battle in which 78,000 men lost to around 75,000 due to the balance tipping slightly after a long struggle, and without being a particularly decisive victory; the trophies were twenty-one cannon and at the most, a few thousand prisoners.

35. Bonaparte

First, the easiest way of understanding Bonaparte's original plan of attack is, as mentioned above, that he moved two-thirds of his army (75,000 men) against Blücher and sent the other third (some 40,000 men) against Wellington to hold up whatever might come from there to aid the Prussian commander. He had presumably calculated that this could not be his [Wellington's] entire army and that 40,000 men led by a man like Ney would buy him enough time to complete his victory over Blücher. On June 15 or the morning of June 16 at Charleroi, the thought that Ney might participate in this battle could not yet have occurred to Bonaparte, for he was still reacting to Blücher's deployment, which had surprised him. Only then did it seem to have given him the idea that Ney would be able to decide the Battle of Ligny if he sent part of his force down the highway from Quatre Bras toward Namur. This idea was mentioned explicitly only in the third of the orders given above. This order was written at 2:15 P.M., and Ney's participation at Ligny was mentioned in it as only a secondary consideration and could only have been so at that time, since Bonaparte could not have known if Ney would have a single man to spare. Furthermore, as the distance between the two battlefields was three hours' march, then it was very uncertain if there would even be time for Ney to intervene. That is why this intervention cannot be regarded as an essential part of Bonaparte's plan, nor (as Bonaparte wanted us to believe) that a quirk of fate prevented the original plan to attack the Prussian army simultaneously from both the front and the rear, so ensuring its destruction.

Second, that Bonaparte, instead of sending a column through Wagnelée and enveloping the exposed Prussian right flank, preferred to send his second column against Ligny, indeed delivering the main blow in that direction. This cannot be regarded as a plan arising from Ney's attack on the enemy rear and acting in concert with it to cause the defeat of the Prussian army. Rather, the reasons he made his main attack here were probably as follows:

a. From Bonaparte's perspective, the Prussian position was with the Prussian army's right flank at St. Amand proper, the center at Ligny, and the left at Sombreffe. St. Amand la Haye appeared to be behind the right flank. He believed that if he attacked St. Amand and sent a division to march on La Haye, he would be enveloping the right flank. His intention was to coordinate this maneuver with the attack on the center, so that the battle would not be conducted in too confined an area, which would have strengthened and prolonged the Prussian resistance. This would appear to be a perfectly simple and normal disposition.
b. As the attack on Ligny would threaten the Prussian right, it was to be expected that it would weaken the defense there. Part of the right flank might possibly be lost as a result of this.
c. The attack on Ligny would threaten the Prussian army's natural line of retreat and lead to substantial losses should it want to hold this line, no matter the cost.
d. Finally, St. Amand and Ligny were the nearest points of attack for the forward units of the French army at Fleurus. A further envelopment via Wagnelée might perhaps have delayed the attack a whole hour, but it was already past noon when Bonaparte reconnoitered the Prussian position, so there was no time to lose.

The existing circumstances would appear to be sufficient motivation for the form this attack took, and existing circumstances are always the ones that are the most influential in war.

Third, yet considering the matter from a more comprehensive standpoint, the first question that must be asked is if it was better for Bonaparte to attack Blücher in a way that drove him back toward Wellington, rather than away from him. The answer has to be that the second course of action more likely would have decided the entire campaign.

Had Bonaparte attacked St. Amand with his right wing and Wagnelée with his left, and had a third column advance along the highway from Brussels, then if the Prussian army had lost the battle, it would have been forced to retreat along the Roman road toward the Meuse, making a union of forces with Wellington in the following days very unlikely, if not impossible.

Fourth, had Bülow arrived that afternoon, which was possible, and had he then been used to stage an attack with Thielemann from the Point du Jour, Bonaparte would have had to fight against a superior enemy in the worst possible position, that is, with both flanks enveloped: the left from Wagnelée, the right from the Point du Jour. As Bülow in fact was expected to arrive from Liège via the Point du Jour, this would have been a further reason for Bonaparte to prefer moving around the Prussian army's right flank.

It is not known if Bonaparte considered these matters or not and if he might have been concerned that despite sending Ney to cover the route from Brussels, he was not certain this would be effective. If this were the case, then the form of his attack is sufficiently justified. But if he had no such concerns and simply attacked according to circumstances, then one could certainly say that this plan was not entirely appropriate and was insufficient for his dangerous situation.

Fifth, the reasons for the movements by the French I Corps are totally unclear. Gamot, Ney's defender, is convinced that Bonaparte ordered it from Frasnes but can offer no proof. Bonaparte believes Ney was indecisive and left it [I Corps] behind to cover his rear. It was most unlikely that Bonaparte ordered it up himself, for its appearance made him believe it might be part of Wellington's army. How would d'Erlon have turned around again and how could there be no mention of this corps in the orders and dispositions issued to Vandamme? Moreover, why did Bonaparte not use d'Erlon's corps to envelop Blücher, when it was at hand? He most probably did not since it was too late. He appeared to have received the report of its approach around 5:30 P.M. It was 7 P.M. when the news arrived that it was d'Erlon. It would have taken an hour before d'Erlon would have received the order and then perhaps another hour before he could reach Brye.

This is only an attempt to clarify the matter, however, and it cannot be denied that the little information available about the movements of this corps points suspicion toward Bonaparte. Gamot named Colonel Laurent as the bearer of the order to d'Erlon, so why has he not come forward with an explanation? It cannot be out of regard for Ney's memory, for even if Laurent had stated that he had not brought an order from Bonaparte for another use for I Corps, then noting this would be of little consequence to Ney. There is simply no other way to explain this lack of clarity, except that mouths that could have spoken were closed out of admiration and affection for the former emperor.

In any case, this useless marching and countermarching by 20,000 men at a moment when they were desperately needed was a cardinal error, some small part of which must always be attributed to Bonaparte, even if he did not recall the corps, even if it could be credible that the instructions given to Ney were not sufficiently clear and definite.

All in all, it could be said that on June 16, Bonaparte did not appear quite equal to his own destiny.

36. The Engagement at Quatre Bras

Where the troops under Ney's command stood on the morning of June 16 is discussed above. Ney left his II Corps at Gosselies and instructed Reille to await Bonaparte's orders while he rushed his advance guard to Frasnes and reconnoitered the enemy that entire morning. They consisted of only the larger part of Perponcher's division and two cavalry regiments, some 6,000 to 8,000 men.

At 11 A.M. General Flahaut,[103] Bonaparte's aide de camp, arrived at Gosselies with the order that Ney should advance and attack

---

103. Gen. Charles-Auguste-Joseph Count Flahaut de la Billarderie (1785–1870). His family emigrated from France during the Revolution, returning in 1797. He joined a regiment of hussars in 1800, fighting at Marengo. After a brief

with his corps. This is probably the order Bonaparte mentioned and that he said Ney received by 11:30 A.M. It would have been 1 P.M. before the Third Division of II Corps reached Frasnes.

At this time, at Frasnes, Ney had three divisions of infantry (II Corps) and three of cavalry (Kellerman and II Cavalry Corps), in all about 23,000 men and forty-eight cannon. He had left the Guard Light Cavalry behind to the rear of Frasnes, for Bonaparte had expressly ordered this and I Corps was still on the march.

On the Allied side, Perponcher's division was facing Ney alone. At this time Wellington was with Blücher.[104] Only when there did he become convinced that the main enemy force was facing Blücher, and only then did he seem to have ordered his reserve divisions, standing at the exit of the Soignes Woods since 10 A.M., to begin moving toward Quatre Bras. It is perfectly understandable how the first of these divisions, Picton's, did not reach Quatre Bras until after 5 P.M., for it is over three [German] miles from Brye to Waterloo, and from there to Quatre Bras, more than two.

The fighting began about 3 P.M. and consisted of three major events:

In the first, Perponcher's division was driven from the ground it occupied roughly halfway between Quatre Bras and Frasnes, losing four guns and partly withdrawing into the Bossu Woods.

In the second, Picton's division arrived around 5 P.M. and resumed the battle, taking up a position along the Namur highway,

---

period in Spain, he fought at Wagram in 1809, then in Russia in 1812. The next year Flahaut joined Napoleon's staff, serving under him in the following campaigns. After Waterloo he sought refuge in Britain, later returning to France. Flahaut returned to favor after the revolution of July 1830 and held various political and administrative posts thereafter.

104. Early in the afternoon of June 16, Wellington met with Blücher at the mill of Bussy, Blücher's headquarters on the Ligny battlefield. The accounts of this meeting fall into two groups: one in which the details of how Wellington would move to assist the Prussians was discussed, and one in which Wellington was supposedly highly critical of the Prussian dispositions and only gave a qualified promise of help. There were a number of witnesses to this discussion, and several accounts have been published. Those from the Prussian side, which contain no mention of any criticisms from Wellington or any qualification to his promise, are largely supported by independent observers from other German states, while Wellington's version has been corroborated only by his aide Sir Henry Hardinge.

then retaking the village of Pierremont on its left.[105] The Duke of Brunswick's troops arrived a little later and advanced down the Charleroi highway, where they occupied some shepherds' huts. Both sides were now roughly equal, as Wellington had around 20,000 men available, though he had no more than 1,800 cavalry to Ney's roughly 4,000.

The battle remained undecided for a couple of hours. The French recaptured Pierremont and maintained their hold on the Gemioncourt farm along the highway. Ney received the later order from Bonaparte urging him to advance and overwhelm his opponent and then, indeed, to take part in the battle at Ligny. He committed his reserve, Jérôme's division,[106] to the battle, and his more numerous cavalry made every effort to advance along the highway to Quatre Bras. It was probably around this time that he sent the order to d'Erlon to hurry to the battlefield, which led to him turning around near Villiers-Perwin about 8 P.M. The French cavalry took six or eight cannon, rode down a couple of battalions, and pushed into parts of Picton's second line. But these efforts did not lead to victory. The fire coming from all sides forced Piré and Kellerman to fall back several times.[107] Despite that, the battle

---

105. The time given for Picton's arrival is a little late. His lead elements reached the battlefield between 3 and 4 P.M.

106. Prince Jérôme Bonaparte (1784–1860), marshal of France, brother of Napoleon Bonaparte. He joined the French navy in 1800, sailing with the fleet that tried to resupply the French forces in Egypt the next year. After spending some years in the colonies and the United States, he returned to Europe and fought on land in the Jena campaign of 1806, during which he commanded a mixed force of Bavarians and Württembergers in the Prussian province of Silesia, now largely in Poland. He became king of Westphalia in 1807, commanding its army in the campaigns of 1809 and 1812. When the French were ejected from Germany in the fall of 1813, Jérôme returned to France. In the following spring he joined Marshal Joachim Murat in Italy. After Waterloo he spent some time living and traveling abroad before being allowed to return to France in 1847.

107. Cavalry Gen. Hippolyte-Marie-Guilliame de Rosnyvinen, Count Piré (1778–1850). Piré initially fled the French Revolution and went into exile, first joining the royal forces, then transferring to the British army. He became involved in a royalist uprising in the Vendée before joining the army of the then first consul, Napoleon Bonaparte. Piré fought at Austerlitz in 1805, Eylau in 1807, and Spain in 1808 before returning to Germany in 1809, where he fought at Aspern-Essling and Wagram. In 1812 he was part of the Grand Army in Russia,

went in favor of the French, and they pushed farther into the Bossu Woods.

Third action: Around 7 or 8 P.M., the divisions of Cook and Alten,[108] the right wing of the Prince of Orange's forces, arrived. Cook's division was used on the right in the Bossu Woods and Alten's on the left against Pierremont. Both overwhelmed the enemy, so deciding the general outcome of the battle. Despite that, the French fought on tenaciously and only around 10 P.M. did the Allies become masters of the Gemioncourt farm. Ney fell back to in front of Frasnes, where he took up positions. Casualties were roughly equal, being around 4–5,000 men on each side.

37. Observations

Bonaparte and all subsequent critics have raised a great hew and cry that Ney failed to seize the position at Quatre Bras before the arrival of a significant Allied force, just as if Quatre Bras were a fortress, once captured, completely fulfilled the objective of the whole operation. Here the expression "position" is one of those terms that, if used blindly, like an algebraic formula, leads to empty phrases and baseless assertions.

Ney's mission was to prevent Wellington from coming to the aid of the Prussians. He could have done this by either driving back the corps attempting to do this or by merely holding it up and preventing it from advancing. The first possibility required significantly superior numbers; the second, a good position.

It would have been difficult for Ney to have estimated the forces moving against him, for they included all the men that could have been concentrated against him not only during June 16 but also up to noon on June 17. As mentioned above, this could have been almost the entire Anglo-Netherlands army, or at least 80,000 men. Initially, he encountered only few of them at Frasnes and Quatre

---

then fought again in Germany in 1813 and then France in 1814. After Waterloo he went to Russia but was allowed to return to France in 1819. Piré held various posts in the army until his death.

108. The lead elements of Alten's division actually started arriving between 5 and 5:30 P.M., with Cooke's Guards beginning to arrive an hour later.

Bras, which was to be expected, as was that they would have been far less than his own force. If he had defeated this smaller force, it would have been but little advantage. But would it have also been so effective an opening move that it could be seen as a guarantee of general victory? That was not possible! Given that on the evening of June 15 or very early on June 16, he had defeated whatever part of Perponcher's division that was in front of him and then advanced, a commander like Wellington would naturally have made his arrangements accordingly, establishing a position somewhat farther to the rear with the first reserves reaching the area, linked up with the defeated division there, and then staged a delaying action so his remaining divisions and corps could concentrate. The farther Ney advanced, the faster Wellington's concentration would be. However astute and fortunate he may have been, this inevitably would have led to a great imbalance of forces and put him in a very dangerous position. To avoid this happening, Ney's attack would have to have shattered Wellington's army, thrown it into confusion, wiped out divisions piecemeal, et cetera, an assumption that could only have been purely illusory.

It could be argued that if, on the evening of June 16 or the morning of June 17, Ney had come up against a superior enemy force, his mission of preventing the enemy from participating in the Battle of Ligny would have been accomplished and that he then could have fallen back. But how could Ney have been so certain that the superior force would not be facing him already on the afternoon of June 16? Having been instructed to advance head down along a road, could he know if, when he lifted his head and eyes, the enemy columns would be firmly established in their positions, on his right and above all, his left? Might not Vandamme's fate in 1813 been on his mind?[109] What commander, indeed, has ever been ordered to advance with 40,000 men between two enemy corps on a single road?

109. After the Battle of Dresden on August 26–27, 1813, Vandamme was put in charge of the pursuit of the defeated Allied forces. He followed up behind part of the Army of Bohemia along one route only to have another part take another route and fall upon his rear. The enemy columns surrounded Vandamme at Kulm on August 30, destroying his force and capturing him, thus reversing the effects of the French victory three days earlier.

Taking this into account, it could well have been the case that Ney never thought his offensive would push back the enemy coming from this direction, but rather that his mission could have been nothing other than to take Quatre Bras, driving off whomever might already be there, and also that Bonaparte had expected nothing more of him. It also follows that Quatre Bras was a very good position that enabled Ney to hold off an enemy superior in numbers on June 16.

But was Quatre Bras such a position? Using the term "position" appears to be assuming it was, but this assumption is entirely gratuitous, for no one has proven it, nor indeed asserted it, nor even discussed it. Such an unfounded assumption cannot be part of any criticism.

To make a judgment about Quatre Bras as a position for Ney, one must have been there, for positions cannot properly be judged from maps, and we do not even have a good map of this area. Generally speaking, however, this sort of crossroads is a disadvantageous position because the line of retreat should not be directly to the rear. But even accepting Quatre Bras as a good position, it was certainly not a strong one, and as Ney did not have time to deploy there accordingly, there was no reason to expect that it would be effective against a stronger enemy.

Bonaparte ordered Ney to Quatre Bras because the two highways met there. Here he could cut the route from Brussels to Namur, that is, from Wellington to the Prussians. Nothing was more obvious than this, and if it had been left to Ney, he would certainly have accomplished it, just as he would have been wrong not to do so. Yet although Ney's appearance at Frasnes nevertheless prevented Wellington from coming to the aid of the Prussians along the Namur highway, this failure has no consequences whatsoever and indeed, in view of the observations made here, it could be simply argued whatever Ney did on the evening of June 15 or the morning of June 16, whatever events he caused or affected, the results would not have been much different than they were or could have been much worse for the French.

Ney fully accomplished his mission of preventing Wellington giving aid. Bonaparte only had the idea of his joining the battle at Ligny later, that is, after reconnoitering Blücher's position and because he had still heard nothing from Ney about a substantial enemy force. By then, however, it was too late to do anything. If he had had this idea on the evening of June 15, it would have been wrong to give Ney so many troops: it would have been better to send a corps down the Roman road into Blücher's rear. First reinforcing Ney then taking these troops away was doing things the wrong way around, for the enemy might well have been weak to start with but was being constantly reinforced.

Bonaparte's hew and cry against Ney is thus nothing more than the wish to represent his plans as more brilliant and grand than they really were at the moment of execution. His orders were much simpler and more usual, and Ney could not possibly have acted according to circumstances that only became apparent later on.

Certainly Ney could have driven off Perponcher early in the morning and held Quatre Bras. He could even have sent a whole corps down the Namur highway against the Prussian right flank without having the events at Quatre Bras turning out much worse for him, but it is only with the benefit of hindsight, taking into account all of the unforeseeable twists of fate, that all he might have done can be seen.

38. Blücher's Movements on June 17

The retreat of the Prussian I and II Corps through Tilly to Wavre was made partly during the night, partly on the morning of June 17. That of III Army Corps, which started only at 4 or 5 A.M., went in the direction of Gembloux and from there to Wavre.

I and II Corps reached Wavre around noon on June 17, taking up positions on both sides of the Dyle River, while leaving part of their cavalry a couple of hours to cover the rear. III Corps remained at Gembloux until 2 P.M. and then went to Wavre, where it arrived that evening. IV Corps had spent the night of June 16–17 in Haute and Basse Baudecet, two hours' march from Gembloux and on June 17 continued to Dion-le-Mont, where it deployed to cover the remaining corps.

While the four Prussian corps were conducting these movements, more or less completing them by noon on June 17, the French pursuit had hardly begun.

That night Bonaparte had assigned the initial pursuit of Blücher to General Pajol,[110] using Pajol's cavalry corps and Teste's division from VI Corps.[111] Pajol set off on the morning of June 17, first seeking the Prussians on the Namur road. It is incomprehensible that the French did not see the Prussian III Corps start out toward Gembloux, since it did not leave until daylight, and still more incomprehensible to assume that Blücher and his whole army would have gone to Namur. One battery from the Prussian II Corps may have given this impression, for it was just arriving from Namur when it heard the battle was lost, attempted to turn back, and was captured en route. It does seem that Grouchy, from whom Pajol received his immediate instructions, was chiefly responsible for this incorrect idea. Grouchy was supposed to follow at once, but since the troops needed a few hours' rest, Bonaparte did not rush to send him off but instead took Grouchy with him to tour the battlefield on the morning of June 17 and did not send him off before noon. He was given the corps of Gérard and Vandamme, Teste's division from VI Corps, Exelmans's cavalry,[112] and half of Pajol's, a total of 35,000 men.

110. Cavalry Gen. Claude-Pierre Count Pajol (1772–1844). Pajol volunteered for the army in 1791 and rose through the ranks. He fought throughout the Revolutionary Wars, mainly in Germany at Ulm and Leoben in 1805. In 1809 he fought at Wagram. Pajol suffered wounds in Russia in 1812 and at Leipzig in 1813 (badly). After Waterloo he went into commerce before participating in the revolution of July 1830, leading Parisian revolutionaries against Charles X.
111. Gen. François-Antoine Baron Teste (1775–1862). Teste joined the army in 1792, rising through the ranks during the Revolutionary Wars. He then participated in the campaigns in Italy at the end of the eighteenth century and held various appointments in the region over the following years. In 1812 he served in Russia and was taken prisoner at Kulm (along with Vandamme) in 1813. After Waterloo he was ordered to defend the left bank of the Loire River. Following the restoration of Louis XVIII, Teste held various senior posts in the army.
112. Rémy-Joseph-Isidore Count Exelmans, marshal of France (1775–1852). Joining the army in 1791 as a volunteer, Exelmans fought in France and Germany during the Revolutionary Wars, then in Italy from 1799 to 1800. He served at Austerlitz in 1805 and in 1807 fought at both Eylau and Friedland. He was taken prisoner in Spain in 1808, escaping in 1811. Wounded in Russia in 1812, Exelmans fought in Saxony in 1813, then in France in 1814. Exiled after Napoleon's second abdication, he was allowed to return to France in 1819 and held several senior posts in the army. In 1830 he was one of the leaders of the Paris revolutionaries. Exelmans was appointed marshal of France in 1851.

As mentioned above, Pajol was already on the move, Exelmans would be sent down the road to Gembloux a little later, but the two corps of Gérard and Vandamme remained in their bivouacs at Ligny and St. Amand until 3 P.M., and it would be evening before Grouchy was able to assemble them at Point du Jour.

Bonaparte's intention was to use Grouchy to pursue Blücher so closely that he would not think of supporting Wellington, while he joined Ney with the remaining 30,000 men, concentrating a force of 70,000 against Wellington, then achieving a second victory against him.

Since Bonaparte's troops had to be left to rest until noon on June 17, he could not face Wellington before the evening of June 17, and this second battle could not take place before June 18.

Bonaparte is supposed to have instructed Grouchy to stay between Blücher and the road from Namur to Brussels, for the second battle was likely to take place along this road, and it was most likely that Grouchy would take part in it. But no such order has been found anywhere other than in Bonaparte's account, which is hardly credible and was written after the fact. Grouchy's account of the movements on June 17 is so plausible that it is difficult not to believe it. According to it, Bonaparte's instructions referred in general terms to pursuing Blücher and contained nothing specific. Bonaparte did send such an order to Grouchy at 10 A.M. on June 18, but how could it be carried out, since it reached Grouchy only when he was already facing Wavre?

In no way did Bonaparte believe, as he stated in his *Mémoires*, that Blücher would go to Wavre to join up again with Wellington. Rather, he automatically assumed that he would, above all, attempt to join up his IV Corps and then move toward the Meuse. Bonaparte thought 35,000 men under a resolute commander would keep the Prussians on the move for several days and that he would therefore be able to fight a battle against Wellington without fearing anything from them.

It is most remarkable that on the morning of June 17, the Prussian army was sought and pursued only in the direction of Gembloux, where one corps had gone, and Namur, where none had gone, but not in the direction of Tilly and Gentinnes, where two had actually gone. There is practically no other explanation for this remarkable fact except that Bonaparte assigned the pursuit specifically to Grouchy, whose two cavalry corps had spent the whole day facing Thielemann toward Gembloux. Had he assigned the pursuit to the Guard cavalry and III Corps, they would have picked up the trail better. His imprecise manner prevented Bonaparte from giving Grouchy more exact instructions. It also seems that Bonaparte himself was so convinced that Blücher would fall back to the Meuse that he never considered another line of march, such as toward Gembloux and along the Roman road. At least there was an indication of this in a message by Gamot from Marshal Soult sent to Ney from Fleurus on June 17 that it was Bonaparte's intention that the pursuit should be along the two roads toward Gembloux and Namur. The intention was evidently to harass the Prussian army on its way to the Meuse, but in no way to block a march toward Wellington. If Bonaparte had had the idea that Blücher might have gone to Wavre, it would have been more reasonable to send a strong force to the left bank of the Dyle.

Pajol's movement, first in the direction of Namur, then toward St. Denis, between Namur and Gembloux, and then back again toward Mazy, remains little understood. Whether Grouchy or Bonaparte ordered this remarkable movement remains uncertain, but the consequence was that Pajol, after wandering around aimlessly with his cavalry and Teste's division for all of June 17, was still at Mazy that evening, close to the battlefield.

As both III and IV Corps marched along one road, even Grouchy was unable to reach Gembloux before 10 P.M., where he had to spend the night, while Exelmans pushed on to Sart-à-Walhain. Yet this corps also required billets, and only two regiments were deployed as a vanguard.

The main results of this day were that the French as good as failed to pursue the Prussian army; Blücher reached Wavre unmolested and was able to concentrate all his corps there on the evening of June 17.

If this seems such a great contrast with the earlier conduct of the French, then the different circumstances should be considered. The exceptionally energetic pursuits that produced such brilliant results for Bonaparte in his earlier campaigns were a result of simply having much superior forces following a totally defeated opponent. Now, however, he had to turn his main force, and specifically his freshest troops, against a new enemy, over whom a victory was yet to be obtained. The forces that were supposed to pursue were III and IV Corps, precisely the troops who had been involved in the bloodiest fighting until 10 P.M. and who now needed some time to reorganize, eat, and replenish their ammunition. The cavalry corps had certainly not suffered losses and so might well have been able to press the Prussian rearguard early on. It may well have been an error not to do so, but cavalry alone would not have been able to bring about the kind of results the general French pursuit had achieved in their earlier victories over Prussia, for the surrounding countryside was too broken up for cavalry alone to be able to achieve much.

Blücher had abandoned his natural line of retreat to maintain contact with Wellington, for as the first battle was more or less a mess, he was resolved to fight a second and let Wellington know he wanted to come to his aid with his whole army.

As his rearguard was not under any pressure and as he did not know what had become of the French, Blücher had naturally thought that Bonaparte had turned against Wellington with his entire force. He thus believed he only had to leave a few troops in the defile at Wavre and could join Wellington with the rest.

This decision by Blücher is unquestionably most praiseworthy. Contrary to all pretenses that rules and false wisdom give rise to in such cases, he simply used his common sense and decided to turn toward Wellington on June 18, preferring to move a little out of his own theater of operations rather than leave the matter half done. The battle he had lost was no defeat. He had lost only about one-sixth of his strength, and with almost 100,000 men, he could turn the battle facing Wellington into an unquestionable victory. He also needed to wash away the stain that the honor of his arms received on June 16 and to earn the glory of standing by a comrade in arms, even beyond all expectations, one who, the day before and contrary to all expectations, had been unable to stand by him. There can be no greater motive for the heart and mind.

Blücher's movements on June 18 will be examined when his part in the battle of that day is considered.

39. Wellington on June 17 and 18

At Quatre Bras on the evening of June 16, Wellington had the Prince of Orange's corps and the Reserve (except Chassé's division and two Netherlands cavalry brigades that remained at Nivelles). During the night and on the morning of June 17, Clinton's division and one brigade of Colville's division arrived from Lord Hill's corps, the right wing. The remainder of the corps concentrated under Prince Frederick of the Netherlands at Halle.

On the morning of June 17, Wellington had 70,000 men at Quatre Bras and Nivelles. He learned of Blücher's retreat around 7 A.M., allowed his troops to cook their breakfast, and around 10 A.M. began the withdrawal to the position at Mont St. Jean in front of the Soignes Woods, where he had found a good position and where he had decided to accept battle, should Blücher be able to come to his aid with two corps, around 50,000 men.

Ney is supposed to have advanced against Wellington's rearguard early that morning, but since Wellington did not leave his position before 10 A.M., Ney could not have done so. As Wellington had his 7–8,000 cavalrymen cover this maneuver, the French did not notice his departure immediately. Ney remained resting in his bivouacs at Frasnes until 1 P.M.

Around noon Bonaparte had sent off VI Corps, the Guard, Milhaud's cavalry, the 1st division of Pajol's cavalry, and Domon's cavalry division from III Corps on the road from Namur to Quatre Bras,[113] that is, his entire force excepting only Girard's division, which according to Bonaparte was intentionally left behind at St. Amand because it had suffered so much, but which was most likely forgotten, which is all the more comprehensible as it was part of

---

113. Cavalry Gen. Jean-Simon Count Domon (1774–1830). He volunteered for military service in 1791, fighting in France, the Netherlands, and the Rhineland during the Revolutionary Wars. Domon participated at Jena in 1806, at Eylau and Friedland in 1807, and at Wagram in 1809. In 1812 he commanded I Cavalry Corps and fought at Borodino. In March 1813 he was appointed commander of the cavalry of the Kingdom of Naples and fought in Germany that fall. Domon was exiled from Paris after Waterloo but was allowed to rejoin the army in 1820, holding various senior posts afterward.

II Corps,[114] so that none of the other corps commanders was concerned with it and General Girard, who had commanded it, was badly wounded. To leave it behind deliberately would have been unquestionably an even greater mistake than to forget it.

Around 2 P.M. this body of troops moved off from the area around the village of Marbais down the highway toward Quatre Bras, while Marshal Ney was chided to move off at the same time. The Anglo-Allied cavalry began its withdrawal, both French columns joined up on the Brussels road and advanced until they encountered strong resistance toward evening at Mont St. Jean, where Bonaparte become convinced that he was facing the entire Anglo-Allied army. Torrential rain and exceptionally poor paths on and next to the highway had delayed the march and exhausted the troops, so there could be even less thought of fighting that day.

Bonaparte positioned his army near Plancenoit and set up his headquarters in Le Caillou.

40. The Battle of Waterloo: Wellington's Deployment

On the morning of June 18, except for the 19,000 men at Halle,[115] Wellington had concentrated all his army, 68,000 strong, at Mont St. Jean.

At the beginning of the battle, his right wing was deployed on the highway to Nivelles, the center behind La Haye Sainte, and the left behind the farms of Smohain, Papelotte, and La Haye.

---

114. The rest of II Corps was with Ney.

115. Historians have since speculated as to why Wellington left such a large force under Prince Frederik at this particular place. Some believe this was to prevent Napoleon from outflanking him on his right and cutting him off from the channel ports, which is often mistakenly seen as his line of retreat should he have lost the battle. In fact he would have retreated through Brussels and then gone on to the great fortified port of Antwerp. It is also possible that this force could have been used to delay any possible French advance on Louis XVIII's court-in-exile in Ghent should Napoleon have won the battle. Another possibility is that Wellington deliberately left a force of Netherlanders out of the firing line at Waterloo so that their army's continued participation in the war after a possible defeat would be guaranteed.

Between the two highways, the ground sloped away gently, and a sunken road left of the Namur highway obstructed frontal attacks. Neither flank had real anchor points, but the right was to some extent protected indirectly by the hamlets of Merbé, Braine, and Braine l'Alleud; the left by the farmhouse at Fischermont. Behind the front, an hour away, stood the Soignes Woods, which Bonaparte and many an armchair critic have regarded as a death-trap for Wellington's army had he lost the battle. Yet it is unlikely this assumption was correct, for otherwise a commander as careful as Wellington would not have taken a position with it so close to his rear. A forest crossed by many paths could actually have been a great source of protection for a defeated army.

Wellington's general deployment was roughly such that his front extended about 5,000 paces, with thirty battalions standing in the first line, around thirteen in the second, sixty squadrons of cavalry in the third and fourth lines, with an additional thirty-eight battalions and thirty-three squadrons stationed at various points farther to the rear or to the flanks in reserve. The deployment could thus be characterized as exceptionally deep.

Before the front were three key points: the farm of Hougoumont, 1,000 paces in front of the right wing; La Haye Sainte, 500 paces in front of the center along the Namur highway; and La Haye, 1,000 paces in front of the left wing. Infantry held all three, and they were to a greater or lesser extent prepared for the defense.[116]

As it was possible that Bonaparte had only left some cavalry behind to deal with Blücher, Wellington had expected the entire French army to attack him. He would then have had to operate with 68,000 men against 100,000 and rely on Blücher's intervention. He had already received a promise of this from him on June 17. For Wellington, everything came down to holding his position long enough for Blücher to arrive. Blücher's intervention would be effective partly by supporting the left wing of the Allies and partly by attacking the right flank of the French. So Blücher's

---

116. The most effort had been put into preparing Hougoumont, whose garrison included elements of the British Guards. La Haye Sainte had also been prepared for the defense, but as the military engineers had been deployed mainly at Hougoumont, measures there remained incomplete. Little seems to have been done to prepare La Haye and Papelotte.

support was in every respect offensive in nature, and it was all the more reasonable that Wellington confined himself entirely to the defensive, seeking to gain every advantage from the ground. Wavre is roughly two [German] miles from Wellington's battlefield. From the moment when Wellington saw the enemy appear to his fore, it would have taken perhaps six to eight hours before Blücher arrived, assuming he had not begun his march earlier. This was too little time for a battle against 70,000 men to be begun, fought, and decided, so there was no reason for Wellington to fear he might be defeated before Blücher arrived.

41. Bonaparte's Plan of Attack

If Bonaparte can be believed, he only let his troops leave their encampments relatively late to give the rain-soaked ground time to dry out. He then lost a couple of hours forming them up in front of Belle Alliance, 2,500 paces from the Anglo-Allied position that consisted of two lines of infantry and a third and fourth of cavalry. Only around 11 A.M. was all this accomplished.

There is something peculiar about this parade-ground deployment, the sight of which still seems to delight Bonaparte's memory. This was quite unusual, for it was not used in any of his other battles. It was entirely useless, because to stage an attack, the troops would have to reform in columns. Instead of concealing his forces from the enemy as much as possible, as is usual, and approaching unnoticed, he deployed them as broadly and systematically as possible, as if it were only a matter of judging a display. Three possible reasons for this come to mind: either he wanted to bolster the courage of his own men, he wanted to impress his opponent, or it was an extravagant bit of playacting by a mind that was no longer quite balanced.

If there was supposed to be a true parallel attack or if it was preferably the center that was supposed to be broken, or a flank taken, cannot be clearly discerned either from the measures taken or from the way the fighting went and least of all from what Bonaparte actually said about his plan.

The deployment of forces and the initial advance indicate that it was a purely parallel attack. The direction of the main effort in the battle indicates that the center was supposed to be broken. This, however, seems to have been more the consequence of immediate necessity than of real planning, and the order of the attack contained the following rather uncharacteristic elements:

II Corps (Reille), supported by Kellermann's cavalry and Guyot's Guard cavalry division,[117] a total of three infantry and four cavalry divisions, attacked the enemy right.

Two divisions of I Corps (d'Erlon), supported by VI (Lobau), which had only two divisions available, and two cavalry divisions; Milhaud's cavalry corps; and one division of Guard Cavalry—a total of four divisions of infantry and five of cavalry altogether—were assigned to the center.

Two infantry divisions from I Corps and one cavalry division were to attack the left wing. The Guard infantry remained in the rear of the center as a reserve.

No other organized thought appears to be behind this attack, at least none that can be understood. Even what Bonaparte said about attacking Wellington's left conflicts with the course of the battle, as will be discussed below.

As all of these arrangements demonstrate, Bonaparte gave no thought whatsoever to Blücher's arrival and participation. Rather, here as at Ligny, he counted to some extent on help from his detached wing. Here too he had given Grouchy, as he had Ney, orders of a kind, but in both cases they were too vague, too late, and, as will be discussed below, paid too little attention to distance, time, and conditions. This is only mentioned here as it affected the plan of battle to some extent, though only to a certain degree, for Bonaparte does not seem to have seriously counted on this help.

---

117. Cavalry Gen. Claude-Étienne Count Guyot (1768–1837). He joined the army in 1790, rising through the ranks during the Revolutionary Wars, when he fought in Germany, the Vendée, and Italy. Guyot also saw action at Austerlitz in 1805, Eylau in 1807, and Wagram in 1809. He commanded the Chasseurs of the Guard in Russia in 1812 and was wounded at Lützen in May 1813. Taken prisoner at Klum, the count was exchanged and fought at Leipzig, then throughout the campaign in France in 1814. Guyot received two wounds at Waterloo.

42. The Key Points of the Battle: Wellington's Defense

The battle can be divided into two separate parts: Wellington's defense and the Prussian attack on the right flank of the French. The battle, that is, Wellington's defense, began around noon, Prussian help arrived around 4:30 P.M., and the fighting ended between 8 and 9 P.M. when darkness fell.

The French attack on Wellington's position could be seen as having consisted of the following phases:

First, around noon, the left-wing division (Jérôme) of Reille's corps attacked the château of Hougoumont, while its other two divisions remained in reserve. The French became masters of the outlying woods, but not the buildings. On Wellington's right, the British Guards (Cooke's division) moved up to support the position. Foy's division (in the center of II Corps) was committed to support the attack, but the French never gained control of the position, so a steady firefight continued. It seemed almost as if this was only supposed to be a feint and that Reille was conserving his forces. In any case, the right-wing division remained in reserve, later being used in the center.

This attack thus accomplished nothing at all, except to use up both lines of infantry on the Allied right as well as the Brunswickers that were used in support.

Second, d'Erlon's corps began its attack two hours later, around 2 P.M., after Bonaparte had learned of Bülow's approach and had already ordered VI Corps and two cavalry divisions (Subervie and Domon)[118] to move against the Prussians. Three divisions undertook the main attack on La Haye Sainte and the part of the Allied center that, from the French perspective, was to the right of the highway and behind the sunken road. The Fourth Division moved

---

118. Cavalry Gen. Jacques-Gervais Baron Subervie (1776–1856). He volunteered for the army in 1792, initially fighting in the Pyrenees before becoming an aide de camp to General Lannes in the Army of Italy. Subervie was part of the Grand Army in Austria, Prussia, and Poland during the campaigns of 1805–1807, then served on the Iberian Peninsula until 1811, and was wounded during the Battle of Borodino in 1812. He commanded a cavalry division in Germany in 1813 and fought in France in 1814. Subervie played a role in the July Revolution of 1830, after which he held various posts in the army.

up to attack La Haye, Papelotte, and Smohain. This attack was of a completely different nature from the one against the center and as such will be considered first.

The skirmishers of Perponcher's Second Brigade occupied these three positions on the far left of the army. At some point they lost these positions, but exactly when is not clear. Yet it is certain that the French never assaulted these outposts. Rather, they engaged them in a continuous firefight. The Netherlanders held on, though evidently only with a few troops, until Bülow pushed on past Fischermont, detached his right wing against them, and drove them off. But as d'Erlon's right-wing division was still largely intact, it regained these positions later on, holding them for a few hours until between 6 and 7 P.M., when Ziethen arrived on the Anglo-Allied left and attacked them.

So there was little difference in what happened with this advanced position on the Anglo-Allied left as with that on the right. What happened there was more of a demonstration, or at any rate covering the flanks of the center, than a serious attack.

Third, regarding the center, as mentioned above, the three remaining divisions of d'Erlon's corps attacked here. As VI Corps and Subervie and Domon's cavalry were already engaged against Bülow, the infantry in the French center consisted only of these three divisions, with nothing else in reserve except the cavalry corps and the Guard.

All accounts agree that d'Erlon's first attack was very tempestuous and hasty, with the second column that struck the First Brigade of Perponcher's division actually breaking through, though the fire of the reserves and charges by the Anglo-Allied cavalry threw it back. Two Anglo-Allied cavalry brigades under Ponsonby[119] and Vandeleur[120] inflicted a considerable defeat that also spread to the

---

119. Maj. Gen. Sir William Ponsonby (1772–1815). He first saw action in Spain in 1811, after service in Ireland and command of the 5th Dragoon Guards. After the Battle of Salamanca in 1812, he replaced the mortally wounded General Le Marchant, leading Le Marchant's brigade at Vittoria. Ponsonby himself was mortally wounded at Waterloo while returning to the Allied lines after having led the charge in question.

120. Maj. Gen. Sir John Ormsby Vandeleur (1763–1849). He joined the 5th Foot as an ensign in 1781, first serving in the West Indies before fighting in

third column. The French cavalry under Milhaud then threw back the Anglo-Allied cavalry, with some considerable losses.

So this first attack seems to have been a kind of warm up that was largely disadvantageous to the French. As this attack was made with no preparations and the opposing forces were not yet exhausted, then a success here would not have decided the battle.[121] But d'Erlon's left column that assaulted La Haye Sainte seems to have brought the fighting there to an immediate halt. The Anglo-Allied army supported this outpost, and it was fought over continuously, changing hands several times.

D'Erlon rallied his forces, and the fight then continued without any overall result or exceptional events until between 5 and 6 P.M. The fighting here consisted of heavy artillery and infantry fire, intermingled with assaults by battalion columns or battalions in line. Occasionally, cavalry was used to cut down battalions trying to retake La Haye Sainte. In this fighting three Allied battalions were lost, and the French cavalry penetrated the Anglo-Allied lines, from which they were always thrown back, however, suffering losses.

After the forces involved had worn each other down considerably in a struggle lasting three or four hours, the Prussians appeared on the battlefield, emerging from the woods. Ney now tried to force a decision against Wellington with the cavalry. As the sunken road to the right of the highway hindered a cavalry attack, he tried to advance left of the highway with Milhaud's cuirassiers and the Guard cavalry division of Lefèbvre-Desnouëttes. They actually reached the rear of the first line of the Anglo-Allied position

---

Flanders in 1794. Two years later he fought against the Dutch in Southern Africa and in 1803 was transferred to India, where he commanded a brigade of cavalry in the Maratha campaigns until 1805. In 1811 Vandeleur was promoted to major general and appointed to command a brigade of the Light Division on the Iberian Peninsula. He was severely wounded when assaulting the breach of Ciudad Rodrigo on January 19, 1812, but was still able to take part in the Battle of Salamanca that June. In 1813 Vandeleur fought at the battles of Salamanca and the Nive.

121. In this context "preparations" means a pre-attack artillery bombardment. The first French assault against the Allied center was conducted without such artillery support.

more than once but had to withdraw every time to regroup. Since these units still did not reach their goal, Kellerman's cuirassiers and the other Guard cavalry division under Guyot were also committed in support. Around this time Bachelu's division of II Corps was probably drawn into the fighting too.[122] The farther Bülow's advance pushed into the rear of the French, the more Ney made his last efforts to break through the front. At this point the entire French army, except the Guard infantry, was engaged in the battle, and the fighting continued for another couple of hours, until around 7 P.M., without real success. In this fighting the opposing sides became more and more exhausted, and it is generally believed that Wellington could hardly have fought off another French assault and was about to abandon the field.

But this belief deserves closer examination. Around 5 or 6 P.M., Wellington probably considered himself so weakened that, if he were to take into account the Guard that was still in reserve and were to expect them to deliver the decisive blow against him, he might have considered he was too weak and the whole army in danger unless the Prussians were diverting them. Yet deducting what was left of the Guard and considering only the part that was engaged in the fighting at around 6 P.M., it seems more likely that Wellington would be more successful than the French. Conceding that the Allied army, consisting of not-so-good troops, may have been substantially more weakened than the French, we still should not forget that Wellington was 68,000 strong, while the part of the French army that fought him was only 45,000. It would also seem that as the French had already committed all their cavalry, their infantry reserves had been entirely exhausted, and taking into account the complete chaos of a few hours later, this can hardly be doubted. But Wellington still seems to have had a lot of troops that had either not fought at all or only a little, such as Chassé's

---

122. Gen. Gilbert-Désiré-Joseph Baron Bachelu (1777–1849). His military career began in the engineers in 1794, and he fought in the Rhineland during the Revolutionary Wars and Etook part in the Egyptian expedition. In 1809 he fought at Wagram and served in Russia in 1812. After the retreat from Moscow, he played an important role in the defense of Danzig, where he remained until its capitulation in 1814. After Waterloo Bachelu was exiled but returned to France in 1817.

division, the British Tenth Brigade ([position] M on the map),[123] Collaert's cavalry division, and so on.

The heavy fighting in the center can be regarded as a tiring wrestling match between the two sides that drove them to such a level of exhaustion that the decisive blow would be all the more decisive and the defeated would be in no position to rally again. The Prussian attack was this decisive blow.

Before moving on to this subject, however, one last act of desperation in the center remains to be mentioned. Bülow was victorious, Plancenoit was lost, the masses of Prussians on the French right were steadily growing, [and] half the Guard was already committed against them with no prospect of winning, as Bonaparte, now full of doubt, still wanted to use his last troops to break Wellington's center. He led the remainder of the Guard down the road to La Haye Sainte toward the enemy position. Four battalions of the Guard vainly undertook a bloody assault. Ziethen's advance had completely broken the French right, the four battalions that had been sent forward had to fall back, and the other eight were in no position to stem the tide of flight and confusion. The entire army fell apart completely, destroying it as an army, with Bonaparte leaving the battlefield to a certain extent on his own.[124]

---

123. Clausewitz refers to the relevant Prussian General Staff map in Wagner, *Plane der Schlachten und Treffen.*

124. In his "Waterloo Dispatch," Wellington is specific about the sequence of events: Just after 7 P.M., the Imperial Guard staged the final attack on his center, he drove it off, and only then did the Prussian intervention begin to take effect. That of course conflicts with the facts—the first Prussian assault on Plancenoit took place hours earlier at 4:30 P.M., and Wellington was very much aware of that. Indeed, Capt. William Siborne, Waterloo historian and maker of the Waterloo models exhibited in the early nineteenth century, suffered severe consequences for challenging the duke on this point. Judging by Wellington's reaction to seeing Lord Liverpool's manuscript translation of Clausewitz's work, it certainly seems he took umbrage to Clausewitz also contradicting him on the point of who actually made the decisive attack at Waterloo. Yet Clausewitz's comments here are not entirely accurate. In fact seven battalions of the Guard took part in the final assault on Wellington's center, not four. When this assault commenced, the Prussians had yet to break out of Plancenoit. Indeed, Napoleon had to stabilize his hold of this village before he could undertake the attack on Wellington. The confusion of battle and the inconsistencies in various eyewitness accounts make it difficult to be entirely certain of the precise sequence of events. Certainly, the Prussians and French were fighting hotly over the possession of

43. The Prussian Attack

When Blücher saw that his forces were not harassed or pursued during the night of June 16 or on June 17, he obviously believed that Bonaparte's whole army had moved against Wellington, so he decided to leave only a few battalions at Wavre and with the rest rush to help Wellington, who was intending to accept battle on this side of the Soignes Woods. This agreement between the two commanders was made on June 17, and Blücher started off the next morning. IV Corps was designated to lead the march and broke camp at 7 A.M., passing through Wavre to St. Lambert, where it arrived at noon and concentrated there. It appeared that the French had noticed.

II Corps was ordered to follow Bülow, and both were ordered to advance against the French right flank, that is, toward Plancenoit, which seriously threatened their line of retreat. I Corps was ordered to march via Ohain toward Wellington's left, as he was concerned about this flank and expressly requested this.[125]

III Corps was ordered to act as the rearguard, leave a few battalions in Wavre, and if no significant opposition appeared, proceed to Couture, that is, toward Plancenoit. If a strong enemy force were to appear at Wavre, however, III Corps was to take up positions there and delay it.

Evidently around 20,000 men were sent directly to support the Anglo-Allied left flank, while 70,000 attacked the enemy's right and rear. The matter could not have been done more simply, naturally and practically. Criticisms that could be made include that I Corps, camping at Bierges, should not have gone with IV Corps to St. Lambert and that as II Corps first had to cross the Dyle, it should have been sent to Ohain, for the two columns held each other up when their paths crossed.

Plancenoit when Wellington drove back the Guard, but it seems unlikely the Prussians actually broke out beyond the village until the Guard was retreating.

125. Müffling, the Prussian liaison officer in Wellington's headquarters, brought this message to Ziethen and urged him to link up with Wellington as a matter of urgency. Blücher had ordered Ziethen to move on Plancenoit, but the general chose to disobey this order, one of the turning points in the battle.

Anyway, due to various unforeseen events, the march was very slow, with IV Corps only reaching Fischermont at 3 P.M., though the distance it had covered up to then was only about 2 1/2 [German] miles. This delay was caused by several defiles, the outbreak of fire in Wavre, the need to close up repeatedly, and very bad roads.[126]

II Corps, following IV Corps, obviously reached the battlefield a few hours later. I Corps, however, arrived later still, owing to other unforeseen events, and only reached Wellington's left flank at 6 P.M.

It could be argued that Blücher's arrival was too late for him to accomplish his actual mission, but this is not how things turned out. Had Bonaparte attacked in the morning, the battle probably would have been decided by this time, in which case, if Blücher had attacked, it would not have been impossible or useless but would have been less certain of success. Yet it should not be forgotten that in such an event, Blücher would have moved more quickly. Most of the failings that may have occurred would take place in the morning, before a single cannonball had fallen on Wellington. Had Wellington been under fire at 8 or 9 A.M., then Blücher's first troops would have arrived at perhaps 12 or 1 P.M.[127]

III Corps also was marching already off when a significant enemy force threatened its rearguard, still on the other side of the Dyle, and a substantial mass of cavalry was sighted, so it took up positions behind the Dyle and awaited developments.

The French claim that by noon they had already observed Bülow's march and his initial deployment at St. Lambert. Bonaparte reacted by having VI Corps and the cavalry divisions of Subervie

---

126. Most of the roads from Wavre were narrow dirt lanes lined by trees. The previous day's deluge had turned them into quagmires, making it difficult particularly for wheeled transport to move. The artillery had first to be dragged cross-country to the top of several ridges that crossed the line of march, then carefully lowered down the other side. While the infantry and cavalry made reasonably good time, the artillery was considerably delayed.

127. Certainly the Prussian infantry and cavalry could have intervened in the battle earlier than they did, but such an intervention would have been without artillery support. As such the advance would have been unlikely to achieve anything other than to attract Napoleon's attention and cause him to deploy a smaller part of his troops to cover the threat to his right. Had Wellington come under pressure earlier, then such a measure could have been undertaken to attempt to relieve him.

and Domon, in reserve behind the French center, advance toward St. Lambert and take up positions on the heights along his right flank. This was before d'Erlon's attack. Nowhere has it been stated if this position had any kind of tactical strength, and merely looking at a map does not help clarify this. Judging by a map, however, they would have been better off farther forward, between Fischermont and Payot, where they could have secured their flanks.

At 3 P.M. Bülow's first two brigades, the Fifteenth and Sixteenth, had reached the Fischermont wood, where they had taken up a concealed position. This, however, could not and did not conceal their presence from the French. Bülow waited for the arrival of the rest of his brigades. Meanwhile, Blücher had seen the French putting the Anglo-Allied center under strong pressure, and fearing they would break through there, he ordered Bülow to attack the enemy VI Corps with his two brigades and the reserve cavalry, which he did around 4:30 P.M. The two remaining brigades followed soon after as reserves for the Fifteenth and Sixteenth, so that thanks to Bülow's superiority in numbers and the little advantage the terrain gave the enemy, initial resistance was not great. Rather, the 12,000 men under Lobau had to undertake a fighting retreat toward La Belle Alliance.[128] Bülow was then ordered to direct his attack more to the left to reach the village of Plancenoit and to make this the objective. But Bülow's right flank was already engaged with the enemy at the village of Smohain, so IV Corps' advance was somewhat deflected, depriving the blow against Plancenoit of the force it might otherwise have had.

Meanwhile Bonaparte, seeing that Lobau had been forced to withdraw to the highway, sent the Young Guard Division to reinforce him. The fighting now came to a halt there, for Bülow could not advance any farther until he gained control of Plancenoit. The battle for the village now ebbed and flowed. One after the other, four battalions of the two other divisions of the French Guard drew up close to the rear of the village, and they were sent into it in support. That is why the battle here was not decided in favor of our troops until II Corps arrived and sent in part of its forces against this village, securing it for us at between 7 and 8 P.M.

---

128. The actual strength of VI Corps was nearer 10,000 men.

While the battle for Plancenoit was underway, the masses of French cavalry made their efforts against the Anglo-Allied center; then Ziethen arrived on the other flank and advanced against the French right flank. Finally, about 8 P.M., the last twelve battalions of the Guard undertook their desperate gamble to decide the battle against Wellington. It would be interesting to know if the Prussians already had Plancenoit firmly in their hands when Bonaparte marched off with these last reserves, hurling them into the open jaws of destruction. Such an action would then seem to have been even more that of a desperate gambler, indifferent to all rational calculations.[129]

44. The Battle of Wavre on June 18 and 19: Grouchy's March

As mentioned above, Grouchy and his two corps only reached Gembloux late in the evening [of June 17]. Pajol's cavalry and Teste's division even spent the night at Mazy. A torrential rainstorm had soaked the routes across the lumpy soil, making marching very difficult then and the following morning. Although Grouchy stated in his defense that he marched off at dawn, Maréchal-de-Champ Berton,[130] who was with Grouchy's forces, asserted most definitely that Exelmans's cavalry did not set off before 8 A.M. and that both army corps had not [begun] to march until between 9 and 10 A.M. The truth probably lies somewhere in between. III Cavalry Corps, which led the march, made contact with the Prussian rearguard in Wavre around 2 P.M. But, as it had to cover three

---

129. As mentioned above, only seven battalions of the Guard participated in the final attack. It also was unlikely that Plancenoit had fallen before this last attack was made, and it was more likely that the Prussians broke out of the village at roughly the same time as the Imperial Guard was pushed back from Wellington's center.

130. Cavalry Gen. Jean-Baptiste Berton (1767–1822). After receiving formal officer training, his active service commenced in 1793 in the Netherlands, then continued in Germany. Berton participated in the campaign of 1806 and fought at Eylau the following year. He was then transferred to the Iberian Peninsula, where he remained until the first abdication. Berton was executed in 1822 for his part in a plot against the state.

[German] miles from Gembloux to there, it probably broke camp at 6 or 7 A.M. The First Division (Hulot) of IV Cavalry Corps may have arrived a few hours later,[131] but the other two arrived only toward evening. The entire force had to march down just one road, which was sufficient explanation for the late arrival, particularly if everything these two corps had done in the last four days is taken into account.

To the right of the main column, Pajol and his column were sent from Mazy through St. Denis and Grand Leez to Tourrines, there to await further instructions. He first had to be brought back from there to Wavre, only reaching Limale, to where he had been ordered, at 8 P.M., when Grouchy became aware he would not break through at Wavre.

There is no doubt that on the morning of June 18, Grouchy still had no clear idea of the direction Blücher had sent his army. Grouchy said so himself, and when he left Gembloux, his immediate objective was only Sart-à-Walhain, not Wavre. Hence Pajol's march in the wrong direction and the fumbling around that delayed it. Only when he made contact with the rearguard of the Prussian II and III Corps in the direction of Wavre did he move in that direction.

This lack of knowledge of the Prussian army's true line of retreat borders on the incomprehensible and is not easy to believe, for it indicates that the French generals were highly incompetent and negligent.

On the contrary, the slowness of Grouchy's movement toward Wavre is not as surprising as most regard it. In modern war, rapid movements are commonplace, with marches that cover five, six, or seven [German] miles in one day being usual. It is regarded as justified to expect marches at such a speed, when it is required. Yet speed comes more from favorable marching conditions than from the urgency of the mission. Only those who have been involved

---

131. Gen. Étienne Baron Hulot (1774–1850). Hulot volunteered for the army during the Revolutionary Wars and fought in France, Germany, Switzerland, and Italy. He was wounded at both Austerlitz in 1805 and Eylau two years later. Hulot served in the Iberian Peninsula from 1808 to 1813, when he was transferred to Saxony, there fighting at Wartenburg and Leipzig. After Waterloo the general held various senior posts in the army.

in such situations and have had to contend with all the difficulties that arise are justified to make such criticisms. Even with the best will in the world, weather and roads, lack of food and shelter, exhaustion of the men, lack of information, and so on can reduce the distance marched to half or indeed a third of what might seem possible on paper. It should be remembered that after the battles of Jena and Auerstedt, when the French were completely victorious, had every reason to accelerate their movements, and were at the peak of their military efficiency, they covered an average of no more than 2 1/2 [German] miles a day during their pursuit.

Assuming that Grouchy's corps did not leave the battlefield at Ligny before 2 or 3 P.M., it is no surprise that they did not reach Wavre before 2 or 3 P.M. the next day, since Wavre is five [German] miles from the Ligny battlefield along the roads over the ridges that Grouchy took, and as is evident, all kinds of setbacks occurred. The cavalry of course could have moved off much earlier, but even if that had not been pointless, it would still not have had the result required from Grouchy's corps in relation to the Battle of Waterloo. The only accusation remaining that can be made against General Grouchy is that he sent his entire force along one road, which resulted in the final divisions of IV Corps arriving in the evening.

45. General Thielemann's Deployment

The Prussian III Army Corps reached Wavre on the evening of June 17. Here the First Brigade of the Reserve Cavalry, detached earlier, rejoined it. Three brigades, the Tenth, Eleventh, and Twelfth, as well as the Reserve Cavalry, had passed through Wavre and camped at La Bawette. The Ninth, having arrived too late, remained on the other side of the Dyle. Along with the Eighth Brigade of II Corps, [the Ninth] was now used to form the vanguard facing Grouchy. On the morning of June 18, when IV Army Corps set out for St. Lambert, Thielemann received the order to act as the rearguard for the other three corps and to follow them if no significant enemy force appeared. He was to head toward Couture, leaving a few battalions behind in Wavre so that French patrols could not harass the Brussels highway while the armies fought at Waterloo. If, however, a significant enemy force were to appear at Wavre, Thielemann was to take up a strong position there on the Dyle and cover the army's rear.

By about 2 P.M., II and III Army Corps had finished marching off from their position at Wavre. As nothing whatever had been seen of the enemy by then, it seemed most likely that Bonaparte had committed his entire force against Wellington. Thielemann then formed up his corps in columns, and his vanguard was about to leave the Brussels highway when the Ninth Brigade, along with the Eighth, which was still on the left bank of the Dyle, engaged the enemy. Thielemann then ordered a halt until he had clarified the situation. Meanwhile, the Eighth Brigade of II Corps moved off. The First, which had stopped for a while, resumed its march, leaving behind a detachment of three battalions and three cavalry squadrons in the village of Limale under Colonel Stengel.[132]

Thielemann now took up positions at Wavre, with the Twelfth Brigade behind the bridge at Bierges, the Tenth behind Wavre to its right, and the Eleventh behind Wavre to its left, on the highway. Three battalions of the Ninth Brigade occupied Wavre, while its remaining units, including the Reserve Cavalry, formed the reserve around La Bawette.

The three brigades holding this position remained in cover as far as it was possible, with most of their troops in brigade columns. Only individual battalions or skirmisher platoons were used to defend the bridges and the river itself, while, except for one battery that was held in reserve, the artillery, twenty-seven guns, was deployed along the edge of the valley and would immediately go into action against the enemy coming down the other side of it. III Corps' front extended from Bierges to Bas-Wavre, a little more than 2,000 paces, and was not exceptionally wide for a force of

---

132. Lt. Col. Rudolf Anton Wenzislaus von Stengel (1772–1831). He joined the Prussian infantry in 1788 as a cadet and fought in the campaigns of 1792–95, including at Valmy. In 1806 he commanded a company of sharpshooters in Silesia. Stengel was part of the Prussian auxiliary corps in Russia in 1812. The next year he fought at Dresden, winning the Iron Cross 2nd Class, and was wounded at Kulm. Stengel was awarded the Iron Cross 1st Class for his role in the fighting at Ligny.

20,000 men. There were four bridges across the river, one at Bas-Wavre, two in Wavre, and one at the mill at Bierges. If necessary, the Dyle could be forded. In contrast, the left side of the valley was fairly high, some fifty or sixty feet, and so steep that it significantly obstructed movement. Nevertheless, it did not hinder effective fire. As the area nearby on the left and right flank was free of obstacles and additional strong points were available farther to the rear, the position could certainly be considered among the strongest that could be taken up immediately without a lot of preparation.

Thielemann's dispositions were designed to risk as few troops as possible, to maintain a firefight with the fewest possible infantry, and to have the artillery do most of work, and thus being in a position to move fresh masses of troops against any enemy attack that might break through anywhere along the edge of the valley. The reserves were preferably to be used against the side of any enemy trying to make a flanking maneuver.

Chance put an end to this plan.

Once the enemy deployed its forces, the Ninth Brigade withdrew through Bas-Wavre, leaving two battalions in Wavre and a third to its rear. The remaining six battalions, two squadrons, and eight guns were sent off with the other army corps and headed for Neuf-Cabaret and Couture, the original destination of Thielemann's corps, instead of remaining in reserve at La Bawette. Nobody noticed this error, because at the moment when General Borcke passed through the position from Bas-Wavre,[133] the enemy's deployment to their front occupied everyone's attention. Only around 7 P.M., when an opportunity to use the reserves might have arisen and some preliminary orders were about to be sent to them, did anyone notice that instead of remaining with the Reserve Cavalry, Borcke had marched off. Officers were sent to see if he had taken up a position anywhere nearby, but when they returned without having located him, Thielemann let the matter rest. As he said, the sound of the heavy artillery fire indicated that a great battle was taking place, and this is where the decision would occur. Nothing happening at Wavre would have any

---

133. Borcke was actually just a colonel at this time.

influence on that decision, so perhaps it was better that one more division had gone there.

That is why on June 18 and 19, Thielemann, with only twenty-four battalions of infantry, twenty-one squadrons of cavalry, and thirty-five guns, in all about 15,000 men, was pitted against Grouchy, whose strength could not be observed because of the woods, of which by 3 P.M. around 10–12,000 men were visible.

46. Grouchy's Attack on June 18 and 19

The Battle of Wavre took place in two different acts: first, from 3 P.M. until nightfall on June 18, the battle along the Dyle; and second, from daybreak until about 9 A.M. on June 19, the fighting on the left bank between the river and the Rixensart Woods.

On June 18 Grouchy wanted to take Wavre with his III Corps, gaining a bridgehead there. III Corps was to the fore, and between 2 and 3 P.M., its main body attacked Wavre, while a detachment attacked the mill at Bierges a little later. But two battalions under Colonel Zepelin,[134] reinforced by two others, held the town and both bridges with determination. The attack on the mill at Bierges was equally unsuccessful. Here the Twelfth Brigade, defending the river crossings just with its skirmish platoons and the artillery, deployed along the left edge of the valley. When IV Corps (Gérard) arrived, part of the First Division (Hulot) was also sent to Bierges. Even though the French generals, finding that they could not break through in Wavre, expected the attacks on the mill at Bierges to succeed, but they did not become masters of this crossing. Later, between 8 and 9 P.M., the First Division withdrew to Limale. The remaining two divisions sent from La Baraque arrived here appreciably later. Pajol was also heading there with his cavalry and Teste's division from VI Corps.

---

134. Col. Konstantin von Zepelin (1771–1848). He joined the Prussian infantry as a cadet in 1787 but first saw action only in 1807, when he fought at Eylau. Zepelin was part of the Prussian Auxiliary Corps in 1812 and saw action throughout the campaigns of 1813–15. After Waterloo he held various senior posts in the army.

All these troops only reached Limale at nightfall and found the town and the river crossing undefended, presumably because Stengel was pulling out and following I Corps. They crossed the Dyle in darkness and pushed forward in dense masses to Delburg on the edge of the valley, where they formed front against Thielemann's right flank.

About 10 P.M. the Twelfth Brigade reported that the enemy was across the river at Limale. Thielemann thought it was a detached column, consisting perhaps of a division, and ordered Colonel Stülpnagel to take all available troops there and throw the enemy back across the river.[135] At the same time, a brigade of reserve cavalry was sent there. Thielemann rushed to the threatened point. The Prussian attack took place in the dark but could not succeed, partly because it ran into a sunken road that disorganized the attacking battalions and partly because the enemy was already too strong.

Stülpnagel had to take up positions close to the enemy, tying them down and preventing them from deploying. With the first glimmer of daylight, the first cannon shots were fired at a distance of five hundred paces. Heavy fighting ensued, in which, under cover of a strong skirmish line, the French methodically pushed their four divisions forward and in which III Corps offered resistance from three different positions. The first was the Twelfth Brigade and Stengel, who was still in the area, around a small wood. Then fourteen battalions of the Twelfth, Tenth, and Eleventh Brigades and the Reserve Cavalry, between Bierges and the Rixensart Woods, while six battalions drew up to the rear of Bierges and Wavre, and four in Wavre.

The defense of the second position lasted the longest, and it was there that Thielemann learned of the victory at Waterloo as well as of the order for II Corps to move via Glabais and La Hutte and attack the rear of the enemy force Thielemann was fighting.

---

135. Col. Wolf Wilhelm Ferdinand von Stülpnagel (1781–1839). He joined the army in 1790 as a cadet and first fought in Poland in 1794–95. He was taken prisoner in Lübeck in 1806. In 1812 he was one of a number of Prussian officers who joined the Russian service rather than fight for Napoleon. In 1814 Stülpnagel was appointed colonel of a regiment in the German Legion, a force recruited from German prisoners of war. After Waterloo he served as a district commander of the militia.

As these places were so far from the battlefield that it would be impossible to intervene, Thielemann could only hope that his opponent had also heard the result of the great battle and would begin his retreat quickly for fear of being cut off. Thielemann had his troops shout a loud hurrah and make other signs of joy. Yet this was in vain. The enemy still pressed forward, forcing Thielemann to fall back farther and finally begin a general retreat and to order Zepelin to evacuate Wavre.

Thielemann withdrew as far as St. Agatha-Rode, three hours from the battlefield toward Louvain, but lost no more than a couple of thousand dead and wounded. III Corps' Ninth Brigade had continued to march to St. Lambert, spent the night of June 18–19 in the woods there, marched back early on June 19 toward the cannon fire at Wavre, and rejoined III Army Corps at Gembloux on June 20, having passed through Limale.

47. The Encounter at Namur

Grouchy first received news of the defeat at Waterloo on the morning of June 19, apparently at just about the time that Thielemann was preparing to retreat. This facilitated his opponent's departure, as Grouchy lost the urge to look around for minor advantages when he was obviously more concerned about his own withdrawal. It was clear to him that he could no longer head for Charleroi and so he decided to go to Namur. At noon he sent off Exelmans's cavalry corps there as a vanguard. It was supposed to have arrived there around 4 P.M., but this is unlikely since the battlefield at Wavre was six [German] miles from Namur. At dusk the infantry followed in two columns, the first on the road via Gembloux, the other cross-country, with the cavalry divisions of Maurin and Soult comprising the rearguard.[136]

---

136. Cavalry Gen. Antoine, Baron Maurin (1771–1830). The baron joined the army in 1792 and fought during the Revolutionary Wars, particularly in Germany. In 1797 he fought in Italy and was posted there again in 1805. Taken prisoner in Portugal in 1808, he returned to France in 1812 but did not rejoin the army until early 1813. Maurin was wounded at Ligny.

The French infantry reached Namur around 8 or 9 A.M. on June 20.

Thielemann reached St. Agatha-Rode around noon on June 19. He had decided under no circumstances to send off his totally exhausted troops in pursuit that day, for they urgently needed rest, and as it was likely that the enemy rearguard would not withdraw before nightfall, nothing could be decided anyway. At daybreak he moved up his troops to join his vanguard at Ottenburg, putting him in good time in a position to pursue the enemy. Assembling the corps took about an hour, and around 5 A.M. the cavalry set off via Gembloux to Namur. The infantry followed.

At Gembloux the cavalry first encountered the enemy horse, which rapidly withdrew. It was followed as quickly as possible along the direct route to Namur, though the enemy was contacted again just three-quarters of an hour away from this town.

While Thielemann's cavalry was on its way to Namur, taking five or six hours to get there, the infantry stayed at Gembloux.

Several enemy battalions, along with some cavalry and artillery, were encountered in front of Namur. They were attacked, lost three guns, and fell back closer to the town.

Several large bodies of enemy troops were on the Brussels to Namur highway, apparently covering a withdrawal. While these were being observed, an enemy division was detected marching in column along the highway. As soon as they saw Thielemann's cavalry, they formed squares, deployed skirmishers and artillery to their left, and continued their march to the town under their cover. This was the last division of the IV Corps that reached Namur somewhat later than III Corps. General Pirch I and the Prussian II Corps were close behind them. After the Battle of Waterloo, Pirch had been ordered to head toward Gembloux and take Grouchy in the rear. He marched all night, passing through Maransart and Bouseval, reaching Mellery on the morning of June 19. He bivouacked there, sending out patrols. As they brought him no news of either the enemy or of Thielemann, he spent the night of June 19 there, setting out toward Gembloux again only at 5 A.M. on June 20, when he received news that the enemy was falling back through the town. This is how he came into contact with the tail of the enemy's left column. After it had fallen back into the town, General Pirch tried to force the Brussels gate. But as a strong force of infantry held it and the remainder of the old city wall, heavy fighting ensued, costing II Corps 1,100 dead and wounded for no result. The action had to be stopped, and the enemy did not leave the town until around 6 P.M., heading toward Dinant, to where, on Blücher's orders, only Colonel Sohr's cavalry brigade followed.[137] Had Pirch continued his march to Namur and had he got there before Grouchy's infantry, which was entirely feasible, Grouchy would not have had a crossing of the Meuse available and would have had to turn toward Charleroi on June 20. By then the Prussian I Army Corps that had followed the beaten French army through Charleroi had already left it and was near Beaumont. On hearing of Grouchy's approach, it would probably have abandoned its march to Avesnes and turned toward Philippeville. That alone made it very unlikely that this corps could have cut off Grouchy's retreat, since he would probably have reached Philippeville first and in the worst case could have continued to Givet. This may have caused heavier losses for Grouchy as odd units would have been cut off, et cetera. The situation would have been entirely different, however, if I Corps had been ordered to remain on the Sambre on June 19 and 20 to stop Grouchy crossing it. Then there would have been 50,000 men concentrated against him on the morning of June 21, so it is hard to see how, hemmed in between two rivers, he could have avoided capitulation in the face of this superior force. Indeed, Bonaparte wrote in a letter to his brother Joseph from Philippeville, "I have heard nothing whatever of Grouchy; if he is not taken, as I fear, I can have 50,000 men in three days." Yet early on June 19, when this disposition would have to have been made, Blücher's headquarters knew too little about Grouchy's position to make cutting him off a major objective of immediate operations.

---

137. Lt. Col. Friedrich Georg Ludwig von Sohr (1775–1845). Sohr joined the Life Hussars as an ensign in 1789. He fought in the campaigns of 1792–95, being wounded both at Valmy and Kaiserslautern. He then joined Marwitz's Free Corps in Pomerania in 1807. Sohr fought throughout the campaigns of 1813–15, being wounded at Möckern, and was awarded the Iron Cross 2nd Class for actions at Haynau and 1st Class for his service at Château-Thierry.

On the one hand, the attack on Namur is hard to justify. If the town had been entered, then little would have been gained, and just after it is the bridge over the Sambre, where all further pursuit would have ended. On the other hand, another way to cross the Sambre probably could have been found. As the highway from Namur to Dinant runs along the left bank of the Meuse, that is, between the two rivers in a valley that continues into a substantial defile, if one gained control of the heights, one could have made the retreat extremely difficult, substantially weakened Marshal Grouchy, above all delayed him, and prevented him from reaching Laon before the Allies. But in war it is seldom the case that everything happens that could happen, and the mission assigned to Pirch I here was in no way normal, but one that required a considerable degree of energy.

48. Reflections on the Battle: Bonaparte

A critical examination of the overall results of the drama of June 17–18 must concentrate on the following issues:

One first needs to consider if Bonaparte could not and should not have attacked on the morning of June 18 instead of at noon. If it was to succeed, his entire offensive against the Allied commanders had to be conducted with the utmost rapidity, because he wanted to fight them individually and not let them combine. Perhaps he could already be criticized for having lost a couple of hours on the sixteenth. The need to rest the troops and take various tactical and strategic measures appears to provide a satisfactory explanation for the fact that the attack at Ligny could not occur earlier on June 16, and generally speaking, criticism made after the events is rarely justified to argue over a couple of hours. On June 18, however, there really does not seem to be any satisfactory justification for delaying half a day. By the evening of June 17, Bonaparte had advanced to Wellington's position, and in his *Mémoires* he complains that he did not have a few more hours of daylight to fight on that day. What was to prevent his columns from moving off at daybreak on June 18, which would have allowed the battle to begin around 6 or 7 A.M.? In such an urgent situation, resting the troops for four or five hours should have been enough.[138] Bonaparte, moreover, now had two matters to fear: the first was the complete concentration of Wellington's army, the second Blücher's participation. The only remedy for both was to attack quickly. But Bonaparte did not believe that:

1. Wellington would accept a battle there if he were still waiting for troops;
2. Still less that Blücher would be able to rush to his aid.

He believed that a few hours would not matter. It was not certain that an attack early in the morning would have led to victory, and it was known that in the course of the day, Wellington actually did not receive any reinforcements. It is likely that if the attack had begun at 6 or 7 A.M., Blücher would probably have arrived three or four hours earlier, still in good time.[139] This may well now be clear, but Bonaparte did not know at the time that both his assumptions regarding Wellington and Blücher had no basis.

---

138. There has been considerable speculation about the reasons for Napoleon delaying the opening of the Battle of Waterloo. The reason most commonly given is that he needed to allow the ground to dry out from the previous day's torrential rain so that his artillery could fire effectively. As Clausewitz points out earlier, the first French assault on the Allied center was carried out without significant artillery preparation, so it seems unlikely that the need to wait for benefit of the artillery was the cause of any delays. Indeed, on the evening on June 17, after the torrential rain, Napoleon had ordered his army to be in position to commence action at 9 A.M. on June 18. So why was there a delay? What seems most likely to have been the cause was a breakdown in Napoleon's supply system. Lacking food and moving through an area that Wellington had passed through twice and stripped of supplies, much of the army dispersed, looking for sustenance. Furthermore, the wagons took their time arriving, so there was a delay in resupplying ammunition. Finally, since the entire army moved up one road in one long column, it needed several hours to deploy into battle formation. Napoleon, of course, came up with a more dramatic reason for his failings—an act of God.

139. Unlike Napoleon, Blücher did not have a paved highway along which he could march to join Wellington. As mentioned above, his artillery literally got stuck in the mud. He too had the option of throwing in infantry without artillery support and could have joined the battle earlier had Wellington's situation demanded it. As it was, the situation demanded that Blücher commit half of Bülow's corps before the other half had joined it, which was not ideal.

REFLECTIONS ON THE BATTLE: BONAPARTE   145

Considering the useless parading around of his army cost Bonaparte two hours, it seems almost credible that he did not want a battle, but rather that this bombastic display would result in the Anglo-Allies withdrawing. Such a wish would have been contrary to his interests and contrary to his previous behavior, so it can only be regarded as the result of a lack of willpower and mental inhibition. This could only have been a fleeting thought, an unfounded suspicion that would hardly have been acceptable if seriously considered, were it not for another matter that will now be examined.

The second issue was the way Bonaparte wanted to engage his right wing in the battle. His entire account of this can be regarded as completely dishonest, a plan conceived only after the fact. Grouchy's situation and the way Bonaparte used it to make excuses greatly resembled the way Ney's actions on June 16 were handled. There, the left wing's original mission was only to delay the Anglo-Allies or perhaps to push back their leading divisions. Only later, when it was obviously too late, did Ney receive the impracticable order to participate in the main battle. Here too, on June 17, the mission of Grouchy's right wing was only to pursue Blücher, to prevent him from rallying after his defeat, from coming to his senses, or even turning back. Only later, and again too late, and again entirely contrary to the nature of the situation, did Grouchy receive the order to participate in the main battle. According to Grouchy, no entry can be found in the chief of staff, Marshal Soult's, order book confirming that such an order was sent to him on June 17. The instructions he received to pursue the Prussians consisted merely of what Bonaparte said to him on the battlefield at Ligny, in the company of General Girard.

But there are two messages from Marshal Soult to Grouchy on June 18, which read as follows:[140]

To Marshal Grouchy
(Carried by Aide de Camp Lenovich)
At the farm of Caillou, June 18, 10 A.M.

---

140. These orders can be found in Marquis Emmanuel de Grouchy, Marshal of France, *Fragments historiques relatifs à la campagne de 1815 et à la bataille de Waterloo. De l'influence que peuvent avoir sur l'opinion les documents publiés par M. le comte Gérard* (Paris, 1829), 137.

To the Marshal: The Emperor has received your last report from Gembloux: you mention to His Majesty only two Prussian columns that passed through Sauvenière and Sart-à-Walhain; however, reports mention a third column moving through St.-Géry and Gentinnes toward Wavre.

The Emperor orders me to inform you that at this moment His Majesty is about to attack the English army, which has taken a position at Waterloo near the forest of Soignes. His Majesty therefore desires you to direct your movements toward Wavre to bring you closer to us, put you in touch with this operation, and make contact to your front with the Prussian army that is moving in this direction and may have come to a halt at Wavre, which you should reach as soon as possible. You are to pursue the enemy columns on your right with several light units to observe their movements and pick off their stragglers.

Inform me at once of your dispositions and movement and of the news you have of the enemy and do not forget to communicate with us. The Emperor wishes to hear from you very soon.

Signed, Chief of Staff, the Duke of Dalmatia

Second Message:

From the battlefield of Waterloo, 1 P.M.

To the Marshal: At 2 A.M., you wrote to the Emperor that you were marching to Sart-à-Walhain; yet your mission was to move to Corbais or Wavre. This movement conforms to His Majesty's dispositions, of which you have been informed.

However, the Emperor orders me to tell you that you should maneuver in our direction. It is for you to judge where we are and determine what steps to take as a consequence, and to secure our communications, as well as to be still in a position to fall upon any enemy troops that might seek to harass our right flank and wipe them out. At this moment the battle has reached the line of Waterloo. The enemy center is at Mont Saint Jean, so maneuver to join our right.

Signed, the Duke of Dalmatia

P.S. A letter just intercepted reports that General Bülow is to attack our flank; we think we see this force on the heights of St.

Lambert, so do not lose a second in returning and joining us and in wiping out Bülow, whom you will catch en flagrant delit.[141]

In contrast, Bonaparte states that he sent an officer to Grouchy at 10 P.M. on June 17:

To inform him that he intended to fight a major battle the next day; that the Anglo-Dutch army was in positions in front of the Soignes Woods, with the village of La Haye on its left; that Marshal Blücher would certainly move in one of three directions:

1. he may retire toward Liège;
2. he may move toward Brussels;
3. he may remain in his positions at Wavre;

that in any case it would be necessary for Grouchy to maneuver past St. Lambert to outflank the left wing of the English army and join up with the French right; but that in the first two cases, he was to execute his maneuver with the majority of his forces combined, and that in the third case, it was not to be done without leaving a detachment, of greater or lesser strength, depending upon the position, that would occupy the front of the Prussian army.

Furthermore, Bonaparte also claims to have sent a duplicate copy of this order early on the morning of June 18. He immediately adds that Marshal Grouchy did not receive either order; the Marshal, however, has stated that they were never given, and if the matter is considered carefully, that is very much how it appears since:

1. There is no such order in the chief of staff's order book.
2. Neither of the two above messages of June 18 referred to it and was not even compatible with it.
3. It is unlikely that two orders should be lost one after the other if officers carried them. Did the officers also disappear?
4. Bonaparte did not name the officers who carried these orders.

---

141. The exact time this postscript was added is a matter of dispute, with some historians considering it likely that it was added well after the event.

5. Bonaparte made the surprising claim that Grouchy did not receive these orders.
6. It was remarkable and suspicious that a similar order also did not reach Ney on June 16.

In any case, Marshal Grouchy was right to say that he could not be responsible for the execution of orders that Bonaparte himself says he did not receive, so that he could only act according to the verbal instructions that Bonaparte gave him around noon on June 17. Bonaparte told him on the evening of June 16, when Grouchy asked for further instructions, that he would give them to him the next morning. Grouchy's account continues:

> I was with him the next day before sunrise, awaiting orders. Around 7:30, he had the chief of staff tell me that he would visit the battlefield and that I should go with him.
> But General Pajol, having been ordered to pursue the Prussians with his light cavalry and a division of infantry, was just sending back some artillery pieces taken on the road to Namur. This event gave the impression that General Blücher was retreating in that direction.[142]
> Between 8 and 9 A.M., Napoleon left Fleurus in a carriage to visit the battlefield. The poor condition of the roads across the field, cut by pits and deep trenches, held him up so much that he decided to mount a horse. Reaching St. Amand, he proceeded along the various routes along which this village had been attacked the previous day. Then he moved around the field of battle, lending comfort and questioning some wounded officers who were still there, and passing in front of the regiments, who formed up without arms on the field where they were bivouacked; and acknowledging their acclamation, he spoke to practically every unit with sympathy and satisfaction at their conduct the day before. He then dismounted and spoke for a long time to General Gérard and myself about the state of opinion

---

142. This would appear to have been the Prussian Horse Battery No. 19 from III Army Corps.

in the chamber in Paris, the Jacobins, and various other topics, completely alien to what would seem to have been the exclusive concerns of a perilous moment.

I enter into these rather minute, parochial details because they serve to show how this morning was employed, the wasting of which had such baleful consequences. It was not until around midday, after having received the report of a patrol that had gone to Quatre Bras, that Napoleon began to concern himself with orders relative to the dispositions he wanted to make. He immediately went into action, ordering the infantry units and the cavalry he wanted to take with him down the road to Quatre Bras, and then gave me the verbal order to assume command of the corps of Generals Vandamme and Gérard and the cavalry of Generals Pajol and Exelmans and to set off in pursuit of Marshal Blücher.

I made the observation that the Prussians had begun their retreat at ten the previous night, so a good deal of time would pass before troops that were so dispersed around the countryside, who had broken down their weapons in order to clean them, were eating, and in no way expected to march that day, could be set in motion, that the enemy would be sixteen to eighteen hours ahead of the units that he was sending after them; that, while the reports of the cavalry were not at all precise about the direction taken by the main body of the Prussian army, it nevertheless appeared that Marshal Blücher's retreat was directed on Namur; so that, in following them, I would find myself cut off from him, outside his circle of operations.

These observations were not well received; he repeated the order that he had given me, adding that it was up to me to discover the route Marshal Blücher had taken; that he would fight the English; that I was to complete the defeat of the Prussians by attacking them wherever they might be found, and that I was to communicate with him via the highway that passed close to our position at Quatre Bras. A few moments' conversation that I then had with the chief of staff dealt only with the distraction that would be caused to the troops when I took the corps under my command to send them toward Quatre Bras.

Taking Grouchy's description of what happened with Bonaparte on the morning of June 17, it is evident that:

1. In all probability Grouchy really had no other instructions about what to do on June 17 except very generally to pursue the Prussians.
2. Bonaparte had no idea that the Prussians were retreating toward the Dyle and did not even consider that they might have headed for Namur and so did not order Grouchy to Wavre.
3. At 10 A.M. Bonaparte indeed had a report that a column of Prussians had gone to Wavre but believed that the main body was nevertheless going in the direction of Liège, thus Grouchy undoubtedly would be able to throw the Prussians out of Wavre and place himself in the path of the main body.
4. Bonaparte actually displayed a kind of lassitude and indifference that neither his circumstances nor his previous conduct can explain, which is in fact the second point that indicates there may have been a change in his personality.

If he did not want his cavalry to continue the pursuit on the evening of June 16, then why did he not have them mount up at daybreak on June 17 to locate the now missing Blücher again and at least get a clear idea of the direction he had taken and, as such, of the best route to assign the forces that were to move against him? Why did he drag around the general responsible for the pursuit for three or four hours without briefing him, and how could his mind be so preoccupied with what might be happening in Paris as to lose sight of the most essential elements of the conduct of war?

In any case, the impression this whole story makes is such that there is no doubt that Bonaparte considered the Prussians to have been dealt with, and he did not even consider that the distant fighting with them could in any way affect the battle he now wanted to bring about with Wellington. He gave no thought whatsoever to Blücher's participation and even less to Grouchy's in the battle that was to take place on the Brussels highway. Bonaparte's claim that he had understood the division of the enemy forces on

June 17 to be a move on Brussels in two columns, the first taking Blücher and Grouchy via Wavre, the second, Wellington and himself via Mont St. Jean, is a view cobbled together after the fact that would not be worth mentioning if many writers had not copied it.

Having shown that, in all probability, the participation of the right wing in what would happen on the left did not occur to Bonaparte on June 17, that is, in good time, the nature of the assistance that was called for much too late on June 18 must again be considered more closely.

If on June 17 Bonaparte had not ordered Grouchy to pursue and force back Blücher on all routes taken but instead to observe him and move between Blücher and the main Allied army, then it might have been possible for Grouchy to help on June 18 either by holding off an advance by Blücher or, in the event Blücher did not advance, by detaching his own forces to Mont St. Jean. Obviously, such a role was entirely different to one of pursuit and harassment. Such orders would have taken Grouchy to the Dyle, since this river ran between the two Allied armies, and not sent him via Gembloux but rather via Tilly, where he could have quickly gained the left bank of the Dyle. If the Prussians stayed on the right bank, then Limale and Wavre were the obvious positions for Grouchy. If, however, he were to hear that the Prussians were heading for Wavre, then the area around Neuf-Cabaret, or any place else on the right bank of the Dyle with a front parallel to the Wavre to Brussels highway, would be an appropriate position from which either to hold Blücher in check, to block him, or to remain in contact with him.

In this position Grouchy was only about one [German] mile from Bonaparte and could have kept in direct contact with him by means of the usual flank patrols, so it was not impossible, even on the day of the battle, for Bonaparte's orders to have guided him.

Yet the route via Gembloux placed him behind Blücher and as such did not block his movement. This was obviously the wrong direction as it not only placed Grouchy's corps far from the main army again but also inevitably made communication between them circuitous and above all uncertain, resulting in an order written at 1 P.M. on June 18 only reaching Grouchy's hands around 7 P.M. This is certainly no surprise, for the chief of staff instructed the officer carrying this order to ride via Quatre Bras and Gembloux, a distance of around seven [German] miles. How then can a force that only received its orders six hours later be considered part of one and the same battle? How can a commander pretend to order such a force to the battlefield on that very day despite the constantly changing situation? Yet that is how it seemed to be, for the end of the second letter states: "At this moment, the battle has reached the line of Waterloo. The enemy center is at Mont St. Jean, therefore maneuver to join our right."

Not to mention the postscript: "A letter that has just been intercepted reports that General Bülow is to attack our flank; we believe we see this force on the heights of St. Lambert; therefore do not lose an instant in returning and rejoining us, and in crushing Bülow, whom you will catch en flagrant delit."

Even if Grouchy had received this order at 4 P.M., which was most unlikely in the circumstances; and even if the marshal had been able to march off at once, he still would not have made it from Wavre to the battlefield before 9 P.M. because 40,000 men cannot march over rough terrain in the presence of the enemy as quickly as a single man can, and Grouchy had to cover over two [German] miles. Taking into account the lost time in carrying out orders in war, which has to be considered an essential element of strategic calculation, this order cannot be regarded as practical. Moreover, what did this order require? It required that Grouchy was not engaged and [was] in a position to march off at once. Furthermore, Grouchy had been ordered to pursue Blücher, and Bonaparte could scarcely assume anything other than that Grouchy was either engaged with Blücher or was spread out across various roads pursuing him. In both events, however, it was most unreasonable to expect him to be ready to march off at once to the Battle of Waterloo. The fact is that on June 18, when Bonaparte received the news that part of the Prussians had gone to Wavre, he should have begun to be concerned that they could support Wellington, but as he considered this column to be only a small part of the Prussian army, he thought Grouchy could scatter them easily. Only now did it start to become apparent to him that he needed to have Grouchy in a position between him and the Prussians, and only now did he start claiming his orders to Grouchy were like those he supposedly sent on June 17, that is, when he arrogantly decided he had already dealt with Blücher. The pressure of the battle led him to think that Grouchy was between him and the Prussians, that Grouchy was in fact the right flank of the line of battle, and that as such could be ordered up to attack the Prussian corps on its way to join Wellington from the rear. Yet armies do not move like thoughts, and when a situation has been visualized incorrectly, then in most cases a price has to be paid.

Bonaparte hardly ever mentions Bülow, as if the Battle of Ligny had made the rest of the Prussians incapable of any further action. That was, however, a foolish assumption, for it did not take into account the outcome of the battle and the small number of trophies taken. As he definitely assumed that what appeared at St. Lambert could only be Bülow and not Blücher, there was even less reason to believe that Grouchy would be ordered up, since he had been sent against Blücher and not against Bülow and had to be regarded as engaged with Blücher and not Bülow.

The results of these considerations are that:

1. On June 17 Bonaparte definitely did not foresee that Blücher and Grouchy would take part in the battle the next day. He gave no thought whatever to the subject and was completely surprised by Blücher's appearance on June 18, as this did not fit into his general scheme.
2. The orders for assistance sent to Grouchy on June 18 appear to be covering his embarrassment and could not possibly have been put into effect.

That covers the relationship between Bonaparte's right wing to the battle. Grouchy's conduct will be examined below.

Regarding the actual battle, the following observations can be made:

[The third issue is that] no mention was made of an actual plan of attack. The approach march and initial advance were parallel to the enemy front, and the distribution of forces was largely uniform along the whole line. Nevertheless, because the attack on the outpost of Hougoumont and the village of La Haye lacked energy, while the attack on the center was so great, it seems that Bonaparte's intention was merely to tie down the flanks while breaking through the center of the Allied army. As the main line of retreat was directly behind the center, and it is generally accepted that the other entrances to the Soignes Woods were not suitable for all arms, a breakthrough in the center indeed would have had the most decisive consequences, and there was certainly no other way than this to bring about a total defeat of the Allied army so quickly. As Bonaparte had placed VI Corps behind his center and the Guard was also to its rear, then such a plan could well have succeeded. If the three divisions of I Corps that attacked the center had sufficiently worn down and almost exhausted the Allied forces in a firefight several hours long, then VI Corps could have advanced to make a decision and actually broken through, with the Guard following in reserve in case Wellington's wings had attempted to improvise an attack on the enemy flanks. Such an impromptu reaction is seldom very sustained or forceful, so the French Guard would probably have been able to withstand the blow, with the victory in the center continuing to develop and threaten Wellington.

Bonaparte's attack could have achieved a brilliant success, though the fundamental causes must not be confused or misplaced.

Against forces in extended positions in hilly country, where it seemed like everything was nailed down and an offensive reaction was, for various reasons, not possible, breaking through in the center would have been the simplest, least dangerous, and most decisive type of attack.

Yet this was not the case in a position where the forces were concentrated or where there was a deep mass of large reserves. Here, breaking through the center, if it succeeded, may still have offered the most decisive success but would have been the most unnatural and dangerous method, because:

1. The attacker did not have greatly superior forces at the decisive point, as on a limited front.
2. He would have been much less able to conceal his intentions and dispositions.
3. If the enemy had gone over to the offensive on the flanks, this would have resulted in the most disadvantageous form of battle.

If battles consisted of a single momentous blow, and if armies could be conceived as brittle bodies, whose crystalline structure could be shattered by such a blow, then the third of these disadvantages would not count for much. But battles lasted a half or a whole day, and taking into account the larger part of the entire effort, consisted of a slow grinding and wearing away of the two armies, which, when their fronts come into contact, are like two hostile elements that destroy each other where they meet. The battle burned like wet powder, slowly, with limited intensity, and only when the greatest part of the opposing forces was burned out like useless cinders would the remainder have achieved the decision. In a fight of this nature, a blow against a reinforced center, like a battering ram against the enemy front, was a very unusual method.

It was often said that the breakthrough in the center was Bonaparte's favorite maneuver. Bold, reckless, overpowering, and arrogant as he was, always thirsting for the greatest results, it is credible that it must have had a particular appeal for him. But an examination of the major battles in which he was the attacker shows that this claim is entirely unjustified.[143]

Perhaps this shows more than anything else how far a blow against the enemy center was contrary to the nature of the situation, and how powerfully the attacker is always drawn toward the flanks.

Regarding a French victory at Mont St. Jean as nevertheless possible, it could only have been so if 70,000 Frenchmen led by Bonaparte and Ney were regarded as markedly superior to 70,000 Allied troops, of whom a third were Hanoverian Landwehr and new formations, and a third newly raised Belgian troops, whose spirit, among officers and men alike, was not entirely reliable. All eyewitnesses indicate that they broke much faster in battle than the French. If Wellington's situation at 5 P.M. was actually very bad already, before a single man of VI Corps and the Guard had fought against him, then this can only be explained by the superiority of the French troops.

---

143. Clausewitz's footnote here reads: "The battles on which this opinion have been based are Marengo, Austerlitz, Eylau, and Wagram. Marengo, Austerlitz, and Wagram, however, were actually defensive [actions] in which Bonaparte [went over to] the offensive."

If it is to be believed that a blow against Wellington's center could have succeeded, it is only:

1. Because the quality of the troops is believed to have been too unequal.
2. Because it does not appear that Wellington had thought of and was prepared to mount a counterattack.

As such, it would be difficult to regard the intended wedge-shaped blow against Mont St. Jean as an error for a commander like Bonaparte, who has to have had his eye on the boldest possible move if he was going to achieve truly brilliant results.

Yet all this was only the case if VI Corps and the Guard had been taken into consideration. When Blücher appeared, the entire VI Corps and half the Guard had to be used against him, so the blow against the center became a hard fight, a wild attempt to overrun the enemy, and exactly the same can be said about the premature and extravagant use of cavalry. From that moment on, nothing was done properly. The French forces attacking the flanks were just as strong as those in the center. There was no superiority of numbers and consequently no basis for success. The fact was that, no matter how worn down Wellington's army may have been, how threatened its position, or how close the French cavalry may have come to its lines, he still had reserves available, and if no large mass of fresh troops followed the French attack, then these exertions were simply a waste of effort. As Bonaparte lacked the forces to prepare the assault on the enemy center, as every attack must be prepared nowadays, and because he also did not have enough time, he had to rush everything.[144] It was no longer a well-thought-out plan, expertly executed, but an action dictated by circumstances—basically, an act of blind desperation.

Blücher's arrival not only snatched the victory from Bonaparte's hands, as it would also have done against Turenne,[145] Frederick

---

144. What Clausewitz refers to here is that Napoleon's first attack on Wellington's center was not preceded by an artillery bombardment and the infantry was sent in without the necessary softening up of the enemy position.

145. Henri de la Tour d'Auvergne, Viscount Turenne (1611–75), marshal of France, was one of the great military commanders of his era.

the Great, or any other great general one might instead mention, it also made him smash his forces to pieces against Wellington in a blind rage as if against a great rock, so bringing about the destruction of his army that ended this remarkable day.

Fourth, most critics claim that Bonaparte would have done better to attack and envelope Wellington's left flank.

Wellington's left was certainly weak, and leaving out Blücher's assistance completely, such an attack has to be considered much easier, though apparently less decisive than one against the center. If Bonaparte regarded Blücher's appearance as simply impossible, then there at least would have been much to say in its favor. But if the possibility of a Prussian advance via Lasnes and St. Lambert was taken into account, then an attack on the Anglo-Allied left would obviously be as good as impossible.

Thanks to the terrain, Wellington's right was stronger than his left, for at Braine l'Alleud and Merbraine, there were substantial hollows that would have made an attack very difficult. Also, an attack from this side, that is, on the right wing and against the right flank, might have taken another couple of hours, which was an unusually important consideration in Bonaparte's situation. Furthermore, he would have completely given up his natural line of retreat, and were he defeated, he would have had to look for one past Mons, on the road to Maubeuge or Valenciennes. Finally, such an attack obviously would be the least decisive, since its success would neither destroy Wellington's army nor separate it from Blücher's. These considerations are so many and so important that in most other cases, the idea of attacking from this direction would have to be discounted. Yet bearing in mind that Blücher's arrival with a significant force (50,000 men) was so likely that it had to be included in the plan of attack in any case and that there was not the least chance of victory in the center or on the left, then the idea of an attack on the right must be accepted, for the first law is the chance of success.

Had Bonaparte deployed the army to his left and advanced against Wellington's right flank via Braine l'Alleud, Wellington would have been forced to form a front to the west. His front there would almost have been even stronger, but the French would gain two advantages. First, in this position it is most unlikely that

Blücher would advance against the French right flank but instead simply support his ally directly from the rear, making the battle less disadvantageous to the French. Second, the Soignes Woods would be on Wellington's right, and since he was always extremely sensitive and concerned about the road to Brussels, Bonaparte could have used the woods to force Wellington to hold the road with more men, dividing his forces so that Bonaparte would have attacked a thinner and not so compact formation, thus encountering less resistance.

Wellington could not have suffered a total defeat this way, though perhaps a blow similar to that Blücher suffered at Ligny. The two Allied commanders might then have become irresolute and gone their own way. Perhaps Grouchy's all-out attack on Blücher's rear, for which there was not enough time on June 18, could then have taken place on June 19. Either way, both commanders would have abandoned their natural lines of retreat, making their situation uncomfortable and weakening their resolve. In short, it was indeed possible that, if both his opponents had not already had victory torn from their hands again on June 18, that on June 19 they would have been forced apart, opening the way to great results.

An attack against the left wing and into the left flank was the least feasible. An attack against the center was the quickest and most decisive. It would have been acceptable had there been a reasonable chance of winning before Blücher arrived. If, however, Blücher's timely and forceful appearance was a required assumption, then the attack on the right still offered the only prospect of victory.

Fifth, Bonaparte may well have made a mistake by not having light troops immediately occupying the ridges at Lasnes and St. Lambert, though it would not have made a noticeable difference to the overall outcome. To deploy a whole corps in this area, such as VI Corps, would have required an entirely different plan and an entirely different point of view than Bonaparte's. Of course, Lobau could have held on for longer at Lasnes and St. Lambert than at Fischermont, but he also would have been engaged much earlier, and if any of Blücher's forces advanced from Couture, he would have been in danger of being completely cut off. Bonaparte then would have had to send additional troops to this area, becoming entangled on a battlefield twice as large, which was not at all to his taste, and on which he would clearly have less control. But it does appear that Lobau's corps would have been better deployed between Fischermont and Payot to mount its main defense there.

Finally, concerning the last comment on Bonaparte's conduct of the battle, that is, the commitment of the last reserves, as already mentioned: a cautious commander, such as Turenne, Eugene,[146] or Frederick the Great, who was not in such an exceptional situation, who either had more to answer for or more to lose, would not have fought the Battle of Waterloo. At noon, when Bülow arrived, he would have broken off the fight and withdrawn. If it were possible to confine the rules for the conduct of war to merely objective conditions, then in this case it was against all the rules to try to attempt to fight this battle. Earlier critics would certainly have confirmed this, adding only that genius certainly cannot be bound by rules. This is not the judgment here. If the conduct of war at the highest level is based on principles, then these must at least encompass every event that can occur in war, above all those that are the most far-reaching and pervasive.

Bonaparte was balancing not only the crown of France but also many other crowns on the tip of his sword, and he tried just with boldness and daring defiance to make his way in a world whose established relationships and order were set against him. How can we measure him by the same standards as a Turenne, who was part of a great political order that he defined far less than it defined him, who can be regarded just as one of its slightly prominent members? How could Bonaparte be blamed for not avoiding a battle just because he saw the flash of the sword that Blücher, thirsting for vengeance, plunged into his side, so that hardly any hope of victory was left for him? Actually, that was the only way to attain his objective: to cling to his last hope, to try to hold on to fortune's weakest threads. When he advanced against Wellington,

---

146. François-Eugène, Prince of Savoy-Carignan (1663–1736), began his military career in the relief of Vienna in 1683 and continued through the Turkish Wars and into the War of the Spanish Succession. He is often regarded as one of history's great commanders.

victory almost certain, 10,000 men appeared on his right flank. There was a hundred-to-one chance that five or six times as many would follow and then the battle could not be won. Yet it was still possible that it could only be a small detachment and that some sort of uncertainty or caution could have prevented it from intervening effectively. Nevertheless, he could have expected nothing other than his inevitable destruction. Should he have let mere danger scare him into this certainty? No, there are situations in which the greatest caution could only be found in the greatest boldness, and Bonaparte's was one of them.

His persistent decision to fight the battle could be judged this way, and viewed from this perspective, it is evident that the sacrifice of his last reserves could only deserve complete disapproval, because it did not take place with the normally required caution. Once Blücher's forces had increased to 50,000 or 60,000 men; once Lobau had been overwhelmed and thrown back to the main line of retreat; once new, black masses under Ziethen had filled in the empty spaces in Wellington's line; once night had fallen, ending any possibility of Grouchy's intervention; from then on, victory was no longer possible, so the only duty and wisdom left for the commander would have been to turn against Bülow with part of his reserves, gaining ground for the retreat, and then to start it immediately, covering it with the remaining reserves. The battle had been lost and perhaps a total defeat could no longer have been avoided, however, for Bonaparte's subsequent negotiations, it obviously would have made an enormous difference whether, defeated by a superior force, he had left the battlefield at the head of a still-undefeated remnant that fought on bravely or he had returned home a fugitive, burdened with the reproach of having led his whole army to destruction and then having left it in the lurch. Bonaparte perhaps never made a greater mistake. Certainly, the commander who cautiously withdrew when the odds turned against him just slightly would win fewer battles, and merely suggesting a fight was in character for Bonaparte's style of warfare. Many battles were only won through perseverance and the expenditure of one's last reserves, but it would be a fair criticism to insist that the commander not seek the impossible, vainly sacrificing forces that can be better used elsewhere. Here,

Bonaparte does not appear to be a great man, but almost as an embittered mediocrity, like someone who had broken an instrument and furiously threw the fragments to the ground.

49. The Allies

The conduct of the Allied commanders at the Battle of Waterloo requires little comment.

Wellington's position was by all accounts very favorable. Whatever may have been said about the danger posed by the proximity of the Soignes Woods in his rear, one would have to investigate the condition of the roads through it to make a judgment. It is very unlikely that access to such a small wood in such a cultivated area would be difficult. If it was not, however, there was clearly an advantage in having it nearby.

One of the great achievements of Wellington's deployment was the numerous reserves, or, to put it differently, the way the narrow position contributed to the strength of the army, allowing many troops to be left in reserve. More might have been done to prepare and fortify the three forward outposts.

Wellington's deployment partly broke up his divisions, presumably because he wanted to mix up the units more and not to leave too many unreliable troops together, specifically not too many Belgians. In fact, this measure seems to have worked when the General Perponcher's battalions fell back before being attacked. If the whole division had been standing there together, the gap might have become too big.[147]

The principle of mixing good and bad troops closely together was certainly better than leaving the bad by themselves and using them at less-important points.

Obviously, Wellington did not consider making a counterattack, because this was down to the Prussians.

---

147. The role of Bijlandt's brigade of Perponcher's division has been the subject of dispute and debate among historians. Some have pointed the finger at "cowardly Belgians" who supposedly ran away at the first opportunity. Others have given more thoughtful accounts of this episode.

Little needs to be said about Blücher's contribution to the victory: it was largely the decision to march to join Wellington. This has already been discussed, along with the simplicity and purposefulness with which it was carried out.

Furthermore, the tireless Prussian pursuit throughout the night deserves a special mention. It can scarcely be calculated how much this contributed to the total dissolution of the enemy army and to the number and brilliance of the trophies that glorify this battle.[148]

50. The Battle of Wavre

Starting with the situation at noon on June 17, when a significant pursuit of the Prussians was not yet under way, the route of their retreat was not actually known but was presumed to be toward the Meuse via Gembloux and Namur. It was only at noon that Grouchy was sent off with Bonaparte's general order to stay on their heels. It is surprising that Grouchy did not think of heading to the Dyle first, then moving down either its right bank or, what would have been far better, down its left. At the very least, a substantial detachment, perhaps a division of infantry and cavalry, might have been sent to Mont St. Guibert to maintain some kind of contact with Bonaparte. But the Dyle was of little importance to the French, partly because they were never wasteful in dividing their forces, preferring instead to have everything in one place, only making the most essential detachments, and partly because

---

148. Clausewitz is understandably proud of the decisive role of the Prussian army at Waterloo. But the pursuit conducted after the battle was minimal, largely because the general exhaustion of the army prevented a large number of troops from being immediately committed to it. The handful of men Gneisenau took on his "wild chase" did achieve an effect greater than might have been expected from their numbers, but it is interesting to note, for instance, that not a single infantry color was captured, which indicates the infantry retired in good order. The narrow bridge at Genappe proved such a bottleneck that much of the wheeled vehicle park of the Army of the North was abandoned there, with a considerable amount of the artillery train being captured. The *pièce de résistance* was the capture of Napoleon's gold-plated, bulletproof coach and the million francs' worth of diamonds it contained.

their attention was always directed toward the Meuse. It is not so surprising that Grouchy followed Blücher via Gembloux, or rather thought he was following him, and only turned toward the Dyle when the Prussian movements drew him there.

Yet when at Gembloux on the night of June 17–18 he discovered that Blücher had turned toward the Dyle, the thought should immediately have entered his mind that this could only be in order to reunite with Wellington, because there was no other reason to abandon his natural line of retreat. From that moment on, his mission should not have been to stay on the heels of Blücher's rearguard but to place himself between Blücher and Bonaparte and so be able to move in front of Blücher should he wish to march off to his right. Accordingly, from Gembloux onward, he should have turned toward the Dyle by the shortest route, more or less via Mont St. Guibert, either to drive off the Prussian forces that might be in this area or, if it was still not occupied, to take positions on the left bank, where he could keep the forces in Wavre at bay. From his position Grouchy should have simply and easily come to this conclusion, and this conclusion, not the cannon fire from Waterloo, should have led him from his original path to the upper Dyle.

Bonaparte and many others have accused Grouchy of not having followed the advice of Exelmans and Gérard, who drew his attention to the heavy cannon fire coming from the main army and urged him to move in that direction immediately. They have relied on Rogniat's hastily fabricated principle that the commander of a detached column should always move toward the place where heavy firing indicates the crisis of a decisive battle.[149] Yet this principle can only apply in those cases where circumstances have placed the commander of a detached column in a doubtful position, obscuring the original clarity and purpose of his mission and where events have overtaken it, as is so often the case in real war. Rather than remain inactive or wander around to

---

149. General Joseph, Viscount Rogniat (1776–1840), served in Germany and Spain during the Revolutionary and Napoleonic Wars. His book *Considérations sur l'art de la guerre* (Paris, 1817) was considered essential reading by aspirant army officers of the era.

no purpose, such a commander would certainly do better to rush to the aid of his neighbor if heavy firing indicated he was in distress. But to expect that Grouchy should have stopped harassing Blücher and marched to where another part of the army was fighting a battle against another enemy would be contrary to all theory and practice. Should Gérard really have given this advice in Sart-à-Walhain in the afternoon of June 18, then that only goes to show that whoever is not responsible for an action does not consider it properly.

Nevertheless, Grouchy never seemed to have realized that Blücher's march to Wavre actually altered his own mission. Instead, he somewhat thoughtlessly took his whole force down the road to Wavre, intending to grab hold of his opponent, so fixing him there. Had he been as strong as Blücher, that might have been feasible, but to pin down an enemy force three times as large by means of a simple frontal attack is impossible. And even the intention to mount a frontal attack would have led Grouchy to divide his forces from Gembloux and to look for a crossing of the Dyle above Wavre with the larger part, taking him to Limale. How could he have expected to force a breakthrough against Blücher along the main road? Even if he did not know that the Dyle around Wavre offered an excellent position, he could have still seen generally from a map that a larger enemy on the other side of the river here could present [him] with considerable problems so that he would have to consider outflanking him. Of course, this flanking maneuver could only be made to the left, because that way he would move closer to the main army.

A supposed lack of energy is said to explain why the attacks on Wavre and Bierges were not more successful, though it should be noted that both Vandamme and Gérard were not the sort to allow them to fail for that reason. A couple of other generals were wounded as well as Gérard, and at one point at Bierges, Grouchy personally took command of a battalion. If these attacks are to be criticized, then it should be for their clumsiness and not any lack of energy. To make a serious attack on Thielemann, the French would have had to cross the Dyle at five or six places, some over bridges, some by fording, and then attempt to storm the heights. Needless to say, there was no easy way to do this, because Thielemann's position could hardly have been better.

Certainly, Grouchy could have inflicted more losses on Thielemann on June 19 if he had made use of his superiority in cavalry (5,000 troopers to 2,000). But the uncertain state of affairs already had left him out on a limb somewhat, hampering his actions. Finally, we come to the question whether Grouchy, had he really arrived at St. Lambert, could have averted Bonaparte's defeat. This is unlikely, but he instead may well have been drawn into the confusion, making the Allied victory much greater, because his troops would not have reached Paris in such strength and in such good order. Wherever Grouchy might have ended up on the left bank of the Dyle at noon on June 18, and however he might have employed his forces against Blücher, he would at most have tied down two Prussian corps, and the other two could have marched to the Battle of Waterloo, which in any case would have decided the issue, since the Prussian forces actually engaged there certainly did not amount to two entire corps.

It is not even likely that Bonaparte personally would have been in a position to reach Grouchy's troops on the evening of June 18, and in all probability his personal situation would have ended up no differently than it did.

51. A Second Battle against Blücher

One major strategic question remains: if on June 17 Bonaparte might not have done better to pursue Blücher with his main force, [thus] either creating panic and confusion with an energetic pursuit, driving him across the Meuse, or, if Blücher wanted to risk a second battle on June 17 or 18, bringing about his total defeat?

Certainly, one of the most important and effective strategic principles is that success, wherever achieved and as far as circumstances permit, should be exploited immediately. Whatever is undertaken when the enemy is in a crisis will have a much greater effect than if there were no crisis, so it is a poor economy of force to let such a favorable situation pass. Furthermore, any use of one's remaining superiority at another point involves losing time and effort spent marching, which, if the situation does not make this diversion necessary, are a waste of effort.

Indeed, it is an important strategic maxim that, when a major decision is at stake, the destruction of the enemy force is the main objective and has to be regarded as the sole means to this end. The more decisive the struggle becomes, the more this is the case, the less it matters where this destruction takes place, since wherever this destruction can be the greatest is where it will be most effective. Of course, other factors still carry a certain weight: for instance, the reputation of the commander and the army, the proximity of the capital city, relationships with allies, et cetera. All these and other such matters have to be evaluated individually as secondary considerations, but it is right to regard the destruction of enemy forces as the main objective.

From this perspective it seems that here too, Bonaparte's main objective was to render ineffective as many of the 215,000 men facing him as possible, and it is almost irrelevant if they were Blücher's, or Wellington's, or both. The moral effect of the overall victory might have been greater if Wellington's unblemished reputation and the excellent British troops were destroyed at the same time, but this is only a small nuance of little importance if a significantly greater destruction of the Allied forces might otherwise have been achieved.

If Bonaparte had been in a position to make a second victory more likely and more successful in a second battle with Blücher rather than Wellington, he unquestionably should have chosen this option, because then, in seeking the second battle, he would not have lost any of the gains already made in the first. The pursuit and the search for a second battle were one and the same operation. Just as two flames that come together have a much greater glow, the first and second victories would have flowed into a larger whole and had a much greater result than separate victories fought against different opponents.

Yet could he be certain he could force Blücher to accept this second battle, as certain, or rather more certain, than Wellington? An army that has not yet lost its balance can fall back without disadvantage, so gaining time. But a beaten army cannot do so. If the pursuer presses hard, the beaten army has to resolve to make a stand or else collapse, suffering great losses and the destruction of its honor. This moral aspect of victory should not be underestimated.

This hopefully shows that if Blücher had wanted to avoid a second battle and pulled back toward the Meuse, Bonaparte's close pursuit would have achieved complete or at least partial compensation for the missing victory. Had he achieved this, driving Blücher back ten or fifteen [German] miles, then it still would have been possible for him to do what he did on June 17 and turn against Wellington with his main army.

What could Wellington have done in the meantime? He would more likely have fallen back than have advanced, but in the best case, that is, he might have inflicted a total defeat on Ney, driving him back across the Sambre. In such a scenario, it is clear that defeating 40,000 men could not possibly bring the same advantages as defeating 115,000. Whatever trophies Wellington would have gained, Blücher probably would have paid for three times over. Of course, there is no doubt Wellington would have beaten Ney, though Bonaparte perhaps may not have destroyed Blücher, but Bonaparte's situation was such that, given a choice between the more likely and the more decisive victory, he always had to choose the latter.

Commanders in wars where equal forces are at play, who do not fear the worst or want the greatest result, can choose the lesser but more certain advantage, but such caution would have been disastrous for Bonaparte.

If the second principle discussed earlier is correct, that when very powerful interests and great decisions make the destruction of the enemy forces the main objective, and that this main objective overwhelms and makes all geographical and geometrical considerations unimportant and ineffective, then the position of the Allied armies in relation to their bases or to geographical points in the area and all its effects is not worth consideration.

For instance, if Wellington had pushed Ney back through Charleroi, he would have been in Bonaparte's rear and cut his lines of communication. That would have been effective if Bonaparte had wanted or indeed needed to remain there, or if Charleroi were Paris. But what difference would it have made to a commander in the full flush of victory if he had lost his communications for a week? What kept Bonaparte from establishing new lines temporarily via Huy to Dinant, providing a line of retreat in an emergency? And if Bonaparte had now turned around and moved against Wellington or even on Brussels, Wellington would immediately have turned back toward that city. Wellington's much greater sensitivity to his lines of communication resides not in the relationship of the mutual lines of communications, nor in Bonaparte's larger base of supplies, but rather in the most general features of their positions as well as in the specific details of their personal situations. What Bonaparte could risk here because he was his own master and had to take risks, and because only through the greatest risks could he survive, could never have been thought defensible by a responsible subordinate commander like Wellington. The result is that Bonaparte, in pursuing Blücher unstintingly, could have been sure of large gains that would have outweighed everything he would have lost in his rear, and that a single move against Brussels would then have snapped Wellington back there like a spring, being for Bonaparte like a splendid overture to a new round of victories.

A retreat by Blücher toward the Meuse is taken as obvious, as Bonaparte assumed it, and as such, his decision could only be fully understood from this perspective. But this possibility must continue to be taken into consideration. What actually happened, that Blücher moved to the Dyle to unite with Wellington, now deserves consideration.

Once the possibility of joining forces after the first battle was possible, it obviously made no difference either to the likelihood or to the scale of Bonaparte's success whether this took place at Wavre or at Waterloo. It all came down to the single question, whether there was more to fear if Bonaparte sought his second battle against Blücher or against Wellington. The latter can be accepted without qualification.

If Blücher had been successful in rallying his forces on June 17 and getting firmly back on his feet again on June 18, so that he could have accepted a battle at Wavre, then this would have been entirely due to the mistakes, failures, omissions, and caution of the pursuer, Grouchy. Had Bonaparte pursued with the main army, he very well could have offered his opponent battle at Wavre early on June 18. It is very questionable whether Blücher was in position to accept it at this time and place, and still more doubtful that Wellington could have gotten there in good time.

It would be pointless to consider all the possibilities that may have arisen. Rather, accepting that it would not have been preceded by a movement from one line to another, a second battle against Blücher could have begun sooner than one against Wellington. Furthermore, as Wellington was uncertain about what had happened to Blücher and what was going to happen to him, Wellington was much less able to decide to aid Blücher than Blücher, in contrast, was to aid Wellington. Blücher was fully aware only of his own situation and knew Wellington was intact, while Wellington knew his own situation, but nothing about Blücher's. Thanks to his characteristic underestimation of his opponents and overestimation of his own abilities, Bonaparte let go of Blücher too soon. Furthermore, the idea of reaching Brussels quickly was attractive. He made the same mistake both in 1813 at the Battle of Dresden[150] and in 1814 after the battles on the Marne.[151] In the first case, he should have pursued the Allied main army beyond Prague, while in the second he should have ruthlessly pursued Blücher as far as the Rhine. There can be little doubt that in both cases, with such a move, he would have dragged the whole force of events with him, completely reversing the situation.

In all three cases, Bonaparte, use to seeing the enemy flee for long distances at the mere sight of him or, like Beaulieu after the Battle of Montenotte,[152] vacillate indecisively, thanks to his characteristic underestimation of his opponents, did not believe the beaten army could rally and turn around so soon.

150. At the Battle of Dresden, August 26–27, 1813, Napoleon defeated the Army of Bohemia. He did not conduct a vigorous pursuit in person after this battle but redirected his main forces toward Blücher's army, which had just crushed Macdonald's force on the Katzbach. Vandamme was sent off to pursue the defeated Allies but was surrounded and utterly destroyed. Napoleon lost his best opportunity of winning the campaign there.

151. Clausewitz is referring to what is often regarded as one of Napoleon's most brilliant performances, when in a series of battles and maneuvers in six days in February 1814 he inflicted four defeats on Blücher's Army of Silesia. There too the emperor did not capitalize on his success, and Paris fell a few weeks later.

152. The Battle of Montenotte was fought on April 12, 1796, when Napoleon defeated an Austro-Sardinian force under Johann von Beaulieu and Eugène-Guillaume Count Argenteau.

This is more an error than a mistake. But in all three cases, it is apparent that Bonaparte's change of direction affected the overall result, and the motives leading to this change were not sufficient to justify deviating from the general principles of this thesis. To that extent, it has to be regarded as a real mistake.

Yet having thoroughly examined the whole course of events, though it is plausible that Bonaparte's conduct was mistaken, a deviation from the rules that determined the course of his star, it is not necessarily the case that it would have been easy to take another course. For a general in normal circumstances and with normal willpower, the decision not to observe Blücher on the Elbe,[153] or Schwarzenberg[154] on the Seine,[155] or Wellington on the Sambre, would have been enormous. But this enormity lay not in the rules of theory, but in the mission at hand; in Bonaparte's perspective that determined the situation of all lines of action. If an object appears enormous, it is either because the draftsman's eye is not yet accustomed to it, or because natural proportions have been transgressed and a mission has been chosen that borders on the impossible.

52. Consequences of the Battle

The French loses in the Battle of Waterloo are given as 25,000 men, including 6,000 prisoners, and for all five days, 41,000 men. Taking this to mean just dead, wounded, and prisoners taken on

---

153. Clausewitz is referring to the fall campaign of 1813, during which, on October 3, Blücher's Army of Silesia was allowed to cross the Elbe at Wartenburg, placing it in a position to link up with the Army of Bohemia and ultimately ensure an Allied victory at Leipzig later that month.

154. Field Marshal Karl Philipp Prince Schwarzenberg (1771–1820) joined the Austrian cavalry in 1788 and first saw action against the Turks. Next he fought during the Revolutionary Wars and commanded the rearguard at Hohenlinden in 1800. In 1812 he took command of the Austrian auxiliary corps in Russia. When the Austrians joined the Allies in the fall of 1813, Schwarzenberg was placed in command of the Army of Bohemia, the largest Allied army operating in Saxony.

155. In late March 1814, when Allied forces approached Paris, Napoleon left his brother Joseph with 20,000 men along with 30,000 National and Imperial Guards to defend Paris against 100,000 attackers. The fall of the city directly caused Napoleon's first abdication.

the battlefield, this estimate may not be too low, but it would be a great mistake to believe that of the 115,000 men who, according to their accounts, took part in the battles, 74,000 remained. The scale of a victory as such, that is, the destructive effect it has on the enemy army, of course has numerous levels. One of these constitutes the main limit and is when the defeated army is no longer capable of forming a rearguard to delay and limit the pursuit. In such an event, the retreat becomes a rout, with the entire army breaking up and considered destroyed for the time being. Prince Hohenlohe at Jena[156] and Bonaparte at Waterloo are examples of this.[157] Such a result is inevitable if the side against which the battle has run still wants to force the tide to turn with a final sacrifice and so commits the reserves that could have formed its rearguard. Bonaparte did this with the last eight battalions of the Guard. The extent to which an army can rally following such a total rout of course varies greatly according to the circumstances. The time of day when the battle ended, the area and ground where it was fought, the moral condition of the army, [and] the political will of the nation and government all influence this. The *Mémoires* of St. Helena claim that 25,000 men from the defeated army rallied at Laon. While this may not have been impossible, there is a great difference between possibility and fact.

The battle ended at nightfall, which led, on the one hand, to the confusion and breaking down of order being much greater. If the darkness had not made any sort of personal intervention

---

156. In the campaign of 1806, Napoleon's pursuit of the defeated Prussian army ensured its total destruction. The only part of the army that escaped this fate was that under Blücher's command, which was forced to capitulate at Lübeck.

157. It is evident that Clausewitz considered the pursuit the Prussians undertook after Waterloo to have been a decisive act. As discussed earlier, the immediate pursuit was limited. Although the Army of the North lost its artillery park, the infantry and cavalry retired in relative good order. Furthermore, Grouchy's wing of the army was still largely intact, and a line of defensive fortifications covered northern France. Napoleon still had a fighting force and a base of operations from which he could have staged a comeback after Waterloo. Part of the reason he did not was the vigorous pursuit undertaken from the day after the battle to the gates of Paris, which gave him little opportunity to rally and captured a number of important fortresses, not the pursuit immediately after the French withdrew from the battlefield.

impossible, Bonaparte might actually have succeeded in forming a rearguard of 10 or 15,000 men and conducted an orderly withdrawal instead of being routed. On the other hand, the darkness made it much easier for individuals to escape, and a couple more hours of daylight would have substantially increased the number of prisoners taken. Under cover of night, all those who still had their legs under them were able to get away. Chaboulon's *Mémoires* notes that Bonaparte passed through Charleroi between 4 and 5 A.M. on June 19, where he tried in vain to rally the fleeing troops and restore order, and thus had to continue his flight to Philippeville.[158] Charleroi is about 3 1/2 [German] miles from the battlefield, so whoever was already there at that time must have ran without stopping.

Fleeing troops had already reached Philippeville on June 19, but they were of little use, so Bonaparte continued to Laon that day. Indeed, what is so remarkable is that at Laon, most probably on the morning of June 21, that is, some sixty hours after the battle ended and twenty [German] miles from the battlefield, Bonaparte was told of the approach of a substantial body of troops. He sent an aide to discover who it was, and it was his brother, Jérôme, along with Generals Soult, Morand, Colbert, Petit, and Pelet de Morvan, approaching with some 3,000 infantry and cavalry that they had rallied. However highly one may regard the French army, this cannot be called anything other than a total rout, one without equal.

It was Jérôme whom Bonaparte had ordered to rally the army at Avesnes, and who, as Bonaparte wrote in his *Mémoires,* already had 25,000 men there on June 21.

According to Bonaparte, Jérôme had brought 50 cannon with him, but all the 240 guns comprising the French artillery were either captured on the battlefield or during the retreat.

On June 28, when, after having brushed aside weak fragments of the beaten army for several days, the pursuing Prussian forces advanced beyond the Oise down the road from Soissons to Paris, they encountered Grouchy. It was impossible for an organized body of 25,000 men to be at either Laon or Soissons, and what was

---

158. Baron Fleury de Chaboulon, *Les cent-jours. Mémoires pour servir à l'histoire de la vie privée, du retour et du règne de Napoléon en 1815,* 2 vols. (London 1820).

there had not joined Grouchy but were fleeing before him toward Paris. Grouchy reported the daily losses and defections from the army to the government commission.[159]

The strength of the army in Paris also proved this. Not counting the National Guard, it amounted to 60,000 men, of whom 19,000 were in the depots, so only 40,000 could have been part of the main army, and of these around 25,000 joined Grouchy, so the remaining 15,000 may be regarded as the residue of the army defeated at Waterloo, a clear indication that this army actually fell apart between the battlefield and Paris.

Strategically, a victory of this scale has to be regarded as in a class of its own that exceptional circumstances had caused and that led to significantly greater results.

The main causes probably include the following:

1. The great effort with which the French army had already fought when the battle was decided. The more the forces are exhausted before the decisive blow comes in a battle, the more effective and successful it will be. Here, as already mentioned, the exhaustion of forces on the French side was total, one might well say more than so, as Bonaparte had committed his last reserves, his true rearguard, to the battle, and even before that, the entire cavalry had been heedlessly thrown into the destruction of the firefight.
   The commitment of the last reserves can be excusable, or rather natural, in a battle that remains almost in balance until the last moment, though not when the scales have already tipped too far in favor of the opponent. This can be regarded as mere bluster and as such shows a lack of true military judgment.
2. Nightfall, which made it impossible to counter the emerging chaos.
3. The envelopment of the Prussian attack.
4. The Allies' great superiority of numbers.
5. The great energy of the pursuit.

159. Ibid., 2:328.

6. Finally, the influence of all the political elements that permeate any war to a greater or lesser extent, but that in this one were obviously more imposing and proved to be liabilities of the worst kind.

The less the intention for a major decision is based on comprehensive and wholly natural conditions and the normal interests of the nation, the more it escalates artificially, the more it is undertaken in a spirit of a daring wager trusting luck, then the more destructive the blow will be by which, in the event of a defeat, all these tensions are released.

In this case, all these factors contributed to the size of the success, and only if several such matters had been present would it be justified in setting one's sights so high.

Yet as far as the consequences of the total destruction of this army were concerned, political factors generally—such as the state of the nation and government, their relations with other nations, and so on—played a greater role, as do the forces, effects, means, and ends of strategy generally affect politics ever more deeply the greater and more comprehensive they become. War can never be regarded as an independent action, but rather simply as a modification of political activity and the implementation of political plans and interests by military means.

In the present case, such a victory would undoubtedly lead directly to Paris and directly to peace. Resistance before Paris was inconceivable, since no enemy forces of the necessary size could be deployed. Even in Paris, all-out resistance was unlikely, because the defense of such a large city, though by no means impossible, always involves great difficulties and requires more favorable conditions than were present. Even if the fighting forces that could have been assembled in Paris were adequate to defend it against Blücher and Wellington for the time being, the rest of the country, so inadequately defended, was open to all the other Allied armies. Moreover, in a few weeks these armies would have arrived at Paris, having conquered half of France on their way. In such circumstances, how could a nation divided by political factions offer further resistance, and would not this impossibility have initiated the internal reaction in Paris?

Everything that Bonaparte and his defenders have said about the great forces that were still available, about the possibility, indeed the ease, of further resistance, was mere blather. By placing the 40,000 men already lost in a purely numerical relationship to existing forces, they wanted to give the impression that they constituted a small part of the whole, but even so they lacked the courage to make this laughable argument out loud. France lost 40,000 men on the fields of Ligny and Waterloo, but an army of 80,000 was destroyed. Furthermore, this army was the keystone of the entire defensive system on which all depended, in which all security lay, and in which every hope was vested. The army was destroyed and the commander that led it, in whose miraculous abilities half of France believed with an enthusiasm bordering on superstition, the great magician was caught, as he himself said of Blücher at Ligny, en flagrant delit. It collapsed along with the structure of the military system that was supposed to secure the borders of France, as well as with the trust in intelligence that led it all.

That is why there has never been a victory with such a tremendous psychological force. Moreover, what was accomplished by that force, that is, the sudden overthrow of the large anti-Bourbon political party and the removal of Bonaparte, whom half of France still worshipped, was hardly noticed or attributable to the actions of individuals that it would have been almost a miracle if matters had turned out otherwise.

Furthermore, on the day after the battle, the two Allied commanders could already see the full extent of this victory, for the trophies consisted of the entire artillery park, some 240 guns, plus the baggage of the supreme commander. Nothing more could be desired, as these were the unmistakable signs of an army that had been totally destroyed and driven from the field.

53. The March on Paris: Initial Pursuit

As such, it was obvious to the Allied commanders that they would encounter no opposition before Paris and that if the enemy could actually meet them again on equal terms there, the rapid approach of the other Allied armies would make a real setback difficult. The march on Paris was thus legitimate, and in strategy whatever is legitimate is necessary. Only such a march could make use of the brilliant victory, worthy of the two commanders and their military achievements. Any lesser venture would have left the victory incomplete and been a waste of energy, for the fruits bought so expensively at Ligny and Waterloo would not have been harvested.

The Allies advanced on Paris as quickly as possible, pursuing the defeated enemy to the city walls. They took more prisoners, hoping to drive isolated units away from the central point of the enemy's power, shattering all organized resistance on the way there, and bringing about terror, confusion, and disunity in Paris itself. Even if they had not taken an appreciable number of new prisoners, even if no enemy forces had been driven off, even if the catastrophe of Bonaparte's fall from power had occurred before the Allied advance on Paris was known there, these intentions remain no less valid from Blücher and Wellington's point of view, because in war, exactly how events will unfold can never been known in advance. But the rapid march on Paris nevertheless hastened the end of major events there, leaving the republican party, which was again starting to rule, with only enough time and energy to attempt to form one new government.

The reasons for the march on Paris have been examined closely here not to justify them, which is not necessary, but because there was no risk involved and military honor alone demanded it. Rather, it has been examined to draw attention to how, in the conduct of war, all the likely consequences of an event have to be thought through and considered, so the relentless advance on Paris appears to the critic as an entirely necessary component of this campaign.

The two Allied commanders agreed on the battlefield itself that since the fighting had not exhausted and weakened it so much and because its line of attack had left it farther forward, the Prussian army would conduct the subsequent pursuit. They also agreed that the Prussian army should take the road through Charleroi to Avesnes and toward Laon, while the Anglo-Allies that via Nivelles and Binche toward Péronnes.

While most of the Prussians marched on with IV Army Corps in the lead, the Anglo-Allied army remained on the battlefield. Lieutenant General von Gneisenau led its point, urging on the pursuit throughout the night. He had infantry drums beaten incessantly to alarm the fleeing enemy, making them believe their pursuers close by, scaring them from their bivouacs, and keeping them constantly on the move.

Bonaparte had left the battlefield with a small entourage, initially intending to remain at Quatre Bras and have Girard's division join him there. It was intended to be the first way station on the retreat, the first rallying point. But Girard's division was nowhere to be found, the terrifying drumbeat of the Prussians drove everything relentlessly to the Sambre.

At daybreak most of the fugitives reached the Sambre at Charleroi, Marchienne-au-Pont, and Châtelet, but it was not possible to stop there either. The Prussian vanguard pressed on to Gosselies, sending its cavalry to the Sambre. The fleeing army continued to Beaumont and Philippeville.

Most of the success can be attributed in all probability to the energetic initial pursuit. It accelerated the flight, the disorder, and the deterioration of the fighting spirit, so scattering the army. The bulk of the captured artillery was certainly found on the roads used in the retreat, because in the haste and confusion of flight, they were all jammed and jumbled together in the defiles, such as the bridge over the Dyle in Genappe. The gunners, knowing it was impossible to save their cannon, simply set the horses free and escaped on them. The rich, glistening trophies taken from the imperial carriage, the existence of which Bonaparte was so reluctant to admit, can also be attributed only to this fortunate decision to conduct a pursuit. It can be called that, because a pursuit following a victorious battle is intrinsically natural in the right circumstances and also because it normally causes numerous difficulties and friction to the machinery, hindering the best decisions. Indeed, in the case at hand, the enormous exertions the Prussian troops made before this victory made thinking so difficult that in the end the force with which Gneisenau pressed on so relentlessly was actually nothing more than a fusilier battalion and its tireless drummer, whom he had put on one of Bonaparte's coach horses.

This is striking proof and certainly a vivid image of the enormously different effects that identical expenditures of energy can have in war.

An army like the French, basking in the glory of a string of victories over more than twenty years that originally had the compact structure, the indestructibility, and, so to say, the brilliance of a gemstone, whose courage and order mere danger in the blazing embers of battle neither broke nor put to flight. Such an army, when the noble forces that gave it its crystalline structure were broken, along with its faith in its commander, in itself, and the sacred discipline of service, fled in breathless terror before the sound of a drum, before a threat from its enemy that bordered on a joke.

In the conduct of war, it is important to correctly evaluate the numerous gradations that lie between these two opposites. What is necessary for this is to have one's own sense of judgment, which can be inborn but, more than any other attribute of a commander, can also be developed through experience, that is, by training. Only to the extent that this sense plays a leading role in war will, in both great and small affairs, in the conduct of a campaign as well as of a patrol, the necessary amount of effort be expended, so that on the one hand, no opportunities are missed, while on the other, no effort is wasted.

Let us return now to the battlefield to examine the positions of the opposing forces more clearly.

Blücher's dispositions on the evening of June 18 were:

IV Army Corps was to pursue the enemy so that he could not
   pause and regroup
II Army Corps was to cut off Marshal Grouchy
I Army Corps was to follow IV in support

Had Blücher known Grouchy's strength on the evening of June 18, he could rightly be criticized for not giving I Corps the same orders as II Corps. As Grouchy was around 30,000 men strong, and as it was only a question of cutting him off, it could well be argued that 20,000 men (II Corps would still have been about this strong if it had been concentrated) were not enough. Indeed,

Thielemann also had about 20,000 men, only it was very uncertain whether these would be to hand at the moment when Grouchy, hastening to his rear, encountered II Corps. But [since] Blücher believed Grouchy was only 12–15,000 strong at that time, as Thielemann's latest reports suggested no more, then the Prussian II Corps would have been strong enough to deal with Grouchy. Moreover, Blücher did not actually think his whole force would be taken prisoner. Rather, he probably thought Pirch I should simply have attacked from the rear and perhaps cut off part of it, for it was naturally assumed that Grouchy had begun his retreat that night and would have gone too far toward Namur to cut him off before he got there.

Taking into account that the result of the Battle of Waterloo forced Grouchy to fall back; that the only place he could cross the Meuse was at Namur, and that there were certainly no pontoons available for him to build a bridge elsewhere; that if he had been denied this place, he would then have to force a crossing of the Sambre, where sufficient troops to hold him up could easily have been available; and that taking even 12–15,000 prisoners was very important, then it must be considered that Blücher made an error by not sending II Corps along the direct route to Namur. If Grouchy could be blocked anywhere, it obviously had to be easiest at the farthest point. The only fear was that it was too far, so that the enemy, hearing of the loss of Namur, could turn toward the Sambre. In such an event, however, it could have been possible to be ready to oppose him there. All of this had not been clearly thought through or carefully considered in the confusion at the close of a battle, with its hundreds of pressing demands, as they can be now in retrospect, which is why things were only half-done.

The dispositions mentioned above resulted in the Prussian forces being located as follows on the night of June 18–19:

I Corps north of Genappe
II Corps marching from Plancenoit via Glabais to Mellery
III Corps at Wavre
IV Corps between Genappe and Gosselies, with the vanguard at Gosselies

Wellington's army remained on the battlefield. Blücher's headquarters was in Genappe; Wellington's headquarters was in Mont St. Jean.

The French army was in flight, crossing the Sambre at Charleroi, Châtelet, and Marchienne, partly en route to Beaumont, partly to Philippeville

Bonaparte was fleeing via Charleroi to Philippeville

Grouchy was at Wavre

On June 19 Blücher's dispositions were as follows:

I Corps is to advance to Charleroi, pushing out its vanguard to Marchienne-au-Pont.

II Corps is to march to Avesnes, pushing out its vanguard to the Sambre and across it over the two bridges at Thuin and Lobbes. Should the enemy wish to hold the Sambre today, the sluices should be opened, so the water can flow away, allowing the river to be forded at a number of points. Should the bridges at Lobbes and Thuin be destroyed, then they must be rebuilt at once.

IV Corps is to advance to Fontaine l'Evêque. This corps is to immediately establish communications with Mons, etc.

From these dispositions it is evident that the only report Blücher had from II Corps was that it was at Mellery but had heard nothing about the enemy, and since he ordered it in a completely different direction, that consequently he completely gave up the idea of it being able to cut off Grouchy. He could not have received any reports from III Corps, because the enemy had just moved between them.

So on June 19, the day when the actual arrangements to cut of Grouchy would have had to have been made, Blücher believed Grouchy already escaped and was all the more set on continuing via Avesnes.

On the evening of June 19, the positions of the opposing armies were:

I Corps at Charleroi, having completed a march of 3 1/2 [German] miles

II Corps at Mellery, which it reached only toward midday
III Corps at St. Agatha-Rode
IV Corps at Fontaine l'Evêque, having also marched 3 1/2 [German] miles
Fifth Brigade of II Corps, which was not with the main body, at Anderlues, not far from Fontaine l'Evêque
The Anglo-Allied army around Nivelles
Blücher's headquarters in Gosselies
Wellington's headquarters in Nivelles
The French main army in Beaumont and Philippeville, some already in the vicinity of Avesnes
Bonaparte reached Philippeville at 10 A.M. and left for Laon around 2 P.M.
Grouchy marched off from Wavre to Namur.

On the evening of June 20:

I Corps at Beaumont, after a march of 4 [German] miles
IV Corps at Colleret, near Maubeuge, after a march of 3 1/2 [German] miles
Fifth Brigade investing Maubeuge
II Corps at Namur
III Corps at Gembloux and Namur
The Anglo-Allied army in the vicinity of Binche
Blücher's headquarters in Merbe-le-Château
Wellington's headquarters in Binche
The main French army partly at Avesnes, partly farther to the rear
Bonaparte in Laon
Grouchy in Dinant

On the evening of June 21:

I Corps investing and bombarding Avesnes
IV Corps between Avesnes and Landrecy, investing Landrecy
II Corps in Thuin
III Corps in Charleroi
Anglo-Allied army between Mons and Valenciennes

Blücher's headquarters in Noyelles-sur-Sambre
Wellington's headquarters in Malplaquet
The defeated army beginning to rally at Laon and Marle
Bonaparte in Paris, where he was forced to abdicate the following day
Grouchy in Philippeville

On June 21 General Ziethen had a battery of six 10-pound howitzers, four 7-pound howitzers, and eight 12-pounders drawn up within six hundred paces of Avesnes and began to bombard it.

The fortress's garrison consisted of 1,700 national guardsmen and 200 veterans. The initial bombardment failed to start a fire, but when it was recommenced that night, a 10-pound shell, the fourteenth shot, hit the fort's main powder magazine, blowing it up and laying waste to a large part of the town, leading to the garrison capitulating the next day.

54. The March on Paris: Critical Comments

The movements on the first three days following the battle have been examined in some detail so that the true results of that catastrophe are clear. After those three days, the battle ceased to have any further consequences. The defeated army had gained the necessary head start, with Grouchy fortunately having avoided being cut off and having directed his withdrawal down the highway to Rheims. An examination of the general situation only requires a description of the main routes of the marches.

The Allied commanders were aware the enemy had made Laon the main point of its withdrawal and rallying. What the enemy could deploy there now was scarcely capable of mounting a significant defense or even of making a second decisive battle necessary. But with rearguard actions it could still delay the Allied advance and force them to make diversions. That is why the Allied commanders decided not to proceed toward Laon but rather along the right bank of the Oise to cross the river between Soissons and Paris, around Compiègne and Pont-Ste-Maxence, hoping in this way to attain the following advantages:

1. To induce the enemy force to remain here for a time, because it would not be threatened and so perhaps get a head start toward Paris.
2. To be able to march unhindered, without expending a lot of energy on tactical precautions, thus marching faster.
3. To march through an area the retreating army had not already crossed, one that was generally fresher and in better condition, making the march easier for their own troops. This was a very important consideration because their earlier exertions were so exceptional, and it would not have been advisable to reach Paris unduly weakened.

As the diversion the nearest Allied column had to make required only about one day's march, that is, the distance it had to cover to reach the Soissons–Paris highway again, and as the uninterrupted movement afterward would undoubtedly make up for it easily, then this plan, which was so obvious, should certainly not be discounted. Yet if the matter is considered closely, the following observations need to be made:

First, it is perhaps an error to believe the enemy would retreat more slowly if it were not pursued. Initially, he might be misled into making a short delay, but a march so close to his side would soon be noticed, which would then lead to him making the appropriate movement.

It may well be obvious that a march without rearguard actions could be much faster, because the rearguard's movements in the face of the enemy have to be made with considerable incidental tactical effort, greatly delaying its retreat. But the rearguard cannot be left to fend for itself every day, and the whole army would need to take part in its delaying actions.

Indeed, Blücher did decide to have the twelve squadrons of Lieutenant Colonel Sohr's vanguard follow the enemy down the road to Laon. Yet so few cavalrymen were not enough to hold up the enemy columns very often or for long. To move around the enemy and force it away from Paris, it would really have been better if I Corps, the most forward, had remained on the Laon highway, keeping steady pressure on the enemy rearguard, while III and IV Corps proceeded along the right bank of the Oise.

It cannot be denied that this way, it was possible that I Corps would have to fight at a disadvantage, but any fighting would have been well rewarded by the time it would have cost the enemy. Perhaps this would have been the only conceivable way of forcing him away from Paris.

Second, taking into account that on the morning of June 22 Grouchy was still fighting at Namur, while Blücher had already reached the vicinity of Beaumont, a direct advance along the road to Laon might have forced Grouchy from there, as well as from Soissons, and consequently prevented him from uniting with the defeated army this side of Paris.

Certainly, not much depended on this, but the main result would have been to cut off Grouchy from Paris, though this depended on first having cut him off from Soissons.

In reality, it is never easy to cut someone off from a large city with only a small lead, least of all if the city lies on one or more rivers, which was the case with Paris. A mere glance at a map will show how considerably the city extended, with the convergence of several excellent highways, and the way the Marne and Seine cut through the terrain still provided the means for a retreating force to reach the city, even if its opponent had reached the outskirts by the most direct route a day or even two days earlier. To fully surround a city like Paris so completely to prevent an opponent from reaching it would require several days and a very substantial force, which would have meant waiting for the arrival of all the other columns, since they could not all arrive at the same moment by the same direct route.

The campaign of 1814 provides two such examples. Marshals Mortier and Marmont,[160] whom Yorck[161] and Kleist[162] had cut off

---

160. Auguste-Frédéric-Louis Viesse de Marmont, Duke of Ragusa, marshal of France (1774–1852). He joined the army in 1790, trained at the artillery school, and then served at the siege of Toulon in 1793. Marmont later fought in Germany and Italy before going to Egypt with Napoleon, where he fought at the Battle of the Pyramids in 1798. Returning to France in 1799, he fought at Marengo in 1800 and Ulm in 1805. During this campaign, he relieved the besieged Italian port of Ragusa. Made a marshal in 1809 just after Wagram, Marmont served on the Iberian Peninsula for several years before returning to Germany early 1813. He fought at several major battles during both the spring and fall campaigns. His

on the road from La Ferté-Gaucher on March 26, reached Paris on that from Provins, while Bonaparte could not have been cut off when he returned from his march to Saint-Dizier if, in the meantime, the city had not gone over to the Allies.

So it is very doubtful, if not most unlikely, whether the Allies, had they been able to push in front of Grouchy at Soissons, would have been in a position to force him completely away from Paris. It then depended on further maneuvering, that is, a march to Meaux, then to Melun, et cetera.

But it was certain that if Grouchy could not have been cut off from Paris at Soissons, it was even less possible to do so if he had been allowed to reach Soissons. Consequently, the hope of a flank march forcing the enemy completely away from Paris did not seem to rest on an absolutely clear understanding of the situation.

The less cutting off Grouchy's force from Paris seemed generally feasible, however, the more important it became to protect

---

surrender to the Allies in 1814 was one of the final acts of the campaign. In 1815 Marmont accompanied Louis XVIII into exile in Ghent.

161. Infantry Gen. Johann David Ludwig Count Yorck von Wartenburg (1759–1830). He joined the Prussian army in 1772 as a cadet in the infantry and first saw action during the War of the Bavarian Succession. After being cashiered for insubordination, he spent several years in Dutch service, fighting in the East Indies. Yorck returned to Prussia in 1786 and rejoined the army the next year. As an officer in the fusiliers, he fought in Poland in 1794–95. In 1799 he was placed in command of the élite Foot Jäger (rifle) Regiment. In 1806 he fought a successful rearguard action at Altenzaun and then surrendered with Blücher at Lübeck. As inspector general of the light troops, Yorck played a leading role in the reconstruction of the Prussian army. He took over command of the Prussian Auxiliary Corps in 1812 and negotiated its neutrality on December 30, thereby sparking Prussia's defection from the alliance with France. He was awarded the Iron Cross 1st Class for his role at the Battle of Lützen in May 1813 and went on to command I Corps of Blücher's Army of Silesia that fall, leading it all the way to Paris the next year. In 1815 Yorck commanded V Army Corps and did not see action.

162. Infantry Gen. Friedrich Heinrich Ferdinand Emil, Count Kleist von Nollendorf (1762–1823). His military career began in 1778, when he joined an infantry regiment as ensign. As a junior staff officer, Kleist saw action in western Germany during the war with France from 1793 to 1795. Four years later he was appointed commander of a grenadier battalion but next saw action at Auerstedt in 1806 as a staff officer. Appointed commander of the Lower Silesian Brigade in 1808, Kleist served in Russia in 1812 as commander of the infantry of the Prussian Auxiliary Corps. In 1813–14 he commanded a corps in France and Germany, defeating Vandamme at Kulm. Due to illness, Kleist did not see action in 1815.

one's own troops; so it can be said that on the whole, the routes chosen for the march to Paris, even now when all of the circumstances are known, do not seem inappropriate.

55. Table of Marches

The table on page 188–189 provides an overview of the main stages of the whole march. This overview shows that:

1. The Prussian army marched in two columns, the left column consisting of I Corps, the right of IV Corps, both only a few miles apart, and III Corps followed the other two as a reserve, sometimes on the same roads, sometimes on others.
2. The left column crossed the Oise at Compiègne, the right at Pont-Ste-Maxence and Creil.
3. The left column made contact with Avesnes, Guise, and La Fère, with 1,900 men occupying Avesnes on June 22 after a bombardment of a few hours. Guise was taken on June 24 without bombardment and occupied by 3,500 men. La Fère was shelled in vain for several hours and then observed by an infantry battalion and a squadron of cavalry.
4. Wellington marched via Cambrai in a third column, following the route of IV Corps a day later at Pont-Ste-Maxence.
5. He attacked the fortresses as Cambrai and Péronne, both of which he took with a simple assault of the outer works, for they were not particularly defensible.
6. The Prussian army's march from the battlefield to Paris lasted eleven days and covered thirty-six [German] miles up to Gonesse, so the speed of the march was certainly very considerable, particularly so since only one day of rest was permitted.
7. Regarding Grouchy's march, it is not certain what route he took from Rethel to Soissons. He linked up there with the remnants of the defeated army and then began to withdraw further toward Paris, when, as is mentioned below, he was

forced off the direct route and had to continue via Meaux. He was still at Wavre on June 19 and reached Paris on June 29. In those ten days he covered about fifty [German] miles and fought several engagements.

While the two allied armies rushed to Paris in three columns, they left part of their forces behind to besiege the nearest fortresses.

The Allies agreed that the Prussians should undertake the siege of all the fortresses on the Sambre and east of this river, the Anglo-Allied army those to the west.

Blücher assigned the Prussian II Corps and the North German Federal Army Corps to the overall command of His Royal Highness, Prince August of Prussia.[163]

Wellington likewise assigned 15,000 men to Prince Frederick of Orange.

After detaching around 60,000 men, the Allied troops marching to Paris amounted to about 70,000 men under Blücher and about 60,000 under Wellington. Deducting say 10,000 men that each of these armies left behind as garrisons and for other purposes, however, they arrived at Paris with no more than 110,000 men.

Had it still been likely that a second decisive battle might have taken place there before the arrival of the other Allied armies, then it would have been a mistake for the two commanders to leave so many troops behind, because nothing compelled them to besiege or invest so many fortresses at the same time. Some 30,000 or 40,000 men would have sufficed to mask those directly on the lines of communications and to observe the others. All that was certain was that even at Paris there was no question of resistance

---

163. Infantry Gen. Friedrich Wilhelm Heinrich August, Prince of Prussia (1779–1843). As the brother of King Frederick William III, he was predestined to a military career, enlisting in the infantry as a captain in 1797. The prince first saw action in 1806 at Jena and then at Prenzlau, distinguishing himself on both occasions. In 1808 he was appointed inspector general of the artillery. He fought in a number of major battles during the campaigns of 1813–14, being awarded the Iron Cross 2nd Class for Lützen. After the first abdication, Prince August was promoted to full general.

Date	I Corps	IV Corps	III Corps	Wellington	Grouchy
19	Charleroi	Fontaine l'Evêque	St. Agatha-Rode	Nivelles	Wavre
20	Beaumont	Colleret nr. Maubeuge	Gembloux	Binche	Dinant
21	Avesnes	Landrecies	Charleroi	Malplaquet	Philippeville
22	Etroeungt	Fesmy-Le-Sart	Beaumont	Le Cateau-Cambrésis	Rocroi
23			Avesnes		Maubert-Fontaine
24	Guise	Bernoville	Le Nouvion		Rethel
25	Cerisy (between St. Quentin and La Fère)	St. Quentin	Homblières	Cambrai	
26	Chauny (between La Fère and Noyon)	Lassigny (between Noyon and the road to Péronne nr. Pont-Ste-Maxence)		Péronne	Soissons

TABLE OF MARCHES

27	Gilacourt (action at Compiègne)	Pont-Ste-Maxence (actions at Creil and Senlis)	Compiègne	Nesle	Villiers-Cotterêts
28	Nanteuil (actions at Villiers-Cotterêts and Nanteuil)	Marly-La-Ville	Crépy	Orvillers	Meaux
29	Aulnay	Le Bourget	Dammartin	Ste-Martin-Langueau	Paris
30	Aulnay	Actions at Aubervilliers and St. Denis	Marching to St. Germain	Louvres	
1	Le Mesnil, downriver from St. Germain	Marching to St. Germain	St. Germain (actions at Versailles and Marly)	Gonesse	
2	Meudon (actions at Sèvres and Issy)	Versailles	Plessis-Piquet		
3	Action at Issy				
4	Convention for the evacuation of Paris				

in the open, let alone a counterattack, and should Paris's garrison be too strong, the arrival of the other armies would have to be awaited. Leaving significant numbers of troops behind, being able to besiege several fortresses simultaneously, thus gaining control of the country sooner would save time. In any case, there was a chance that some of these fortified places might have surrendered due to the shock alone.

The army engaged in marching to Paris first encountered the enemy again when it crossed the Oise on June 27.

I Corps' vanguard did so at 3 A.M. at Compiègne. Hardly had it entered the town on the left bank of the river when d'Erlon attacked it, but the fighting was insignificant. As d'Erlon seemed only to have a weak force and in any case had arrived too late, he soon withdrew, and I Corps advanced along the Soissons–Paris road as far as Gilacourt, while sending forward the Second Brigade, reinforced by a regiment of dragoons, to seize control of the highway at Villiers-Cotterêts and cut off from Paris any French troops that might still be in Soissons.

IV Corps had found both Pont-Ste-Maxence and the bridge at Creil unguarded. But its vanguard encountered a weak enemy detachment at Creil, which withdrew immediately.

When the vanguard of IV Corps reached Senlis, it found the enemy occupying the town and engaged it, gaining possession at 10 P.M.

All these detachments seem to have come from the defeated army, and their obvious weakness, their limited resistance, and their failure to occupy the Oise bridges suggested that these remnants were certainly not going to be found in appreciable strength and in a decent state of readiness.

Toward evening on June 27, the utterly exhausted troops of Grouchy's IV Corps arrived at Villiers-Cotterêts and those of III Corps at Soissons. He distributed his troops to the nearby villages so they could be provided with the food and rest needed as quickly as possible. At 2 A.M. on June 28, he decided to continue the march to Nanteuil. At Villiers-Cotterêts it was probable that he received reports of that morning's battle at Compiègne, thus it was risky for him to continue the march on the road from Soissons to Paris. It would have made better sense for him to have turned immediately toward Meaux, via Ferté Milon, because at Nanteuil he could have run into three Prussian corps and been destroyed within sight of Paris. It was most likely that he rejected the thought of taking his weary troops on a further detour over very poor roads but still hoped to get through on a good, straight highway. As he was forced to abandon the highway, he did not actually achieve his objective but then did not suffer a potential catastrophe, because the Prussian forces were not sufficiently concentrated to mount a concerted attack on him.

As mentioned above, Pirch I and his Second Brigade were sent off toward Villiers-Cotterêts, spending the night of June 27–28, until about 1 A.M., at Longpré, about an hour away. He allowed his troops some rest and broke camp again at 2 A.M. He first encountered a train of horse artillery, consisting of fourteen guns and twenty ammunition wagons, that were trying to reach the highway from their camps at Viviers, Montgobert, and Puisieux. As it was moving with virtually no escort, it was captured immediately. After this, Pirch I advanced to attack Villiers-Cotterêts itself.

Grouchy assembled his troops, 9,000 strong (presumably Gérard's corps), and fought back. Vandamme moved up on the other side, coming from Soissons with III Corps. The sound of cannon fire on the Paris highway immediately caused a panic-stricken terror to set in, with cries that they might be cut off leading most of the troops there to strike out at once for Meaux by way of La Ferté Milon. Vandamme nevertheless succeeded in advancing up the road with about 2,000 men, coming to Marshal Grouchy's assistance. General Pirch I only had five weak battalions, three squadrons of cavalry, and thirteen cannon. Ziethen and most of the Prussian II Corps were still marching from Gilocourt to Crépy, around three hours away, [and] so were not near enough to provide support. Vandamme advanced against Pirch I's left flank, while Grouchy maneuvered against his right. In such circumstances Pirch I correctly decided that a bold assault was ill advised [and] so began to retreat toward Compiègne, later turning toward Crépy by way of Fresnoy.

Ziethen had yet to assemble his troops at Crépy, so when Grouchy's force passed by, only the Third Brigade and half the Reserve Cavalry moved toward the highway. The artillery fired on the village of Lévignen, through which the French passed and the rearguard was pursued to Nanteuil, where two cannon were captured.

The French now presumably learned that the previous day, another Prussian corps already crossed the Oise at Creil and Pont-Ste-Maxence, thus did not consider it advisable to continue along the Soissons–Paris highway but instead turned left via Assi to Meaux, and from there via Claye to Paris, where evidently in a rather weakened condition, they arrived on June 29. In those two days, as well as the two guns, the Prussians took about a thousand prisoners.

On June 29 the Prussian army stood before Paris, with its right wing behind St. Denis and its left by the Bondi Woods. Wellington's army was supposed to have arrived on the evening of June 30, when Blücher intended to have his right march off, crossing the Seine somewhere below St. Denis, to march around the south side of the city, or rather to establish a position there from which he could attack.

Meanwhile, to make the most of the initial panic, during the night of June 29–30, a brigade from I and IV Corps was to attempt an attack against the enemy pickets and outposts behind the Ourq Canal, with both corps advancing in support. The attempt took place, resulting in the vanguard of IV Corps being involved in a lively fight at Aubervilliers. Generally, however, the enemy was found to have good morale.

When Blücher learned that since being forced to abdicate on June 22, Bonaparte was in seclusion at Malmaison, he ordered Major von Colomb of the 8th Hussars to establish if the bridge at Chatou, on the Paris–St. Germain road, might still be intact and if so to proceed to nearby Malmaison and take Bonaparte into custody. If he found the bridge already demolished, he was to take the one at St. Germain. The bridge at Chatou in fact was destroyed, so it was this detachment that gave the Prussian army control of the bridge at St. Germain that was also supposed to have been demolished and that was very important for crossing the Seine, making this [crossing] possible a day or two earlier.

At 5 A.M. on June 30, III Army Corps, five hours from Dammartin, broke camp and reached Gonesse at noon but was forced to continue marching around Paris that evening, while I and IV Corps stood facing the enemy, waiting for Wellington's army to arrive. It moved from St. Denis via Argenteuil to St. Germain, where it arrived at 3 A.M., having covered seven [German] miles in less than twenty-four hours. It remained at St. Germain.

Lieutenant Colonel von Sohr, with six squadrons of the Brandenburg and Pomeranian Hussars, about six hundred sabers, had been ordered to push on past St. Germain and Versailles toward the Orleans road. He crossed the Seine before III Corps and was in Versailles when this corps reached St. Germain.

At 11 P.M. I Corps followed III Corps, crossing the Seine below St. Germain at Le Menil, which it reached at 7 P.M. and where it remained.

At noon on July 1, IV Corps moved off to St. Germain, arriving there that night.

Sohr had his horses fed at Versailles, with his detachment remaining there for several hours. The French, having learned of this, lay in wait for him with two regiments of cavalry and some infantry in the woods between Versailles and Marli. Around noon, Sohr left Versailles on the road to Plessis-Piquet, when he encountered some enemy dragoons that hastily departed. The Prussians pursued them impetuously, following them to near Plessis-Piquet, where four regiments under Exelmans attacked them, driving them back through Versailles. They had already suffered heavy losses when they fell into the trap on the other side and were completely scattered. Despite this, amazingly, a couple hundred horses from the detachment were available again the next day. Thanks to this engagement, the French advanced that evening as far as Marly, where they encountered the Ninth Brigade, Thielemann's vanguard, and fought a significant engagement with it.

As Sohr's detachment was not the vanguard of a larger force, and as such could expect no support, instead being sent off several miles ahead as a raiding party, he should have behaved with all the caution of a guerrilla, never feeding his horses in a place like Versailles, making his existence known, and encouraging the plan for his encirclement.

On June 1 the three Prussian corps gathered at St. Germain and marched off the next day.

III Corps advanced through Versailles, reaching Plessis-Piquet without encountering a significant enemy force.

I Corps' route led to Sèvres, which was strongly garrisoned. It was courageously defended for several hours against attacks by the First Brigade before finally being abandoned when Ziethen's right wing gained the heights of Meudon. The defenders retreated to Issy. The First Brigade followed through Moulineaux, where it fought a second brisk engagement on the road to Issy. The First Brigade attacked this village at 7 P.M. The enemy held it in force, so the Second Brigade was forced to support the First's attack. Even then, the fighting lasted until around midnight, when the French pulled back.

As early as 3 A.M., two columns under Vandamme, coming from Vaugirard and Montrouge, returned to attack Issy, possession of which was contested for more than an hour, albeit in vain for the French. The First and Second Brigades held on, with the French falling back to their positions beyond Vaugirard and Montrouge.

The Convention of St. Cloud was concluded the same day, so this was the final act of the war.

56. The Situation in Paris

Paris was in an unusual situation.

On June 21 Bonaparte arrived and set himself up in Elysée Palace. He had his ministers called in to report on the situation. In this meeting he received a declaration from the Chamber of Deputies in which, having been informed of recent events by Bonaparte's "Bulletin," they had declared themselves in permanent session and ordered the ministers to appear before them without delay. Bonaparte immediately understood that an abyss had opened under his feet and all at once, his spirit seemed to be crippled and his courage broken. He was no longer the reckless soldier of Vendemiaire and Brumaire,[164] who could win everything and lose nothing, who boldly cut through political factions with his sword,

---

164. Clausewitz was referring here to the coup d'état in November 1799 by which Napoleon overthrew the Directory, replacing it with the Consulate.

dispelling a popular rising or overwhelming a Chamber of Deputies like an outpost. Among the thousand counterweights that always acted in so many ways to restrain and moderate the actions of princes and commanders, who operated within and depended on a fixed order of affairs, one of these thousand counterweights had already attained great significance for him: it was the question of his son and his dynasty.

Neither France nor Paris was entirely pro-Bourbon. The republicans and revolutionaries were the party that ruled in the Chamber. Lafayette was the ringleader,[165] and many other well-known names from that period were to be found within it. Bonaparte had high hopes of satisfying this party, but it now opposed him abdicating in favor of his son. He had imagined that the manifold revolutionary interests of this group would give it the energy to move against the Bourbons and that whoever the leader was to be in this situation, he could become the center of the whole nation's political opposition to the will of the Allied powers.

This must obviously be regarded as half-fantasy. Bonaparte was no less than inwardly reconciled to this idea and expected that the rebellious factions would destroy France's last resistance, hastening the reversal he hated so much. But that possibility prevented him from gathering a few hundred loyal supporters and using force against the Chamber. So after some futile opposition, he consented to abdicate.

After sending first his minister Regnauld[166] and then his brother Lucien[167] to the Chamber of Deputies and trying in vain to pacify it, after the Chamber spoke out more and more, after they finally gave him only an hour more to consider a choice between

---

165. Marie-Joseph-Paul-Yves-Roch-Gilbert du Motier (the Marquis de Lafayette until 1790) (1757–1834) was a French military officer and former aristocrat who participated in both the American and French revolutions. He came out of retirement with the first restoration and was a deputy until 1824.

166. Michel Louis Étienne Regnauld de Saint-Jean-d'Angély (1761–1819). A politician and participant in Napoleon's coup of 1799, he suggested to Napoleon on June 21, 1815, that he should abdicate in favor of his son.

167. Lucien Bonaparte (1775–1840). Napoleon's younger brother, their relationship was often stormy. Lucien rallied to the imperial cause during the Hundred Days, which led to him being proscribed on the second restoration.

abdication and removal, after first Regnauld, then Bassano[168] and Caulaincourt,[169] and finally Joseph[170] and Lucien advised him to give up, on the morning of June 22, after about twelve hours of this struggle, he signed the abdication in favor of his son.

Then the two chambers named a government commission of five members, with Quinette[171] and Caulaincourt from the lower chamber and Carnot,[172] Fouché,[173] and Grenier[174] from the upper. Fouché was the commission's president.

Bonaparte's abdication in favor of his son did not resolve the factional struggle.

The true Bourbon loyalists were totally against recognizing the son, while the republicans and revolutionaries were not entirely for it either. A third party, led by Fouché, and which in fact wanted the Bourbons, though only under certain conditions, also saw this abdication as a great obstacle to compromise. Furthermore, the proponents of these three different points of view distrusted each other, so they could not come to a consensus. What was most important was that they all feared the remnants of the Bonapartist party that was still influential in Paris and that could count on strong support from the army and the armed forces in the suburbs. This resulted in the initial opposition to Napoleon II being

168. Hugues-Bernard Maret, Duke of Bassano (1763–1839). A lawyer by training, Bassano supported Napoleon's coup in 1799 and then held various posts in his government. In 1815 he was Napoleon's private secretary.
169. Armand Augustin Louis de Caulaincourt (1773–1827), a French general and politician. He was Napoleon's foreign minister in 1815.
170. Joseph Bonaparte (1768–1844). Napoleon's elder brother, king of Naples and Sicily (1806–1808) and king of Spain (1808–13).
171. Nicolas-Marie Quinette, Baron de Rochemont (1762–1821). A politician and supporter of Napoleon, he was exiled after the Hundred Days.
172. Lazare Nicolas Marguerite Count Carnot (1753–1823). Best known for his role as "Organizer of the Revolution," he served as Napoleon's minister of the interior during the Hundred Days.
173. Joseph Fouché, 1st Duke of Otranto (1763–1820). Very much an opportunistic politician, Fouché made the most of every change of government in France during this period. In 1814 he was in close contact with the Allies and plotted against Napoleon. Made minister of police during the Hundred Days, he played an astute game of double-dealing during this time (see below).
174. Gen. Paul Grenier (1768–1827). A member of the Provisional Government in 1815, he fought during the Revolutionary Wars, at Wagram in 1809, and in Italy against the Austrians in 1813.

suppressed and matters being left in a state of uncertainty. Fouché and his party, being the real leaders, still found a way amid this unresolved crisis to guide it in their own direction.

Fouché was president of the government, he was in secret contact with Wellington and the Bourbons, besides which his personality and his earlier connections suited him to play the leading role.[175] He should be regarded as the head of the government, though the other members of the commission and the chambers, of course, watched him anxiously, constraining his actions greatly, limiting them to intrigue and obstruction. After him, Davoût was

---

175. Fouché's devious behavior had a significant effect on the outcome of the Hundred Days. He claimed to have promised to provide Wellington with the French plan of campaign but then had the agent carrying it held up at the border. As he related in his memoirs:

In such a decisive moment, my situation became just as delicate as difficult; I did not want Napoleon any more; and if he had been victorious, I would have suffered his yoke along with the rest of France, as he would have prolonged the disastrous situation. On the other hand, I had commitments to Louis XVIII, which I was not only inclined to keep, but also which prudence required me to guarantee. Furthermore, my agents had promised both Metternich and Wellington to move mountains. The generalissimo [Wellington] required that I at least obtain the plan of campaign for him.

My first thoughts? But the voice of my nation, the glory of the French army which was in my mind as much as the nation, finally the cry of honor horrified me with the idea that the word "traitor" must never appear on the epithet of the Duke of Otranto, so I resolved to be pure. Sides had to be taken, however, [and] in such circumstances, was a statesman to be allowed no resources? This is what I decided. I had certain knowledge that the unexpected invasion by Napoleon would most likely take place between [June] 16 and, at the latest, [June] 18. Napoleon wanted to fight a battle with the English army on [June] 17, separating it from the Prussians, after having pushed the latter back. He expected to be all the more successful with his plan, as Wellington, on the basis of false information, believed he would be able to put back the commencement of the campaign until July 1. The success of Napoleon's undertaking thus depended on surprise. I made my moves accordingly; on the day of Napoleon's departure [from Paris to the front], I sent Madame D . . . with a message in cipher containing the plan of campaign. At the same time, I laid a number of obstacles at the place she would have to cross the border, so that she could only reach Wellington's headquarters after the event. This accounts for the inexplicable uncertainty of the generalissimo, which has surprised everybody and caused much speculation.

Fouché, *Mémoires*, 2:341ff.

Certainly Wellington's hesitation on the outbreak of hostilities deserves explanation, but he never provided a credible one. He was livid, however, when Scottish historian Sir Archibald Alison published Fouché's story.

the most important person at this time.[176] He was minister of war and had been appointed chief of the army after Soult and Grouchy refused. Furthermore, he fully shared Fouché's position, the one that had the greatest chance of prevailing. It was largely these two who brought about the Convention of July 3.

Taking into account the political situation in Paris and the nature of the authority wielded by the government, at a time when the retreating armies were rushing to the city and the Allied commanders, hot on their heels, were appearing at the gates, it is understandable how difficult it must have been to consider organized resistance, of exhausting all the means still available, so this point needs to be dwelt on for a moment.

Bonaparte remained at the Elysée from June 22 to 25, secluded in drab, empty rooms; accompanied only by a few friends; and watched over by a single sentry from a detail of old grenadiers. Of course his proximity must have caused fear of unrest breaking out either for or against him, which could have led to a catastrophe. On June 25 the government commission forced him to move to Malmaison to wait there for the passport for a journey to America Wellington had requested.

The government commission then sent the well-known delegation consisting of Lafayette, Sébastiani,[177] Benjamin Constant,[178]

---

176. Louis-Nicolas Davoût, Duke of Auerstaedt, Prince of Eckmühl, marshal of France (1770–1823). His military career began as an officer in the Royal Champagne Cavalry Regiment until 1789, when he lost his commission. Davoût commanded a battalion of volunteers in 1792 and worked his way up the ranks during the Revolutionary Wars, serving on the Rhine. He accompanied Napoleon to Egypt and fought at Marengo in 1800. His corps played an important role at Austerlitz in 1805, while his actions at Auerstedt in 1806 became legendary. Davoût distinguished himself at Wagram in 1809 and commanded a corps during the Russian campaign of 1812. He ruled Hamburg with an iron fist during the siege of 1813–14, only capitulating after Napoleon's first abdication. As minister of war, Davoût remained in Paris during the Hundred Days.

177. Horace François Bastien Sébastiani de La Porta (1771–1851). He was a soldier, diplomat, and politician who joined the French army in 1792, rose through its ranks, and became a supporter of Napoleon. Sébastiani fought in his native Corsica in 1793, then in the Alps and at Marengo in 1800. He conducted a number of diplomatic missions but continued to hold field commands, fighting at Ulm and Austerlitz in 1805, and later spent several years on the Iberian Peninsula. Sébastiani then commanded a cavalry division in Russia in 1812; fought

Pontécoulant,[179] d'Argenson,[180] and Laforest[181] to the Allied headquarters to announce Bonaparte's removal and appeal for a ceasefire. What they and all the parties in Paris wished for was to prevent an occupation of the city, partly to prevent various sacrifices and dangers, and partly to be able to use this kernel of resistance as a bargaining chip in later negotiations, so obtaining better terms in a final agreement.

At first, even Fouché and Davoût shared this view, but when they saw the increasing threat of their opponents taking action as the army reached the city and were confronted by their Bonapartist spirit and their hate of the Bourbons, and who clearly regarded them as the Bourbons' secret tools, they tried to promote the surrender of Paris and the removal of the army to beyond the Loire.

Bonaparte's removal was also important to them. On June 28, when he heard the cannon fire coming from Villiers-Cotterêts, he was obviously exalted. All the passions of war and battle were reawakened and drove him to offer his services as a general to the government commission. He succeeded in getting General

---

at Lützen, Bautzen, and Leipzig in 1813; and helped defend France in 1814. He accepted the Bourbon Restoration but was quick to rejoin Napoleon during the Hundred Days, when he organized contingents of the National Guard. After the second abdication, Sébastiani pursued a career in politics.

178. Henri-Benjamin Constant de Rebecque (1767–1830). A Swiss-born liberal politician and one of the great thinkers of his time, Constant opposed Napoleon's martial appetite. From 1815 to 1830 he was a leader of the Independents, the liberal-left party in the French National Assembly.

179. Louis Gustave le Doulcet, Count Pontécoulant (1764–1853). A royalist army officer and politician, he favored certain aspects of the French Revolution. But some regarded him as a royalist, so Pontécoulant spent time in exile and out of office until Napoleon's coup of 1799. Louis XVIII made him a peer of France in 1814.

180. Marc-René de Voyer de Paulmy d'Argenson (1771–1842). A supporter of the French Revolution, d'Argenson joined the army as a staff officer in 1792. He later entered politics, becoming the prefect Deux-Néthes from 1809 to 1813. Refusing office under Louis XVIII, d'Argenson represented Belfort during the Hundred Days.

181. Antoine-René-Charles-Mathurin Count Laforest (1756–1846). Laforest was a diplomat in the United States when the revolution broke out in France. Returning in 1795, he worked in the foreign ministry, undertaking a number of missions abroad. Laforest was foreign minister for a short period after the first restoration and a deputy during the Hundred Days.

Beker,[182] who was charged with watching him, to rush to Paris with this offer and had the few horses remaining saddled up. But Fouché and Davoût received his offer with derision. They both saw that it was high time to get rid of him, if they did not want to run the risk of suddenly seeing him take center stage once more. Added to that, Blücher's attempt to have him seized at Malmaison became known, which made Bonaparte somewhat more eager to begin his journey. So at 5 P.M. on June 29, accompanied by Beker, he made his way to Rochefort, where he intended to take the first opportunity to sail for America.

On June 26 the delegation sent to the headquarters of the Allied commanders was directed to the headquarters of the monarch, the ceasefire rejected, and as such negotiations ended.

In the week between Bonaparte's arrival and that of the beaten army, that is, from June 22 to 29, nothing much was done to organize resistance, at least nothing that could have fundamentally changed the situation. The available guns were moved into place and the nearest depots troops called up, but nothing was done to equip appreciable new forces or [to do] any serious work on the city's fortifications.

On June 28 the army corps under the command of Reille arrived, followed by Grouchy's force on June 29. The Prussians not only followed right on their heels but, as mentioned above, were at St. Germain on the left bank of the Seine the next day, threatening Paris from its unfortified side. This forced the French army to divide into two immediately, occupying the southern side of the city with half its men.

There was no clear and definite information on the fortifications that were supposed to provide security for the capital. Most of them were on the north side of the city, with the main works being in Montmartre, just as in 1814, only this time more

---

182. Cavalry Gen. Nicolas-Léonard Bagert Beker, Count of Mons (1770–1840). Beker joined a dragoon regiment in 1786, fought with the Army of the North in 1792–93, and was one of the few unfortunate enough to have been wounded at Valmy. He was actively involved in several campaigns and actions during the Revolutionary Wars before commanding a division at Austerlitz. He served at Aspern-Essling in 1809 but fell into disgrace and returned to France. Beker entered politics with the first restoration and later escorted Napoleon to the *Bellerophon*, the ship that took the defeated emperor into exile after the Hundred Days.

complete. From there the lines extended toward Vincennes. St. Denis should be regarded as an outpost. Some reports describe these fortifications as having fortress-like strength, others, namely those of the delegation sent from Paris, represent them as insignificant. The following facts, however, are indisputable:

1. The front to be covered on the north side of the city ran from the Seine at Charenton back to the Seine again at Chaillot, two [German] miles without taking St. Denis into account. If the defensive line between La Villette and St. Denis was to be held, the front would not be less.
2. At a council of war the governmental commission held on June 30, Soult declared that as the Prussians had taken Aubervilliers, even thinking of defending the right bank of the Seine was very dangerous because, if the line of the canal joining St. Denis and La Villette were breached, then it would not be possible to stop the enemy moving against the French troops at the gate at St. Denis, which indicates that this position was not of fortress-like strength.
3. All accounts agree, as does this one, that the works on the left bank have to be regarded as largely insignificant. The village of Montrouge was superficially prepared for the defense, but as it had stone houses and walls, exceptional resistance was certainly possible. Moreover, as it was directly in front of the center on the south side, it could well have become an objective of the main attack, costing an enormous amount of blood to take. Yet such a position would not be able to secure the area half a [German] mile to its left or right, and in the end it would have been realized that Paris could have been taken without having taking Montrouge, or even Montmartre, and then the French would have been limited merely to defense by force of arms, without appreciable cover.
4. The front on the south side, from the Seine back to the Seine again, which also lacked defenses and would have to be manned by sufficient troops, was 5,000 toises long,[183] that is, almost 1 1/2 [German] miles.

183. A "toise" was a linear measurement of exactly two meters.

The French army thus had to hold a line of 13,000 toises or 39,000 paces long,[184] only in part fortified and in part incomplete. It should be noted that these fortifications did not offer a particularly good refuge or support for a defeated army.

Including the 20,000 men from the depots, the French army was 60,000 strong. A further 20,000 men were available in the armed suburbs, and they were normally allocated to the defense of Paris. The fortifications were armed largely with iron and other dismounted guns available in Paris, making probably a sufficient number of cannon available for the fixed defenses. Regarding the field artillery, however, the Army of the Loire took no more than seventy guns with it. That was obviously very few, especially for the southern side, where the fighting would take place more or less in the open, and far too few to think of mounting [an] effective defense. What could seventy guns have done, spread out over 1 1/2 [German] miles?

The Allied armies, as mentioned above, reached Paris with about 50,000 men under Wellington, 60,000 under Blücher. This was almost double that with which the French could oppose them in front of Paris. But what the French could not have known was how the Allies would divide their forces on the two banks of the Seine, so they still had to man their fortifications on the right bank with appreciable numbers. Wellington held a bridge at Argenteuil and had an outpost at Courbevoie, allowing him unhindered contact with Blücher. Furthermore, as the intense cultivation broke up the countryside, the French could never know how many of his troops had moved directly to the left bank of the Seine. This made it quite possible for the Prussians to accept a battle on the plain of Montrouge since the French, with 40,000 men and seventy guns while leaving 20,000 men in their fortifications, would have faced 80,000 men with three hundred guns, which was not likely to have produced a favorable result. It should also be noted that on July 1, Davoût's headquarters was still in La Villette. As the last council of war would be held there on the night of July 1–2, the larger part of the French army must still have been in the north of the city.

Having examined the situation, it would be useful to present the resolution of the final council of war verbatim. It would now

---

184. A "pace" was a linear measurement of around 2.5 feet.

make more sense and also summarize the results of the observations made [above] in a single passage.

It was held under Davoût's chairmanship and included all those officers of exceptional reputation then in Paris, including Marshals Masséna,[185] Lefebvre,[186] Soult, and Grouchy, Generals Carnot, Grenier, and many others.

Questions asked by the Government Commission to the Council of War Assembled at La Villette, July 1, 1815:
1. What is the state of the fortifications erected for the defense of Paris?

Answer: The state of the fortifications and their armaments on the right bank of the Seine, though incomplete, is generally satisfactory. On the left bank, the fortifications can be regarded as nonexistent.

2. Is the army capable of covering and defending Paris?

Answer: It can do so, but not indefinitely. It should not be exposed [in the open field] due to a lack of provisions and a place to retreat.

3. If the army were attacked at all points, could it prevent the enemy from penetrating into Paris on one side or the other?

---

185. Jean-André Masséna, 1st Duke of Rivoli, 1st Prince of Essling (1758–1817), marshal of France. After spending his youth at sea, Masséna enlisted in the army in 1775. Unable to rise beyond the noncommissioned ranks due to his humble origins, he left the army in 1789. Rejoining two years later, Masséna rose to the rank of colonel by 1792. He fought extensively during the Revolutionary Wars but fell out of favor with Napoleon in 1800 due to his excessive looting. In 1804 he was made a marshal and fought the Austrians in Italy the next year but was dismissed again for his excesses. Reinstated to the army in 1809, Masséna commanded a corps at Aspern-Essling and fought at Wagram. He led the ill-fated invasion of Portugal in 1810 but did not serve again. Masséna did not commit to either side in 1815.

186. François Joseph Lefebvre (1755–1820), Duke of Danzig, marshal of France. Son of a hussar, Lefebvre joined the French army at age eighteen and became a sergeant in the royal guard. He supported the revolution, rose rapidly through the ranks, and fought as a general at Fleurus in 1794. In 1799 he commanded the garrison of Paris and supported Napoleon's coup. Made a marshal in 1804, Lefebvre commanded the Imperial Guard in 1806 and successfully besieged Danzig in 1807. After a brief sojourn on the Iberian Peninsula, he commanded the Bavarian army at Wagram. Defeated that year by Andreas Hofer in the uprising in the Tyrol, he was replaced. From 1812 to 1814 he commanded the Old Guard. Lefebvre voted for Napoleon's deposition in 1814 but rallied to him during the Hundred Days.

Answer: It is difficult for the army to be attacked at all points simultaneously, but if that were to happen, there would be little hope of resistance.
4. In the event of a defeat, could the general in chief reserve or rescue sufficient means to oppose an entry into the city by brute force?
Answer: No general can answer for the outcome of a battle.
5. Is there sufficient ammunition available for several engagements?
Answer: Yes.
6. Finally, could the capital be left and for how long?
Answer: There are no guarantees in this regard.
Signed: Marshal Davout, Minister of War, Prince of Eckmühl, 3 A.M., July 2.

Taking all this into account, the following conclusions can be drawn:

1. Accepting a defensive battle within the walls of Paris would not have been absolutely impossible for the French, but in all probability the battle would have been lost. This would have risked [France] being forced to submit to much worse terms.
2. If the battle were won, that is, the attack repelled, the result would be nothing more than a few weeks' reprieve until the other armies arrived, but this reprieve would not have achieved a different outcome, nor any change in the situation, because no major effort of any kind had been made to organize other resistance, nor could it have been, given the condition of the government. The French would then have fought it only for the honor of their arms.
3. Attacking the Prussian army in its position between Meudon and Plessis-Piquet, if it had not been expected, perhaps would have offered more advantages, but the position was very strong, so it would have been difficult to overwhelm a much stronger enemy. If, however, a kind of siege ensued, this would again have led to nothing, for the French either had to retreat toward Paris or move toward

the Loire. Any march to the Loire would have become a kind of retreat.

It is thus obvious, given the facts of the situation, that provided it was not allowed to withdraw, the army confined in Paris could have been forced to accept any terms and as such, to lay down its arms.

This [voluntary withdrawal] too would only have been to provide honor of arms, because in the current circumstances, it [the French army] could have no further influence on the terms of the peace.

And accelerating the surrender of the capital city could have accelerated the surrender of a number of fortresses too, and the possession of the fortresses was of great importance as a guarantee.

It was clearly in the interests of the two parties to conclude the Convention made between representatives of the two Allied commanders and of the City of Paris on July 3 at St. Cloud. In it a ceasefire was declared, while the French army handed over the city and withdrew to the Loire. Their march was made on July 4, 5, and 6; the Prussian I Corps entered Paris on July 7; and Louis XVIII arrived the next day.

57. Advance of the Remaining Armies into France

In mid-June Schwarzenberg's Army of the Upper Rhine was deployed as follows:

Wrede between Mannheim and Kaiserslautern[187]
The Crown Prince of Württemberg behind the Rhine as far as Bruchsal[188]

---

187. Field Marshal Carl Philipp Josef, Count and 1st Prince von Wrede (1767–1838). In 1799 he raised a volunteer corps in the Palatinate, then under Bavarian rule. Wrede commanded an infantry brigade at Hohenlinden in 1800 and fought against the Austrians in 1805 and 1809. Bavaria joined the Allies just before the Battle of Leipzig in 1813, but Wrede's attempt to block Napoleon's retreat at Hanau was unsuccessful.

188. Wilhelm Friedrich Karl, Crown Prince of Württemberg (1781–1864).

The Austrians under Colloredo,[189] the Prince of
Hohenzollern,[190] and Archduke Ferdinand[191] between Basel
and Lake Constance

On June 23, when it heard the news of events in the Netherlands, the Army of the Upper Rhine marched off. The same day, after a brief fight on the Saar, Wrede marched through Saarbrücken and Saareguemines, while the Crown Prince of Württemberg crossed the Rhine at Germersheim. On June 25 the Austrian force passed through Basel.

Wrede marched on Nancy, while the Crown Prince of Württemberg moved upstream along the Rhine toward Strasbourg. One Austrian corps under Colloredo pushed back Lecourbe and then continued to Belfort, while the other under the Prince of Hohenzollern crossed the Rhine downstream and also marched on Strasbourg. The reserves under Archduke Ferdinand marched on Nancy.

On June 28 the Crown Prince of Württemberg engaged General Rapp at Strasbourg, forcing him to withdraw into the fortress, which the Crown Prince then invested.

At the end of July, the Russian army under General Barclay reached the Rhine.[192]

---

189. Field Marshal Hieronymus Karl Count von Colloredo-Mansfeld (1775–1822). He enlisted in the Austrian army in 1792 and fought in Flanders in 1793–94. In 1796 the count participated in the Italian campaign and in 1800 fought as a colonel at Hohenlinden. In 1809 he held a command in Italy and in 1813 led a corps during the fall campaign.

190. Field Marshal Hermann Otto, Prince of Hohenzollern-Hechingen (1776–1838).

191. Archduke Ferdinand Karl Joseph of Austria-Este (1781–1850). Born in Milan, he attended the military academy in Wiener Neustadt and then joined the Austrian army. His command was surrounded at Ulm in 1805, but the archduke managed to escape to Bohemia, where he raised new forces. In 1809 he led an Austrian army into Poland.

192. Field Marshal Prince Michael Andreas Barclay de Tolly (1761–1818). A German-speaking descendent of the Scottish clan Barclay, he was born in Lithuania. He enlisted in a cavalry regiment in 1767. Barclay fought both the Turks and Swedes, then in 1794, the Poles. He commanded Bagration's rearguard with distinction in 1806–1807 and fought at Eylau. Barclay fought in the Russo-Swedish War of 1808–1809 before becoming Russian minister of war in 1810. His scorched-earth policy in the face of Napoleon's invasion of Russia in 1812 made

On June 15 the French under Marshal Suchet also began hostilities in Upper Italy, attempting to reach the Alpine passes before the Austrians. But the Austrians arrived first, and together with the Sardinians, in two columns under Frimont's command,[193] some 50–60,000 men, advanced into Savoy. Meanwhile, a third column, composed of Sardinian troops, moved against Marshal Brune in the county of Nice.[194]

The right column, under Frimont, crossed the Simplon Pass and moved through Meillerie, Geneva, Fort de l'Écluse, and Bourg-en-Bresse to Mâcon. Bubna's column moved via Mont-Cenis, Montmélian, Les Échelles, and Lyon.[195]

Grenoble fell on July 3, and both columns reached the Saône on July 10, following several tough fights with Marshal Suchet's troops.

58. The Capture of the Fortresses

Prince Frederick of the Netherlands took the fortresses at Valenciennes, Le Quesnoy, and Condé.

---

him unpopular, and Kutuzov replaced him. He returned to senior command in the spring of 1813 and fought at Kulm and Leipzig in the fall. Barclay commanded Russian forces in France in 1814.

193. Field Marshal Johann Maria Philipp Frimont, Count of Palota, Prince of Antrodoco (1759–1831). He enlisted in the Austrian cavalry in 1776 and fought in the War of the Bavarian Succession, the Turkish wars, and the Revolutionary Wars. Frimont distinguished himself at Marengo in 1800 and fought in Italy both in 1805 and 1809. In 1812 he commanded the cavalry of the Austrian auxiliary corps. Frimont further distinguished himself during the campaign of 1814 in France, then became governor of the fortress of Mainz.

194. Guillaume Marie Anne Brune (1763–1815), marshal of France. Appointed to command a brigade in 1793, he fought under Napoleon in Italy in 1796, and in 1799 Brune defended Amsterdam against an Anglo-Russian expedition. His republican sympathies led to him leaving the army in 1807, but he returned to active service in 1815. Brune was murdered by royalists during the White Terror.

195. Field Marshal Ferdinand Count von Bubna and Littitz (1768–1825). He enlisted in the Austrian army in 1784 and fought against the Turks between 1788 and 1790 and against France from 1792 to 1797. At Austerlitz he accompanied Prince Liechtenstein to Napoleon's headquarters. Bubna commanded the Austrian Second Light Division at Leipzig in 1813.

The Prussian II Army Corps, under His Royal Highness Prince August, took Maubeuge, Landrecy, Mariembourg, Philippeville, Rocroi, and Givet, though not Charlemont.

The North German Corps under the command of Lieutenant General Hake took Charleville, Mezières, Montmédy, and Sedan.

Men of the garrison of Luxembourg under the command of His Excellency Prince Ludwig of Hesse-Homburg took Longwy.[196]

Most of these conquests took place more as a result of investment than of actual sieges, and any sieges only lasted a few days. None of these fortifications had adequate garrisons and armaments.

On September 20 the order to cease these operations was given, and the remaining fortified places in France went over to Louis XVIII. But those that had been captured were used by the army of occupation as secure bases.

---

196. Prince Ludwig Wilhelm of Hesse-Homburg (1770–1839). He first fought in the Rhineland in 1793 and was taken prisoner by the French in 1806. After his release the prince was appointed major general in the Prussian army and was wounded at Leipzig in 1813. After the Hundred Days he became commander of the federal fortress of Luxembourg.

Epilogue

Peter Hofschröer

Very little German-language material on the Waterloo campaign has ever been used in English histories of Waterloo. The first British historian to use German sources was Capt. William Siborne, whom Wellington then accused of having been "humbugged" by the Prussians. Col. Charles Chesney refers to Clausewitz in his analysis, but these two works would appear to be the only accounts written in English during the nineteenth century that have referred directly to German sources, and it was close to the end of the twentieth when my two-volume work on the campaign, containing considerably more material from German sources, was published. This translation of Clausewitz is the only German text on the subject translated into English and published in full since General Müffling's account more than 150 years ago. Furthermore, as Clausewitz not only fought in this campaign but also taught its lessons to subsequent generations of Prussian officers, this treatise is of value to the historian for both its content as well as the insight it gives into the military education of the Prussian officer corps during the early nineteenth century. The clarity of Clausewitz's analysis and the authority of what amounts to his teaching notes indicate how thoroughly these officers were instructed in military history.

Despite this, Clausewitz's work was not highly rated by his contemporaries in the Prussian high command. Other accounts published in the immediate post-Waterloo era include those by the senior general staff officer Karl Wilhelm Georg von Grolman (written up by Carl von Damitz) and the official history written by August Wagner and published by the Prussian General Staff. Karl von Plotho's earlier account appears to have been based on official sources. This all leads one to wonder why greater prominence was not given to the work produced by one of the leading teachers of the officer corps. The fact that Clausewitz did not hail from the landed gentry and military nobility may have played a role. As his manuscripts were not given official sanction and published by E. S. Mittler by appointment to the King of Prussia, Clausewitz's widow was forced to seek the services of Berlin publisher Ferdinand Dümmler, a former member of the rather dubious Lützow Freikorps, which added to the rather questionable nature of this enterprise.

Anglophone historians have tended to draw a line under the events of June 18, 1815, considering the campaign of the Hundred Days as having ended with Napoleon's defeat. Siborne was one of the few British Waterloo historians who have mentioned events after this fateful day, though his coverage of the race to Paris and the sieges of the fortresses in northern France is somewhat scant. Clausewitz, as with most German historians, devotes greater attention to these events, particularly since they proved as decisive as the great battle of June 18, if not more so. Furthermore, as he participated in the Battle of Wavre, his account of this affair and its consequences remains of particular interest.

Finally, other than to make implausible excuses and to distort the record, British Waterloo historians have rarely mentioned the discrepancies in Wellington's accounts of the outbreak of hostilities and the events immediately afterward. The facts are that Napoleon "humbugged" the duke, stole a march on him, and left the Allied commander floundering in the Netherlands, mistakes that could well have proved fatal had Wellington not had the nerve to use an unwitting Blücher to buy back the lost time. Rather than critically examine such issues, though, these historians have instead regurgitated and even embellished a long-established liturgy of dubious excuses and favored myths. Perhaps the availability in English of Clausewitz's account of the 1815 campaign and his penetrating analysis will help begin to correct these errors, appealing to those who wish to discover historical fact rather than to repeat misinformed legend.

APPENDIX A

Order of Battle of the Prussian Army at Waterloo, June 18, 1815

Commander in Chief: Field Marshal Prince Blücher von Wahlstadt

I Army Corps: Lieutenant General von Ziethen

First Brigade: Major General von Steinmetz
  12th Infantry Regiment, 3 battalions
  24th Infantry Regiment, 3 battalions
  1st Westphalian Landwehr Infantry Regiment, 3 battalions
  3rd and 4th Companies, Silesian Schützen Battalion
  1st Silesian Hussar Regiment No. 4, 4 squadrons
  6-pounder Foot Battery No. 7: (6) 6-pounders; (2) 7-pound howitzers

Second Brigade: Major General von Pirch II
  6th (1st West Prussian) Infantry Regiment, 3 battalions
  28th Infantry Regiment, 3 battalions
  2nd Westphalian Landwehr Infantry Regiment, 3 battalions
  1st Westphalian Landwehr Cavalry Regiment, 4 squadrons
  6-pounder Foot Battery No. 3: (5) 6-pounders; (2) 7-pound howitzers

Third Brigade: Major General von Jagow
  7th (2nd West Prussian) Infantry Regiment, 3 battalions
  29th Infantry Regiment, 3 battalions
  3rd Westphalian Landwehr Infantry Regiment, 3 battalions
  1st and 2nd Companies, Silesian Schützen Battalion
  6-pounder Foot Battery No. 8: (6) 6-pounders; (2) 7-pound howitzers

Fourth Brigade: Major General von Henckel von Donnersmarck
  19th Infantry Regiment, 3 battalions
  4th Westphalian Landwehr Infantry Regiment, 3 battalions
  6-pounder Foot Battery No. 15: (6) 6-pounders; (2) 7-pound howitzers

Reserve Cavalry: Lieutenant General von Roeder
FIRST BRIGADE: MAJOR GENERAL VON TRESKOW
  5th (Brandenburg) Dragoon Regiment Prince William, 4 squadrons
  2nd (1st West Prussian) Dragoon Regiment, 4 squadrons
  3rd (Brandenburg) Uhlan Regiment, 4 squadrons
  4th Hussar Regiment, 3 squadrons
  Horse Battery No. 2: (6) 6-pounders; (2) 7-pound howitzers
SECOND BRIGADE: LIEUTENANT COLONEL VON LÜTZOW
  6th Uhlan Regiment, 4 battalions
  1st Kurmark Landwehr Cavalry, 4 squadrons
  2nd Kurmark Landwehr Cavalry, 4 squadrons
  Horse Battery No. 7: (6) 6-pounders; (2) 7-pound howitzers

Reserve Artillery: Lieutenant Colonel von Rentzell
  12-pounder Foot Battery No. 2: (6) 12-pounders; (2) 10-pound howitzers
  12-pounder Foot Battery No. 6: (6) 12-pounders; (1) 10-pound howitzer
  6-pounder Foot Battery No. 1: (6) 6-pounders; (2) 7-pound howitzers
  Horse Battery No. 10: (6) 6-pounders; (2) 7-pound howitzers
  7-pound Howitzer Battery No. 1: (8) 7-pound howitzers
  Pioneer Company No. 1

II Army Corps: Lieutenant General von Pirch I
  Fifth Brigade: Major General von Tippelskirch
  2nd (1st Pomeranian) Infantry Regiment, 3 battalions
  25th Infantry Regiment, 3 battalions
  5th Westphalian Landwehr Infantry Regiment, 3 battalions
  Feldjäger Company
  1st and 2nd Squadrons, 11th Hussar Regiment

THE PRUSSIAN ARMY AT WATERLOO 213

   6-pounder Foot Battery No. 10: (6) 6-pounders; (2) 7-pound howitzers

Sixth Brigade: Major General von Krafft
   9th (Colberg) Infantry Regiment, 3 battalions
   26th Infantry Regiment, 3 battalions
   1st Elbe Landwehr Infantry Regiment, 3 battalions
   3rd and 4th Squadrons, 11th Hussar Regiment
   6-pounder Foot Battery No. 5: (6) 6-pounders; (2) 7-pound howitzers

Seventh Brigade: Major General von Brause
   14th Infantry Regiment, 3 battalions
   22nd Infantry Regiment, 3 battalions
   2nd Elbe Landwehr Regiment, 3 battalions
   1st and 3rd Squadrons, Elbe Landwehr Cavalry Regiment
   6-pounder Foot Battery No. 34: (6) 6-pounders; (2) 7-pound howitzers (British guns)

Eighth Brigade: Major General von Bose
   21st Infantry Regiment, 3 battalions
   23rd Infantry Regiment, 3 battalions
   3rd Elbe Landwehr Infantry Regiment, 3 battalions
   2nd and 4th Squadrons, Elbe Landwehr Cavalry Regiment
   6-pounder Foot Battery No. 12: (6) 6-pounders; (1) 7-pound howitzer

Reserve Cavalry: Major General von Wahlen-Jürgass

FIRST BRIGADE: MAJOR GENERAL VON THÜMEN
   1st (Queen's) Dragoon Regiment, 4 squadrons
   6th (Neumark) Dragoon Regiment, 4 squadrons
   2nd (Silesian) Uhlan Regiment, 4 squadrons
   Horse Battery No. 6: (6) 6-pounders; (2) 7-pound howitzers

SECOND BRIGADE: LIEUTENANT COLONEL VON SOHR
   3rd (Brandenburg) Hussar Regiment, 4 squadrons
   5th (Pomeranian) Hussar Regiment, 4 squadrons

THIRD BRIGADE: COLONEL VON DER SCHULENBURG
   4th Kurmark Landwehr Cavalry Regiment, 4 squadrons
   5th Kurmark Landwehr Cavalry Regiment, 4 squadrons

Reserve Artillery: Major Lehmann
 12-pounder Foot Battery No. 4: (6) 12-pounders; (2) 10-pound howitzers
 12-pounder Foot Battery No. 8: (6) 12-pounders; (2) 10-pound howitzers
 6-pounder Foot Battery No. 37: (6) 6-pounders; (2) 7-pound howitzers
 6-pounder Horse Battery No. 5: (6) 6-pounders; (2) 7-pound howitzers
 6-pounder Horse Battery No. 14: (6) 6-pounders; (2) 7-pound howitzers
 Pioneer Company No. 7

III Army Corps: Lieutenant General von Thielemann

Ninth Brigade: Major General von Borcke
 8th (Life) Infantry Regiment, 3 battalions
 30th Infantry Regiment, 3 battalions
 1st Kurmark Landwehr Infantry Regiment, 3 battalions
 1st and 2nd Squadrons, 3rd Kurmark Landwehr Cavalry
 6-pounder Foot Battery No. 18: (6) 6-pounders; (2) 7-pound howitzers

Tenth Brigade: Colonel von Kemphen
 27th Infantry Regiment, 3 battalions
 2nd Kurmark Landwehr Infantry Regiment, 3 battalions
 3rd and 4th Squadrons, 3rd Kurmark Landwehr Cavalry
 6-pounder Foot Battery No. 35: (6) 6-pounders; (2) 7-pound howitzers

Eleventh Brigade: Colonel von Luck
 3rd Kurmark Landwehr Infantry Regiment, 3 battalions
 4th Kurmark Landwehr Infantry Regiment, 3 battalions
 1st and 2nd Squadrons, 6th Kurmark Landwehr Cavalry

Twelfth Brigade: Colonel von Stülpnagel
 31st Infantry Regiment, 3 battalions
 5th Kurmark Landwehr Infantry Regiment, 3 battalions
 6th Kurmark Landwehr Infantry Regiment, 3 battalions
 3rd and 4th Squadrons, 6th Kurmark Landwehr Cavalry

Reserve Cavalry: Major General von Hobe

FIRST BRIGADE: COLONEL VON DER MARWITZ
 7th Uhlan Regiment, 4 squadrons
 8th Uhlan Regiment, 4 squadrons
 12th Hussar Regiment, 4 squadrons

SECOND BRIGADE: COLONEL COUNT VON LOTTUM
 5th Uhlan Regiment, 3 squadrons
 7th Dragoon Regiment, 3 squadrons
 9th Hussar Regiment, 3 squadrons
 Horse Battery No. 20: (6) 6-pounders; (2) 7-pound howitzers

Reserve Artillery: Major von Grevenitz
 12-pounder Foot Battery No. 7: (6) 12-pounders; (2) 10-pound howitzers
 12-pounder Foot Battery No. 12: (6) 12-pounders; (2) 10-pound howitzers
 Horse Battery No. 18: (6) 6-pounders; (2) 7-pound howitzers (Russian guns)
 Horse Battery No. 19: (1) 6-pounder; (2) 7-pound howitzers (Russian guns)
 4th and 5th Pioneer Companies

IV Army Corps:
Lieutenant General Graf Bülow von Dennewitz

Thirteenth Brigade: Lieutenant General von Hake
 10th (1st Silesian) Infantry Regiment, 3 battalions
 2nd Neumark Landwehr Infantry Regiment, 3 battalions
 3rd Neumark Landwehr Infantry Regiment, 3 battalions
 1st and 2nd Squadrons, 2nd Silesian Landwehr Cavalry Regiment
 6-pounder Foot Battery No. 21: (6) 6-pounders; (2) 7-pound howitzers

Fourteenth Brigade: Major General von Ryssel
 11th (2nd Silesian) Infantry Regiment, 3 battalions
 1st Pomeranian Landwehr Infantry Regiment, 3 battalions
 2nd Pomeranian Landwehr Infantry Regiment, 3 battalions

3rd and 4th Squadrons, 2nd Silesian Landwehr Cavalry Regiment
6-pounder Foot Battery No. 13: (6) 6-pounders; (2) 7-pound howitzers

Fifteenth Brigade: Major General von Losthin
18th Infantry Regiment, 3 battalions
3rd Silesian Landwehr Infantry Regiment, 3 battalions
4th Silesian Landwehr Infantry Regiment, 3 battalions
1st and 2nd Squadrons, 3rd Silesian Landwehr Cavalry Regiment
6-pounder Foot Battery No. 14: (6) 6-pounders; (2) 7-pound howitzers

Sixteenth Brigade: Colonel von Hiller
15th Infantry Regiment, 3 battalions
1st Silesian Landwehr Infantry Regiment, 3 battalions
2nd Silesian Landwehr Infantry Regiment, 3 battalions
3rd and 4th Squadrons, 3rd Silesian Landwehr Cavalry Regiment
6-pounder Foot Battery No. 2: (6) 6-pounders; (2) 7-pound howitzers

Reserve Cavalry: Major General Prince Wilhelm (William?) of Prussia

First Brigade: Colonel Graf von Schwerin
6th (2nd Silesian) Hussar Regiment, 4 squadrons
10th Hussar Regiment, 4 squadrons
1st (West Prussian) Uhlan Regiment, 4 squadrons
Horse Battery No. 1: (6) 6-pounders; (2) 7-pound howitzers

Second Brigade: Major General von Watzdorff
8th Hussar Regiment, 3 battalions
Horse Battery No. 12: (6) 6-pounders; (2) 7-pound howitzers

Third Brigade: Lieutenant Colonel von Sydow
1st Neumark Landwehr Cavalry Regiment, 4 squadrons
2nd Neumark Landwehr Cavalry Regiment, 4 squadrons
1st Pomeranian Landwehr Cavalry Regiment, 4 squadrons
2nd Pomeranian Landwehr Cavalry Regiment, 4 squadrons

1st Silesian Landwehr Cavalry Regiment, 4 squadrons

Corps Reserve Artillery: Major von Bardeleben
12-pounder Foot Battery No. 3: (6) 12-pounders; (2) 10-pound howitzers
12-pounder Foot Battery No. 5: (6) 12-pounders; (2) 10-pound howitzers
12-pounder Foot Battery No. 13: (6) 12-pounders; (2) 10-pound howitzers
6-pounder Foot Battery No. 11: (6) 6-pounders; (2) 7-pound howitzers
Horse Battery No. 11: (6) 6-pounders; (2) 7-pound howitzers (British guns)

5th Pioneer Company

The approximate strength of Prussian forces marching to Waterloo was about 75,000 men with 134 guns. Of these, about 48,000 reached the battlefield during the duration of the fighting, and about 28,000 were effectively engaged.

APPENDIX B

Order of Battle of the Anglo-Allied Army at Waterloo, June 18, 1815

Commander in Chief: Field Marshal Duke of Wellington

Cavalry: Lieutenant General Earl of Uxbridge

First (Household) Brigade: Major General Lord Somerset
  1st Life Guard Regiment
  2nd Life Guard Regiment
  Royal Horse (Blues) Guard Regiment
  1st (King's) Dragoon Guard Regiment

Second (Union) Brigade: Major General Ponsonby
  1st Royal Dragoon Regiment
  2nd Royal North British Dragoon Regiment
  6th (Inniskilling) Dragoon Regiment

Third Brigade: Major General Dörnberg
  23rd Light Dragoon Regiment
  1st King's German Legion [KGL] Light Dragoon Regiment
  2nd KGL Light Dragoon Regiment

Fourth Brigade: Major General Vandeleur
  11th Light Dragoon Regiment
  12th (Prince of Wales's) Light Dragoon Regiment
  16th (Queen's) Light Dragoon Regiment

Fifth Brigade: Major General Grant
  7th (Queen's Own) Hussar Regiment
  15th (King's) Hussar Regiment
  2nd KGL Hussar Regiment (detached & not in battle)

THE ANGLO-ALLIED ARMY AT WATERLOO

Sixth Brigade: Major General Vivian
  10th (Prince of Wales's Own Royal) Hussar Regiment
  18th Hussar Regiment
  1st KGL Hussar Regiment

Seventh Brigade: Colonel von Arentsschildt
  13th Light Dragoon Regiment
  3rd KGL Hussar Regiment

First Hanoverian Cavalry Brigade: Colonel von Estorff
  Duke of Cumberland's Hussar Regiment
  Prince Regent's Hussar Regiment
  Bremen & Verden Hussar Regiment

Netherlands Heavy Cavalry Brigade: Major General Baron Trip van Zoutelande
  1st Carabineers
  2nd (South Netherlands) Carabineers
  3rd Carabineers

First Netherlands Light Cavalry Brigade: Major General van Ghigny
  4th Light Dragoons
  8th (South Netherlands) Hussars

Second Netherlands Light Cavalry Brigade: Major General van Merlen
  5th (South Netherlands) Light Dragoons
  6th Hussars

Brunswick Cavalry
  2nd Hussars Regiment
  2nd Squadron, Uhlans

Royal Horse Artillery (attached to the cavalry): Lieutenant Colonel Frazer
  Bull's Troop Horse Artillery: (5) 6-pounders; (1) 5.5-inch howitzer
  Gardiner's Troop Horse Artillery: (5) 6-pounders; (1) 5.5-inch howitzer

Mercer's Troop Horse Artillery: (5) 9-pounders; (1) 5.5-inch howitzer
Ramsay's Troop Horse Artillery: (5) 9-pounders; (1) 5.5-inch howitzer
Webber-Smith's Troop Horse Artillery: (5) 6-pounders; (1) 5.5-inch howitzer
Whinyates Troop Horse Artillery: (5) 6-pounders; 2nd Rocket Troop
Petter's (Netherlands) Horse Half-Battery: (3) 6-pounders; (1) 5.5-inch howitzer
Gey van Pittius's (Netherlands) Horse Half-Battery: (3) 6-pounders; (1) 5.5-inch howitzer)

First (British) Division: Major General Cooke

FIRST (BRITISH) BRIGADE: MAJOR GENERAL MAITLAND
    2nd Battalion, 1st Foot Guard Regiment
    3rd Battalion, 1st Foot Guard Regiment

SECOND (BRITISH) BRIGADE: MAJOR GENERAL SIR BYNG
    2nd Battalion, 2nd (Coldstream) Guard Regiment
    2nd Battalion, 3rd (Scots) Guard Regiment

ARTILLERY: LIEUTENANT COLONEL ADYE
    Sandham's Battery, RFA: (5) 9-pounders; (1) 5.5-inch howitzer
    Kuhlmann's Battery, 2nd KGL: (5) 9-pounders; (1) 5.5-inch howitzer

Second (Anglo-Hanoverian) Division: Lieutenant General Clinton

THIRD (BRITISH) BRIGADE: MAJOR GENERAL ADAM
    1st Battalion, 52nd (Oxfordshire) Regiment
    71st (Highland) Light Infantry Regiment
    3rd Battalion, 95th Rifles, 2 companies
    2nd Battalion, 95th Rifles, 6 companies

FIRST (KGL) BRIGADE: COLONEL DU PLATT
    1st Line Battalion, KGL
    2nd Line Battalion, KGL
    3rd Line Battalion, KGL
    4th Line Battalion, KGL

THIRD (HANOVERIAN) BRIGADE: COLONEL HALKETT
  Bremervörde Landwehr Battalion
  Osnabrück Landwehr Battalion
  Quakenbrück Landwehr Battalion
  Salzgitter Landwehr Battalion

ARTILLERY: LIEUTENANT COLONEL GOLD
  Bolton's Battery, RFA: (5) 9-pounders; (1) 5.5-inch howitzer
  Sympher's Battery, KGL: (5) 9-pounders; (1) 5.5-inch howitzer

Third (Anglo-Hanoverian) Division: Major General Alten

FIFTH (BRITISH) BRIGADE: MAJOR GENERAL HALKETT
  2nd Battalion, 30th (Cambridgeshire) Regiment
  2nd Battalion, 33rd (West Riding) Regiment
  2nd Battalion, 69th (South Lincoln) Regiment
  2nd Battalion, 73rd (Highland) Regiment

SECOND KGL BRIGADE: COLONEL VON OMPTEDA
  1st Light Battalion, KGL
  2nd Light Battalion, KGL
  5th Line Battalion, KGL
  8th Line Battalion, KGL

FIRST HANOVERIAN BRIGADE: MAJOR GENERAL COUNT VON KIELMANSEGGE
  Bremen Field Battalion
  Verden Field Battalion
  Duke of York's First Field Battalion
  Lüneburg Light Battalion
  Grubenhagen Jäger Battalion
  Kielmansegge Feldjäger-Korps

ARTILLERY: LIEUTENANT COLONEL WILLIAMSON
  Lloyd's Battery, RFA: (5) 9-pounders; (1) 5.5-inch howitzer
  Cleeve's Battery, KGLFA: (5) 9-pounders; (1) 5.5-inch howitzer

Fourth (Anglo-Hanoverian) Division: Lieutenant General Colville

FOURTH (BRITISH) BRIGADE: COLONEL MITCHELL
  3rd Battalion, 14th (Buckinghamshire) Regiment
  1st Battalion, 23rd (Royal Welsh) Fusiliers Regiment
  51st (2nd West Riding) Light Infantry Regiment

SIXTH (BRITISH) BRIGADE: MAJOR GENERAL JOHNSTONE (DETACHED & NOT IN BATTLE)
    2nd Battalion, 35th (Sussex) Regiment
    1st Battalion, 54th (West Norfolk) Regiment
    2nd Battalion, 59th (2nd Nottinghamshire) Regiment
    1st Battalion, 91st Regiment

SIXTH (HANOVERIAN) BRIGADE: MAJOR GENERAL LYON (DETACHED & NOT IN BATTLE)
    Lauenburg Field Battalion
    Calenberg Field Battalion
    Nienburg Landwehr Battalion
    Hoya Landwehr Battalion
    Bentheim Landwehr Battalion

ARTILLERY: LIEUTENANT COLONEL HAWKER
    Broome's Battery, RFA (detached): (5) 9-pounders; (1) 5.5-inch howitzer
    Rottenberg's Battery, KGL: (5) 9-pounders; (1) 5.5-inch howitzer

Fifth (Anglo-Hanoverian) Division: Lieutenant General Picton

EIGHTH (BRITISH) BRIGADE: MAJOR GENERAL KEMPT
    1st Battalion, 28th (North Gloucestershire) Regiment
    1st Battalion, 32nd (Cornwall) Regiment
    1st Battalion, 79th (Cameron) Regiment
    1st Battalion, 95th Rifles Regiment, 6 companies

NINTH (BRITISH) BRIGADE: MAJOR GENERAL PACK
    3rd Battalion, 1st (Royal Scots) Regiment
    1st Battalion, 42nd (Black Watch) Regiment
    1st Battalion, 44th (East Essex) Regiment
    1st Battalion, 92nd (Gordon) Highlanders Regiment

FIFTH (HANOVERIAN) BRIGADE: MAJOR GENERAL VON VINCKE
    Hameln Landwehr Battalion
    Hildesheim Landwehr Battalion
    Peine Landwehr Battalion
    Gifhorn Landwehr Battalion

Artillery: Major Heisse
  Rogers Battery, RFA : (5) 9-pounders; (1) 5.5-inch howitzer
  Braun's Battery, Hanoverian FA: (5) 9-pounders; (1) 5.5-inch howitzer

Sixth (Anglo-Hanoverian) Division: Lieutenant General Cole

Tenth (British) Brigade: Major General Lambert
  1st Battalion, 4th (King's Own) Regiment
  1st Battalion, 27th (Inniskilling) Regiment
  1st Battalion, 40th (2nd Somersetshire) Regiment
  2nd Battalion, 81st (Loyals) Regiment (detached)

Fourth (Hanoverian) Brigade: Colonel Best
  Verden Landwehr Battalion
  Lüneburg Landwehr Battalion
  Osterode Landwehr Battalion
  Münden Landwehr Battalion

Artillery: Lieutenant Colonel Brückmann
  Unett's Battery, RFA: (5) 9-pounders; (1) 5.5-inch howitzer (detached)
  Sinclair's Battery, RFA: (5) 9-pounders; (1) 5.5-inch howitzer

British Reserve Artillery: Major Drummond
  Ross's Battery, RHA: (5) 9-pounders; (1) 5.5-inch howitzer
  Bean's Battery, RHA: (5) 9-pounders; (1) 5.5-inch howitzer
  Morrison's Battery, RFA: (4) 18-pounders (at Vilvoorde)
  Hutchesson's Battery, RFA: (4) 18-pounders (at Ostende)
  Ibert's Battery, RFA: (4) 18-pounders (at Ostende)

Netherlands Reserve:
  Battery Bois: (8) 12-pounders (at Braine-Le-Comte)

Netherlands Reserve Park:
  3rd Battery, 2nd Artillery Battalion (at Louvain)
  Kaempfer's Foot Battery: (6) cannon; (2) howitzers (at Zottegem)

First Netherlands Division: Lieutenant General Stedmann (detached)

FIRST BRIGADE: MAJOR GENERAL D'HAUW
   4th (South Netherlands) Line Battalion
   6th Line Regiment
   16th Jäger Battalion
   9th Militia Battalion
   14th Militia Battalion
   15th Militia Battalion

SECOND BRIGADE: MAJOR GENERAL DE EERENS
   1st (South Netherlands) Line Battalion
   18th Jäger Battalion
   1st Militia Battalion
   2nd Militia Battalion
   18th Militia Battalion

Second Netherlands Division: Lieutenant General de Perponcher-Sedlnitzky

FIRST BRIGADE: MAJOR GENERAL BIJLANDT
   7th (South Netherlands) Line Regiment
   27th Jägers
   5th Militia Battalion
   7th Militia Battalion
   8th Militia Battalion

SECOND BRIGADE: MAJOR GENERAL VON SAXE-WEIMAR
   1st Battalion, 2nd Nassau Regiment
   2nd Battalion, 2nd Nassau Regiment
   3rd Battalion, 2nd Nassau Regiment
   1st Battalion, Orange-Nassau Regiment
   2nd Battalion, Orange-Nassau Regiment
   Nassau Jägers, 1 company

ARTILLERY: MAJOR VAN OPSTAL
   Bijlveld's Battery, HA: (6) 6-pounders; (2) 5.5-inch howitzers
   Stievenaar's (South Netherlands) Battery, FA: (6) 6-pounders; (2) 5.5-inch howitzers

Wijnand's Foot Battery, FA: (6) 6-pounders; (2) 5.5-inch howitzers

Third Netherlands Division: Lieutenant General Baron Chassé

FIRST BRIGADE: MAJOR GENERAL DETMERS
  2nd Line Battalion
  35th (South Netherlands) Chasseurs Battalion
  4th Militia Battalion
  6th Militia Battalion
  17th Militia Battalion
  19th Militia Battalion

SECOND BRIGADE: MAJOR GENERAL D'AUBREMÉ
  3rd (South Netherlands) Line Battalion
  12th Line Battalion
  13th Line Battalion
  36th (South Netherlands) Chasseurs Battalion
  3rd Militia Battalion
  10th Militia Battalion

ARTILLERY: MAJOR VAN DER SMISSEN
  De Bichin's Horse Battery, HA: (6) 6-pounders; (2) 5.5-inch howitzers
  Lux's Battery, FA: (6) 6-pounders; (2) 5.5-inch howitzers

Netherlands Indian Brigade: Lieutenant General Anthing (detached)

  5th East Indian Regiment, 3 battalions
  10th West Indian Chasseurs
  11th West Indian Chasseurs
  Flank companies of 19th and 20th Line Regiments
  Riesz's Battery, FA: (6) 6-pounders; (2) 5.5-inch howitzers

Brunswick Contingent: Duke of Brunswick

ADVANCED GUARD: MAJOR VON RAUSCHENPLAT
  2nd Squadron, Uhlans (detached)
  Avantgarde Battalion

FIRST (LIGHT) BRIGADE: LIEUTENANT COLONEL VON BUTTLAR
  Life Guard Battalion
  1st Light Infantry Battalion
  2nd Light Infantry Battalion
  3rd Light Infantry Battalion

SECOND (LINE) BRIGADE: LIEUTENANT COLONEL VON SPECHT
  1st Line Infantry Battalion
  2nd Line Infantry Battalion
  3rd Line Infantry Battalion

ARTILLERY: MAJOR MAHN
  Heinemann's Horse Battery, HA: (8) 6-pounders
  Moll's Foot Battery, FA: (8) 6-pounders

Nassau Contingent: Major General von Kruse
  1st Battalion, 1st (Duke of Nassau) Regiment
  2nd Battalion, 1st (Duke of Nassau) Regiment
  Landwehr Battalion, 1st (Duke of Nassau) Regiment
  Approximate strength of Anglo-Allied forces at Waterloo (excluding detachments) totaled 68,000 men and 159 pieces of artillery, comprising:
  24,000 British troops
  6,000 King's German Legionnaires
  20,000 German contingent troops
  18,000 Netherlands troops

APPENDIX C

Order of Battle of the French Army of the North at Waterloo, June 18, 1815

Commander in Chief: Emperor Napoleon I

Imperial Guard: Marshal Mortier, Duke of Treviso / Division General Drouot

Old Guard: Division General Count Friant
  1st Grenadiers, 2 battalions
  2nd Grenadiers, 2 battalions
  1st Chasseurs, 2 battalions
  2nd Chasseurs, 2 battalions

Middle Guard: Division General Count Morand
  3rd Grenadiers, 2 battalions
  4th Grenadiers, 1 battalion
  3rd Chasseurs, 2 battalions
  4th Chasseurs, 2 battalions

Young Guard: Division General Count Duhesme
  1st Tirailleur Regiment, 2 battalions
  1st Voltigeur Regiment, 2 battalions
  3rd Tirailleur Regiment, 2 battalions
  3rd Voltigeur Regiment, 2 battalions

Guard Cavalry: Marshal Mortier, Duke of Treviso

LIGHT CAVALRY DIVISION: DIVISION GENERAL COUNT LEFÈBVRE-DESNOËTTES
  1st Lancers Regiment, 1 squadron
  2nd Lancers Regiment, 4 squadrons
  Horse Chasseurs, 5 squadrons

Heavy Cavalry Division: Division General Count Guyot
  Horse Grenadiers, 4 squadrons
  Empress Dragoon Regiment, 4 squadrons

Artillery of the Guard: Division General Desvaux de St. Maurice
  6 Old Guard Foot Batteries: (48 guns)
  4 Old Guard Horse Batteries: (24) 6-pounders
  4 Line Foot Batteries: (6) 6-pounders; (2) 5.5-inch howitzers (each)
  1 Line Horse Battery: (4) 6-pounders; (2) 5.5-inch howitzers
  1 Young Guard Foot Battery: (6) 6-pounders; (2) 5.5-inch howitzers

I Corps: Division General d'Erlon

First Division: Division General Allix

First Brigade: Brigade General Quiot
  54th Line Regiment, 2 battalions
  55th Line Regiment, 2 battalions

Second Brigade: Brigade General Bourgeois
  28th Line Regiment, 2 battalions
  105th Line Regiment, 2 battalions

Artillery: Captain Hamelin
  20th Battery, 6th Foot Artillery: (6) 6-pounders; (2) 5.5-inch howitzers

Second Division: Division General Donzelot

First Brigade: Brigade General Schmitz
  13th Light Regiment, 3 battalions
  17th Line Regiment, 2 battalions

Second Brigade: Brigade General Aulard
  19th Line Regiment, 2 battalions
  31st Line Regiment, 2 battalions

Artillery: Captain Cantin
  10th Battery, 6th Foot Artillery: (6) 6-pounders; (2) 5.5-inch howitzers

Third Division: Division General Marcognet

FIRST BRIGADE: BRIGADE GENERAL NOGUÈS
21st Line Regiment, 2 battalions
46th Line Regiment, 2 battalions

SECOND BRIGADE: BRIGADE GENERAL GRENIER
25th Line Regiment, 2 battalions
45th Line Regiment, 2 battalions

ARTILLERY: CAPTAIN EMOM
19th Battery, 6th Foot Artillery: (6) 6-pounders; (2) 5.5-inch howitzers

Fourth Division: Division General Durutte

FIRST BRIGADE: BRIGADE GENERAL PÉGOT
8th Line Regiment, 2 battalions
29th Line Regiment, 2 battalions

SECOND BRIGADE: BRIGADE GENERAL BRUE
85th Line Regiment, 2 battalions
95th Line Regiment, 2 battalions

ARTILLERY: CAPTAIN BOURGEOIS
9th Battery, 6th Foot Artillery: (6) 6-pounders; (2) 5.5-inch howitzers

First Cavalry Division: Division General Jacquinot

FIRST BRIGADE: BRIGADE GENERAL BRUNO
7th Hussar Regiment, 3 squadrons
3rd Horse Chasseur Regiment, 3 squadrons

SECOND BRIGADE: BRIGADE GENERAL GOBRECHT
3rd Light Lancer Regiment, 3 squadrons
4th Light Lancer Regiment, 2 squadrons

ARTILLERY: CAPTAIN BOURGEOIS
2nd Battery, 1st Horse Artillery: (4) 6-pounders; (2) 5.5-inch howitzers

Reserve Artillery: Dessales
  11th Battery, 6th Foot Artillery: (6) 12-pounders; (2) 6-inch howitzers
  2nd Battalion, 1st Engineers, 5 companies

II Corps: Division General Reille

Fifth Division: Division General Bachelu

First Brigade: Brigade General Husson
  3rd Light Regiment, 4 battalions
  61st Line Regiment, 2 battalions

Second Brigade: Brigade General Campi
  72nd Line Regiment, 2 battalions
  108th Line Regiment, 3 battalions

Artillery: Captain Deshaulles
  18th Battery, 6th Foot Artillery: (6) 6-pounders; (2) 5.5-inch howitzers

Sixth Division: Division General Bonaparte

First Brigade: Brigade General Baudin
  1st Light Regiment, 3 battalions
  2nd Light Regiment, 2 battalions

Second Brigade: Brigade General Soye
  1st Line Regiment, 3 battalions
  2nd Line Regiment, 3 battalions

Artillery: Captain Meunier
  2nd Battery, 2nd Foot Artillery: (6) 6pounders; (2) 5.5-inch howitzers

Seventh Division: Division General Girard

First Brigade: Brigade General de Villiers
  11th Light Regiment, 2 battalions
  82nd Line Regiment, 1 battalion

Second Brigade: Brigade General Pait
  12th Light Regiment, 3 battalions

4th Line Regiment, 2 battalions

ARTILLERY: CAPTAIN BARBAUX
3rd Battery, 2nd Foot Artillery: (6) 6-pounders; (2) 5.5-inch howitzers

Ninth Division: Division General Count Foy

FIRST BRIGADE: BRIGADE GENERAL MARBAIS
92nd Line Regiment, 2 battalions
93rd Line Regiment, 2 battalions

SECOND BRIGADE: BRIGADE GENERAL JAMIN
100th Line Regiment, 3 battalions
4th Light Regiment, 3 battalions

ARTILLERY: CAPTAIN TACON
1st Battery, 6th Foot Artillery: (6) 6-pounders; (2) 5.5-inch howitzers

Second Cavalry Division: Division General Piré

FIRST BRIGADE: BRIGADE GENERAL BARON HUBERT
1st Horse Chasseur Regiment, 4 squadrons
6th Horse Chasseur Regiment, 4 squadrons

SECOND BRIGADE: BRIGADE GENERAL GAUTHIER
5th Lancer Regiment, 3 squadrons
6th Lancer Regiment, 4 squadrons

ARTILLERY: CAPTAIN GRONNIER
2nd Battery, 4th Horse Artillery: (4) 6-pounders; (2) 5.5-inch howitzers

Reserve Artillery: Brigade General Le Pelletier
7th Battery, 2nd Foot Artillery: (6) 12-pounders; (2) 6-inch howitzers
1st Battery, 1st Horse Artillery: (4) 6-pounders; (2) howitzers
4th Battery, 1st Horse Artillery: (4) 6-pounders; (2) howitzers
(Horse artillery was detached)

1st Battalion, 1st Engineers, 5 companies

Third Cavalry Division: Division General Domon

FIRST BRIGADE: BRIGADE GENERAL DOMMAGNET
    4th Horse Chasseur Regiment, 3 squadrons
    9th Horse Chasseur Regiment, 3 squadrons

SECOND BRIGADE: BRIGADE GENERAL VINOT
    12th Horse Chasseur Regiment, 3 squadrons

ARTILLERY: CAPTAIN DUMONT
    4th Battery, 2nd Horse Artillery: (4) 6-pounders; (2) 5.5-inch howitzers

III Corps: Division General Vandamme

Eighth Division: Division General Lefol

FIRST BRIGADE: BRIGADE GENERAL BELLARD
    15th Light Regiment, 3 battalions
    23rd Line Regiment, 3 battalions

SECOND BRIGADE: BRIGADE GENERAL CORSIN
    37th Line Regiment, 3 battalions
    64th Line Regiment, 2 battalions

ARTILLERY: CAPTAIN CHAUVEAU
    7th Battery, 6th Foot Artillery: (6) 6-pounders; (2) 5.5-inch howitzers

Tenth Division: Division General Habert

FIRST BRIGADE: BRIGADE GENERAL GENGOULT
    34th Line Regiment, 3 battalions
    88th Line Regiment, 3 battalions

SECOND BRIGADE: BRIGADE GENERAL DAPREYROUX
    22nd Line Regiment, 3 battalions
    70th Line Regiment, 2 battalions
    2nd Swiss Infantry Regiment, 1 battalion

ARTILLERY: CAPTAIN GUERIN
    18th Battery, 2nd Foot Artillery: (6) 6-pounders; (2) 5.5-inch howitzers

Eleventh Division: Division General Berthezène

FIRST BRIGADE: BRIGADE GENERAL DUFOUR
12th Line Regiment, 2 battalions
56th Line Regiment, 2 battalions

SECOND BRIGADE: BRIGADE GENERAL LAGARDE
33rd Line Regiment, 2 battalions
86th Line Regiment, 2 battalions

ARTILLERY: CAPTAIN CHEANNE
17th Battery, 2nd Foot Artillery: (6) 6-pounders; (2) 5.5-inch howitzers)

Reserve Artillery: Division General Dorureau
2 Foot Batteries: (6) 6-pounders; (2) 5.5-inch howitzers (each)
1 Foot Battery: (6) 12-pounders; (2) 6-inch howitzers

2nd Battalion, 1st Engineer Regiment, 4 companies

IV Corps: Division General Gérard

Twelfth Division: Division General Pêcheux

FIRST BRIGADE: BRIGADE GENERAL ROME
30th Line Regiment, 2 battalions
96th Line Regiment, 2 battalions

SECOND BRIGADE: BRIGADE GENERAL SCHAEFFER
63rd Line Regiment, 2 battalions

ARTILLERY: CAPTAIN FENOUILLAT
2nd Battery, 5th Foot Artillery: (6) 6-pounders; (2) 5.5-inch howitzers

Thirteenth Division: Division General Vichery

FIRST BRIGADE: BRIGADE GENERAL LE CAPITAINE
59th Line Regiment, 2 battalions
76th Line Regiment, 2 battalions

SECOND BRIGADE: BRIGADE GENERAL DESPREZ
48th Line Regiment, 2 battalions

69th Line Regiment, 2 battalions

ARTILLERY: CAPTAIN SAINT-CYR
1st Battery, 5th Foot Artillery: (6) 6-pounders; (2) 5.5-inch howitzers

Fourteenth Division: Division General Hulot

FIRST BRIGADE: BRIGADE GENERAL HULOT
9th Light Regiment, 2 battalions
111th Line Regiment, 2 battalions

SECOND BRIGADE: BRIGADE GENERAL TOUSSAINT
44th Line Regiment, 2 battalions
50th Line Regiment, 2 battalions

ARTILLERY:
3rd Battery, 5th Foot Artillery: (6) 6-pounders; (2) 5.5-inch howitzers

Sixth Cavalry Division: Division General Maurin

FIRST BRIGADE: BRIGADE GENERAL VALLIN
6th Hussar Regiment, 3 squadrons
8th Horse Chasseur Regiment, 3 squadrons

SECOND BRIGADE: BRIGADE GENERAL BERRUYER
6th Dragoon Regiment
16th Dragoon Regiment

ARTILLERY: CAPTAIN TORTEL
1st Battery, 5th Horse Artillery: (4) 6-pounders; (2) 5.5-inch howitzers

Reserve Artillery: Brigade General de Pouilly
5th Battery, 5th Foot Artillery: (6) 12-pounders; (2) 6-inch howitzers

2nd Battalion, 2nd Engineer Regiment, 3 companies

VI Corps: Division General Count de Lobau

Nineteenth Division: Division General Baron Zimmer

FIRST BRIGADE: BRIGADE GENERAL BARON DE BELLAIR
  5th Line Regiment, 2 battalions
  11th Line Regiment, 3 battalions

SECOND BRIGADE: BRIGADE GENERAL JAMIN
  27th Line Regiment, 2 battalions
  84th Line Regiment, 2 battalions

ARTILLERY: CAPTAIN PARISOT
  1st Battery, 8th Foot Artillery: (6) 6-pounders; (2) 5.5-inch howitzers

Twentieth Division: Division General Jeanin

FIRST BRIGADE: BRIGADE GENERAL BONY
  5th Light Regiment, 2 battalions
  10th Line Regiment, 2 battalions

SECOND BRIGADE: BRIGADE GENERAL TROMELIN
  47th Line Regiment, 1 battalion
  107th Line Regiment, 2 battalions

ARTILLERY: CAPTAIN PAQUET
  2nd Battery, 8th Foot Artillery: (6) 6-pounders; (2) 5.5-inch howitzers

Twenty-first Division: Division General Baron Teste

FIRST BRIGADE: BRIGADE GENERAL LAFITTE
  8th Light Regiment, 3 battalions
  40th Line Regiment, 3 battalions

SECOND BRIGADE: BRIGADE GENERAL PENNE
  65th Line Regiment, 3 battalions
  75th Line Regiment, 3 battalions

ARTILLERY: CAPTAIN DUVERREY
  3rd Battery, 8th Foot Artillery: (4) 6-pounders; (2) 5.5-inch howitzers

Reserve Artillery: Division General Noury
  4th Battery, 8th Foot Artillery: (6) 12-pounders; (2) 6-inch howitzers
  [?] Horse Artillery: (6) 6-pounders; (2) howitzers

  1st Battalion, 3rd Engineers, 2 companies

I Cavalry Corps: Division General Count Pajol

Fourth Cavalry Division: Division General Soult

First Brigade: Brigade General de Saint-Laurent
  1st Hussar Regiment, 4 squadrons
  4th Hussar Regiment, 4 squadrons

Second Brigade: Brigade General Ameil
  5th Hussar Regiment, 4 squadrons

Artillery: Captain Cotheraux
  1st Battery, 1st Horse Artillery: (4) 6-pounders; (2) 5.5-inch howitzers

Fifth Cavalry Division: Division General Subervie

First Brigade: Brigade General de Colbert
  1st Light Lancer Regiment, 4 squadrons
  2nd Light Lancer Regiment, 4 squadrons

Second Brigade: Brigade General Merlin
  11th Horse Chasseur Regiment, 3 squadrons

Artillery: Captain Duchemin
  3rd Battery, 1st Horse Artillery: (4) 6-pounders; (2) 5.5-inch howitzers

II Cavalry Corps: Division General Exelmans

Ninth Cavalry Division: Division General Strolz

First Brigade: Brigade General Burthe
  5th Dragoon Regiment, 4 squadrons
  13th Dragoon Regiment, 4 squadrons

SECOND BRIGADE: BRIGADE GENERAL VINCENT
  15th Dragoon Regiment, 4 squadrons
  20th Dragoon Regiment, 4 squadrons

ARTILLERY: CAPTAIN GODET
  4th Battery, 1st Horse Artillery: (4) 6-pounders; (2) 5.5-inch howitzers

Tenth Cavalry Division: Division General Chastel

FIRST BRIGADE: BRIGADE GENERAL BONNEMAINS
  4th Dragoon Regiment, 4 squadrons
  12th Dragoon Regiment, 4 squadrons

SECOND BRIGADE: BRIGADE GENERAL BERTON
  14th Dragoon Regiment, 4 squadrons
  17th Dragoon Regiment, 4 squadrons

ARTILLERY: CAPTAIN BERNARD
  4th Battery, 4th Horse Artillery: (4) 6-pounders; (2) 5.5-inch howitzers

III Cavalry Corps: Division General Kellermann

Eleventh Cavalry Division: Division General l'Héritier

FIRST BRIGADE: BRIGADE GENERAL PICQUET
  2nd Dragoon Regiment, 4 squadrons
  7th Dragoon Regiment, 3 squadrons

SECOND BRIGADE: BRIGADE GENERAL GUITON
  8th Cuirassier Regiment, 3 squadrons
  11th Cuirassier Regiment, 2 squadrons

ARTILLERY: CAPTAIN MARCILLAC
  3rd Battery, 2nd Horse Artillery: (4) 6-pounders; (2) 5.5-inch howitzers

Twelfth Cavalry Division: Division General d'Hurbal

FIRST BRIGADE: BRIGADE GENERAL BLANCHARD
  1st Carabineer Regiment, 3 squadrons
  2nd Carabineer Regiment, 3 squadrons

SECOND BRIGADE: BRIGADE GENERAL DONOP
  2nd Cuirassier Regiment, 2 squadrons
  3rd Cuirassier Regiment, 4 squadrons

ARTILLERY: CAPTAIN LEBAU
  2nd Battery, 2nd Horse Artillery: (4) 6-pounders; (2) 5.5-inch howitzers

IV Cavalry Corps: Division General Count Milhaud

Thirteenth Cavalry Division: Division General Wathier

FIRST BRIGADE: BRIGADE GENERAL DUBOIS
  1st Cuirassier Regiment, 4 squadrons
  4th Cuirassier Regiment, 3 squadrons

SECOND BRIGADE: BRIGADE GENERAL TRAVERS
  7th Cuirassier Regiment, 2 squadrons
  12th Cuirassier Regiment, 2 squadrons

ARTILLERY: CAPTAIN DUCHET
  5th Battery, 1st Horse Artillery: (4) 6-pounders; (2) 5.5-inch howitzers

Fourteenth Cavalry Division: Division General Delort

FIRST BRIGADE: BRIGADE GENERAL FARINE
  5th Cuirassier Regiment, 3 squadrons
  10th Cuirassier Regiment, 3 squadrons

SECOND BRIGADE: BRIGADE GENERAL VIAL
  6th Cuirassier Regiment, 4 squadrons
  9th Cuirassier Regiment, 3 squadrons

ARTILLERY:
  4th Battery, 3rd Horse Artillery: (4) 6-pounders; (2) 5.5-inch howitzers
  Approximate strength of French forces at Waterloo were 73,140 men and 252 guns.

Published Works of Carl von Clausewitz

"Bemerkungen über die reine und angewandte Strategie des Herrn von Bülow." *Neues Bellona* 9, no. 3 (1805).

"Historische Briefe über die grossen Kriegsereignisse im Oktober 1806." *Minerva* 1, 2 (January–February, April 1807).

"Kriegsartikel für die Unter-Officiere und gemeinen Söldaten (der königl. preussischen Armee). . . . Verordnung wegen der Militär-Strafen. Verordnung wegen Bestrafung der Officiere. . . . Reglement über die Besetzung der Stellen der Port-epée Fähnriche und über die Wahl zum Officier. . . ." *Jenaische Allgemeine Literatur-Zeitung* 238 (October 11, 1808).

Übersicht des Sr. Königl. Hoheit dem Kronprinzen . . . ertheilten militärischen Unterrichts. N.p., 1812.

"Nachruf" [obituary of Scharnhorst]. *Preussischer Correspondent*, July 12, 14, 1813.

Der Feldzug von 1813 bis zum Waffenstillstand. Glatz, 1813.

"Über das Leben und den Charakter von Scharnhorst." *Historisch-politische Zeitschrift* 1 (1832).

Hinterlassene Werke des Generals Carl von Clausewitz über Krieg und Kriegführung. 10 vols. Berlin, 1832–37.

Vols. 1–3: *Vom Kriege.*

Vol. 4: *Der Feldzug von 1796 in Italien.*

Vols. 5–6: *Die Feldzüge von 1799 in Italien und in der Schweiz.*

Vol. 7: *Der Feldzug von 1812 in Russland; Der Feldzug von 1813 bis zum Waffenstillstand; Der Feldzug von 1814 in Frankreich.*

Vol. 8: *Der Feldzug von 1815 in Frankreich.*

Vol. 9: *Gustav Adolphs Feldzüge von 1630–1632; Historische Materialien zur Strategie; Turenne; Die Feldzüge Luxemburgs in Flandern von 1690–1694; Einige Bemerkungen zum spanischen Erbfolgekriege. . . .*

Vol. 10: *Sobiesky; Krieg der Russen gegen die Türken von 1736–1739; Die Feldzüge Friedrich des Grossen von 1741–1762; Der Feldzug des Herzogs von Braunschweig gegen die Holländer 1787; Übersicht des Krieges in der Vendée 1793.*

"Über das Fortschreiten und den Stillstand der kriegerischen Begebenheiten." *Zeitschrift für preussische Geschichte und Landeskunde* 15 (1878).

"Nachrichten über Preussen in seiner grossen Katastrophe." In *Kriegsgeschichtliche Einzelschriften,* vol. 10. Berlin, 1888.

"Zwei Denkschriften von Clausewitz 1830/31." *Militär-Wochenblatt* 29–31 (1891).

"Betrachtungen über den künftigen Kriegsplan gegen Frankreich." *Moltkes Militärische Werke,* 1st ser., 4 (1902).

"Ein kunsttheoretisches Fragment des Generals Carl von Clausewitz." *Deutsche Rundschau* 173, no. 3 (1917).

(With Marie von Karl und Marie von Clausewitz). *Ein Lebensbild in Briefen und Tagebuchblättern.* Edited by K. Linnebach. Berlin, 1917.

"Ein Brief von Clausewitz an den Kronprinzen Friedrich Wilhelm aus dem Jahre 1812." *Historische Zeitschrift* 121, no. 2 (1920).

Politische Schriften und Briefe. Edited by Hans Rothfels. Munich, 1922.

Strategie aus dem Jahr 1804, mit Zusätzen von 1808 und 1809. Edited by Eberhard Kessel. Hamburg, 1937.

"Zwei Briefe des Generals von Clausewitz: Gedanken zur Abwehr." Special issue, *Militärwissenschaftliche Rundschau* 11 (1937).

"Clausewitz über den Gedanken eines Ländertauschs zur Verbindung der Ost- und West-Masse der Preussischen Monarchie nach den Befreiungskriegen." *Forschungen zur Brandenburgischen und Preussischen Geschichte* 51 (1939).

Geist und Tat. Edited by W. M. Schering. Stuttgart, 1941.

Schriften—Aufsätze—Studien—Briefe. Introduction by Werner Hahlweg. Göttingen, 1966.

"An Anonymous Letter by Clausewitz on the Polish Insurrection of 1830–1831" [letter printed in *Zeitung des Grossherzogtums Posen,* July 21, 1831]. *Journal of Modern History* 42, no. 22 (1970).

"Verstreute kleine Schriften." Collected, edited, and introduced by Werner Hahlweg. Osnabrück, 1979.

Bibliography

The first published account of the Battle of Waterloo was the "Waterloo Despatch" written by the Duke of Wellington in his headquarters in the village of Waterloo on June 19, 1815, the morning after the battle. He completed it in Brussels later that morning before sending it to London, where it was published in the *Times*. Not surprisingly, Wellington's version of events has formed the basis of most Anglophone accounts of the battle in the years since, and many indeed followed, with at least seventy works published in 1815 alone. Most of these earlier histories were put together with some haste to make the most of the business opportunity at hand. Later accounts were often produced to complement the various panoramas, exhibitions, and reenactments that formed a stable of early nineteenth-century entertainment in Britain. All religiously toed Wellington's line until Capt. William Siborne's *History of the War in France and Belgium, 1815,* first published in 1838. Siborne differed from his contemporaries in that he undertook original research, corresponding with many survivors of the campaign, including members of the various German contingents, though his attempts to contact various French veterans were politely ignored. His account varies with Wellington's on several important issues, and Siborne suffered the duke's wrath, dying a broken and impoverished man. The Rev. George Gleig reiterated the official line, and he was a man very much in the Wellington camp, so the duke's version prevailed in later histories, such as those by Maj. Gen. Sir C. W. Robinson, E. L. A. Horsburgh, and Capt. A. F. Becke. The only work published in nineteenth-century Britain other than Siborne's to use sources other than those in English was Col. Charles C. Chesney's, so there were just two voices in this wilderness. With just a few exceptions, all Anglophone works on the subject published during the twentieth century and into the first decade of the twenty-first consist largely of embellishments of Wellingtonian mythology.

Siborne irritated Wellington particularly with his detailed examination of the issue of when the duke actually first received news of the outbreak of hostilities on June 15. In the "Waterloo Despatch" Wellington states that it was that evening, though he later conceded privately that he did receive a report to that effect from the Prince of Orange at 3 P.M., the memorandum he wrote first mentioning this being published only after his death. Robinson, Horsburgh, and Becke all fell into line with this amendment to the record without mentioning the discrepancy. All ignored Siborne, who in the third edition of his *History* went so far as to state that Wellington actually first received the news at 9 A.M.

Napoleon had his version written while in his final exile on the isolated Atlantic island of St. Helena. Full of excuses, it is of little historical value save as a study of Napoleonic propaganda, though many of Napoleon's myths have found their way into later histories. Not surprisingly, little was said and less published on the matter in France during the years and indeed decades following the end of the Napoleonic era. The first authoritative history of the campaign in French was that by Jean Baptiste Adolphe Charras, originally published in 1857, though it was as late as 1869 before it was first published in France. Much of what has followed in French can only be described as Bonapartist propaganda, with the incessant repetitions of the cause of Napoleon's defeat being errors supposedly made by Ney at Quatre Bras as well as his handling of the assault on Wellington's center at Waterloo and Grouchy's failure to prevent the Prussians from reaching Waterloo. In both cases Napoleon's subordinates were merely following their master's orders.

The approach Prussian historians took on the subject could not have been more different. All Prussian commanders were required to write an after-action report that was then deposited in the War Archives and used as the basis of subsequent histories, the first of these being that written by Plotho and published in

1818, though this was not an official history. The first official history was written by Wagner, an officer on the Prussian General Staff, with the Waterloo volume appearing in 1825, though the sources used were largely Prussian. In contrast, Hans Oskar von Lettow-Vorbeck's later official history, written during the golden age of military historiography, referred to all relevant authorities, using source materials in English, French, and German. Presumably Clausewitz had access to the Prussian War Archives, but what is certain is that the few footnotes given in his account of the campaign indicate that he was well read on the subject, referring to accounts published in French.

The following is a list of works consulted while preparing this translation.

Manuscripts

Journal of Constant Rebecque. Coll. 66. Algemeen Rijksarchief, The Hague, Netherlands.

Books

Becke, Capt. A. F. *Napoleon and Waterloo—The Emperor's Campaign with the Armée du Nord, 1815—A Strategical and Tactical Study.* 2 vols. London, 1914.

Blesson, L. *Beitrag zur Geschichte des Festungskrieges in Frankreich im Jahre 1815.* Berlin, 1818.

Bornstedt, Major von. *Das Gefecht bei Wavre an der Dyle am 18. und 19. Juni 1815.* Berlin, 1858.

Charras, Jean Baptiste Adolphe. *Histoire de la campagne de 1815. Waterloo.* 2 vols, Paris, 1869.

Chaboulon, Baron Fleury de. *Les cent-jours. Mémoires pour servir à l'histoire de la vie privée, du retour et du règne de Napoléon en 1815.* 2 vols. London, 1820.

Chesney, Col. Charles C., R.E. *Waterloo Lectures: A Study of the Campaign of 1815.* 3rd ed. London, 1907.

Ciriacy, F. von. *Der Belagerungs-Krieg des Königlich-Preussischen zweiten Armee-Korps an der Sambre und in den Ardenne.* Berlin, 1818.

Clausewitz, Carl von. *Der Feldzug von 1815 in Frankreich.* Vol. 8 of *Hinterlassene Werke des General Carl von Clausewitz über Krieg und Kriegführung.* Berlin, 1835.

Conrady, Emil von. *Leben und Wirkung von Karl von Grolman.* Pt. 2. Berlin, 1895.

Dalton, Charles. *Waterloo Roll Call.* London, 1890.

Damitz, Carl von. *Geschichte des Feldzuges von 1815 in den Niederlanden und Frankreich.* 2 vols. Berlin, 1837–38.

De Bas and T'Serclaes de Wommersom. *La campagne de 1815 aux pays-bas.* 3 vols. Brussels, 1908.
De Bas, F. *Prins Frederik der Nederlanden en zijn tijd.* Pt. 3, vol. 2. Schiedam, 1904.
Fouché, Joseph. *Mémoires de Joseph Fouché, due d'Orante.* 2 vols. Paris, 1824.
Gamont, M. *Refutation, en ce qui concern le m[aréch]al Ney, de l'ouvrage ayant pour titre: Campagne de 1815, ou relation des operations militaires qui ont lieu pendant les cent fours, par le general Gourgaud, ecru a Sainte-Helene.* Paris, 1818.
Gleig, Rev. G. R. *History of the Life of Arthur Duke of Wellington.* Vol. 2. London, 1858.
———. *Story of Waterloo.* London, 1847.
Gourgaud, Gaspard. *La campagne de dix-huit cent quinz.* Paris, 1818.
Grosser Generalstab. *Das Preussische Heer in den Jahren 1814 und 1815.* Berlin, 1914.
Grouchy, Emmanuel de, Marquis, Marshal of France. *Fragments historiques relatifs à la campagne de 1815 et à la bataille de Waterloo. De l'influence que peuvent avoir sur l'opinion les documents publiés par M. le comte Gérard.* Paris, 1829.
Gurwood, John, ed. *Dispatches of Field Marshal the Duke of Wellington.* 12 vols. London, 1837–39.
Hofmann, General von. *Zur Geschichte des Feldzuges von 1815.* Berlin, 1851.
Horsburgh, E. L. S. *Waterloo—A Narrative and a Criticism.* London, 1900.
Houssaye, Henry. *1815.* 3 vols. Paris, 1914.
Hyde Kelley, W. *The Battle of Wavre and Grouchy's Retreat.* London, 1905.
Leach, *Rough Sketches of the Life of an Old Soldier.* London, 1831.
Lettow-Vorbeck, Major General von, *Napoleons Untergang 1815.* Berlin, 1904.
Müffling, Freiherr Friedrich Carl Ferdinand von. *Aus meinem Leben.* Berlin, 1851.
Ollech, General von. *Geschichte des Feldzuges von 1815.* Berlin, 1876.
Pflugk-Harttung, Julius von. *Belle Alliance.* Berlin, 1915.
———. *Das Preussische Heer und die Norddeutschen Bundestruppen.* Gotha, 1911.
———. *Vorgeschichte der Schlacht bei Belle Alliance. Wellington.* Berlin, 1903.
Plotho, Carl von. *Der Krieg des verbündeten Europa gegen Frankreich im Jahre 1815.* Berlin, 1818.
Renouard, C. *Das Norddeutsche Bundes-Korps im Feldzuge von 1815.* Hanover, 1865.
Robinson, Maj. Gen. Sir C. W. *Wellington's Campaigns Peninsula—Waterloo 1808–15.* Pt. 3, *1815—Waterloo.* 6th ed. London, 1927.
Schwartz, Karl. *Leben des Generals Carl von Clausewitz.* Berlin, 1878.
Siborne, William. *History of the War in France und Belgium, 1815.* 4th ed. London, 1894.
Six, Georges. *Dictionnaire Biographique des Généraux & Admriaux Français de la Révolution et de l'Empire (1792–1814).* Paris, 1934.
Stafford, Alice, Countess of, ed. *Personal Reminiscences of the Duke of Wellington by Francis the first Earl of Ellesmere.* London, 1904.
Stanhope, Philip Henry, 5th Earl. *Notes of Conversations with the Duke of Wellington, 1831–1851.* London, 1888.
Thurn und Taxis, Prinz August von. *Aus drei Feldzügen 1812 bis 1815.* Leipzig, 1912.

Voss, Generalmajor von. *Napoleons Untergang 1815*. Vol. 2, *Von Belle-Alliance bis zu Napoleons Tot*. Berlin, 1906.
Wagner, August. *Plane der Schlachten und Treffen wlche von der preussischen Armee in den Feldzügen der Jahre 1813, 14, und 15 geliefert worden*. Vol. 4. Berlin, 1825.
Wellington, 2nd Duke of. *Despatches, Correspondence, and Memoranda of Field Marshal Arthur, Duke of Wellington*. N.s., 8 vols. London, 1867–80.
———. *Supplementary Despatches, Correspondence, and Memoranda of Field Marshal Arthur, Duke of Wellington*. 16 vols. London, 1857–72.

Articles

Militärisches 1 (Leipzig, January 1896).
Nostitz, Graf von. "Das Tagebuch des Generals der Kavallerie Grafen von Nostitz." Pt. 2 in *Kriegsgeschichtliche Einzelschriften*, vol. 6. Berlin, 1885.
Pflugk-Harttung, Julius von. "Das I. Korps Zieten bei Belle-Alliance und Wavre." *Jahrbücher für die deutsche Armee und Marine* (January–June 1903).
———. "Zu Blüchers Brief an den König von Preussen vom 17 Juni 1815." *Jahrbücher für die deutsche Armee und Marine* (1904).
———. "Das I. preussische Korps bei Belle-Alliance." *Jahrbücher für die deutsche Armee und Marine* (July–December 1905).
———. "Zu den Ereignissen des 18. Juni 1815." In *Forschungen zur Brandenburgischen und Preussischen Geschichte*, vol. 19. Leipzig, 1906.
———. "Von Wavre bis Belle-Alliance." *Jahrbücher für die deutsche Armee und Marine* (1908).

Index

Alexander, Tsar of Russia, 10, 45
Alten, Sir Charles Count von, 51, 80, 81, 112; order of battle, 221
Anthing, Carl Heinrich Wilhelm, 51, 80; order of battle, 225
Arbuthnot, Charles, 15, 16, 24
Army of the North (Napoleon's forces), 69n, 77n79, 162n, 171n157; order of battle, 227–37
Army of the North (Revolutionary Wars), 200n
Aspern-Essling, Battle of, 4, 111n107, 200n,
Aubervilliers, 201; action at, 192; table of marches, 189
Austerlitz, Battle of, 4, 15, 34n, 36n12, 49n28, 49nn30–32, 50nn35–36, 89nn94–95, 97n, 111n107, 116n, 124n112, 134n, 155n, 198nn176–77, 200n
Avesnes, 69, 142, 172, 176, 180, 181, 182, 186, 196; table of marches, 188

Bachelu, Gilbert-Désiré-Joseph Baron, 128; order of battle, 220
Berton, Jean-Baptiste, 133; order of battle, 227
Bierges, 130; action at, 136–39, 164
Blücher (von Wahlstatt), Gebhardt Leberecht Prince, 6, 7, 11, 12, 17–22, 25, 27–29, 37, 38, 40, 42, 46, 53–58, 60–62, 64–68, 70–75, 79, 81, 83–88, 90, 93–96, 98–103, 106, 108, 110, 114–20, 122–24, 130–32, 134, 142, 144, 145, 147–53, 156–60, 162–71, 174–76, 178–85, 187, 192, 200, 202, 210; order of battle, 211
Bonaparte, Jérôme, 71, 89, 111, 125, 172
Bonapartist, 36, 37, 242
Bonapartist Party, 44, 196
Bossu Woods, 110, 112, 120
Braine l'Alleud, 122, 157
Brune, Guillaume-Marie-Anne, 37, 207
Brye, 83, 90, 91, 92, 94, 95, 105, 109, 110; meeting at, 84
Bülow (von Dennewitz), Friedrich Wilhelm, Count, 54, 66, 70, 79, 82, 85, 87, 101–103, 108, 125, 126, 128–32, 144, 146, 147, 152, 153, 159, 160; order of battle, 215

Cavalry Reserve (Wellington's Army), 53
Central Europe, 4
Charleroi, 18, 19, 20, 22, 27, 53, 56, 57, 58n66, 64, 66, 67, 69, 71, 73, 74, 81, 89, 90, 106, 111, 140, 142, 167, 172, 176, 177, 180, 181; engagement at, 75–79; table of march, 188
Chassé, David Hendrik, 51, 52, 55, 80, 81, 120, 124, 128; order of battle, 225
Châtelet, 75, 76, 77, 79, 177, 180
Chatou, 192
Clauzel, Bertrand, Count, 37

247

INDEX

Clinton, Sir Henry, 50, 58, 67, 80, 120; order of battle, 220
Collaert, Baron Jena-Marie-Antoine-Philippe de , 52, 55, 129
Colville, Sir Charles, 50, 55, 80, 120; order of battle, 221
Compiègne, 182, 186, 190, 191; table of marches, 189
Cooke, Sir George, 51, 80, 81, 112, 125; order of battle, 220
Couture, 130, 135, 137, 158

Davoût, Louis-Nicolas, 9, 197–200, 202, 204
Decaen, Charles-Mathieu-Isidore, 37
Decken, Friedrich von der, 52, 53, 55
d'Erlon, Jean-Baptiste Drouet, Count, 49, 78, 90, 100, 108, 109, 111, 124–27, 132, 190; order of battle, 228
Diebitsch, Johann Karl Friedrich Anton, 10, 11
Domon, Jean-Simon Count, 120, 125, 126, 132; order of battle, 232
Dörnberg, Wilhelm Caspar Ferdinand Baron von, 20, 28, 71; order of battle, 218
Douro River, 5

Egerton, Francis, first earl of Ellesmere, 16, 17, 24, 25
Exelmans, Rémy-Joseph-Isidore Count, 116–18, 133, 140, 149, 162, 192; order of battle, 236
Eylau, Battle of, 4, 49n32, 111n107, 116n112, 120n, 124n, 133n130, 134n, 138n, 155n, 206n192

Fischermont, 122, 126, 131, 132, 158, 159
Fleurus, 66, 73, 82, 84, 86, 87, 90, 91, 92, 107, 118, 148; 1794 Battle of, 203; action at, 76–79
Fontaine l'Evêque, 76, 180, 181; table of marches, 188
Frasnes, 20, 27, 72, 78, 79, 81, 92, 93, 100, 108, 109, 110, 112, 114, 120

French Revolution (the Revolution), 3, 49, 53, 109, 111, 195, 199, 203

Genappe, 25, 26, 27, 162, 177, 179, 180
Gérard, Maurice-Étienne, Count, 49, 86, 88, 97, 103, 116, 117, 138, 148, 149, 163, 164, 191; order of battle, 233
Gilly, 76, 77, 79
Gneisenau, August Wilhelm Antonius Neidhardt von, 7, 10–13, 38, 72, 162, 177
Gonesse, 186, 192; table of marches, 189
Gosselies, 76, 78, 79, 86, 89, 93, 109, 177, 179, 181
Grolman, Karl Wilhelm Georg von, 10, 209
Guard and Grenadier Corps; (Royal) Guard (Pr), 48n, 54n58, 98n
Guards (British), 27, 51, 52, 112n, 122n, 125, 126; order of battle, 218–20
Gurwood, John, 15, 17, 18
Guyot, Claude-Étienne Count, 124, 128; order of battle, 228

Hannut, 66, 68, 70
Hanoverian Landwehr Brigade (reserve), 52, 55
Hardinge, Sir Henry, 21, 110n104
Hesse-Kassel, 54n57, 71
Hill, Rowland, 50, 57, 58, 120
Hougoumont, 122, 125, 153
Hulot, Étienne Baron, 86n89, 134, 138; order of battle, 234
Hundred Days, the (Napoleon's return from exile, culminating with Waterloo), 4, 31, 36, 37, 195n167, 196nn171–73, 197n175, 198nn176–77, 199n180–81, 200n, 203n186, 208n, 210

Imperial Guard (French), 36, 41, 47, 48, 49, 50, 68, 69, 70, 79, 86, 89, 92, 95, 96, 97, 98, 99, 100, 103, 110, 120, 124, 126, 127, 128, 129, 130n,

INDEX

133, 154, 155, 156, 170, 171, 203; order of battle, 227–28
Iron Cross (1st and 2nd Class), 77n80, 95n98, 98n, 136n, 142n, 185n161, 187n
Issy, 194; table of marches, 189

Jagow, Friedrich Wilhelm Christian Ludwig von, 97, 98, 105; order of battle, 211
Jena, Battle of, 4, 34n, 36n12, 49nn31–32, 51n40, 54n54, 71n, 78n82, 93, 95n99, 111n106, 120n, 135, 171, 187
Johnstone, George, 50; order of battle, 222
(Wahlen-)Jürgass, Alexander Georg Ludwig Moritz Konstantin Maximilian von, 94, 95, 98, 104; order of battle, 213

Kiesewetter, Johann Gottfried Karl Christian, 9
Königsberg, 9, 11

La Bawette, 135–37
La Fère, 186; table of marches, 188
La Haye, 147, 153
La Haye Sainte, 121, 122, 125, 127, 129
Lamarque, Jean-Maximilien, Count, 37
Lambert, Sir John, 52, 80; order of battle, 223
Lambusart Woods, 77
Landwehr (German militia), 33, 48, 52, 55, 75n, 105, 155; Hanoverian order of battle, 221–23; Nassau, 226; Prussian order of battle, 211–17
Laon, 49, 68, 143, 171, 172, 176, 181–84
Le Caillou, 121
Lecourbe, Claude-Jacques, Count, 36, 206
Lefèbvre-Desnouëttes, Charles Count, 89, 92, 127
Leipzig, Battle of, 4, 6, 32, 50n38, 54n58, 77n80, 78n82, 78n84, 95n98, 98n, 116n110, 124n, 134n, 170n153, 199n177, 205n187, 207n195, 208n
Liège, 54, 56, 66, 70, 108, 147, 150
Ligny, Battle of, 12, 22, 25, 29, 53n53, 58n65, 69, 71, 80–87, 94, 97–101, 103–107, 110, 111, 113, 114, 117, 124, 135, 136, 140, 143, 145, 153, 158, 175, 176
Ligny Brook, 64, 99, 103
Lille, 49, 56, 57, 58, 65, 67, 68, 69
Limale, 134, 136, 138, 139, 140, 151, 164
Lobau, Georges Mouton, Count of, 49, 124, 132, 158–60; order of battle, 235
Louis XVIII, 4, 31, 116, 121, 185, 197, 199, 205, 208

Malmaison, 192, 198, 200
Malplaquet, 182; table of marches, 188
Marbais, 92, 121
Marchienne(-au-Pont), 75–79, 81, 86, 177, 180
Marwitz, Friedrich August Ludwig von der, 95, 96, 98, 142n; order of battle, 215
Maurin, Antoine, Baron, 140; order of battle, 234
Mellery, 141, 179–81
Meudon, 194, 204; table of marches, 189
Meuse River, 46, 47, 56, 62, 63, 65, 67, 73, 74, 84, 102, 108, 117, 118, 142, 143, 162, 163, 165, 167, 168, 179
Military Academy (Berlin), 9, 12, 13, 14, 94, 206
Mons, 20, 22, 53, 56, 57, 65, 71, 85, 88, 94, 99, 124, 126, 157, 180, 181, 200n
Mont Potriaux, 84, 103
Mont St. Jean, 120, 121, 151, 152, 155, 156, 180
Mortier (Duke of Treviso), Adolphe-Edouard-Casimir-Joseph, 49, 50, 184; order of battle, 227

Müffling, Friedrich Carl Ferdinand Baron von, 20, 22–24, 27, 29, 72, 130, 209

Napoleonic Wars, 3, 4, 32n6, 73n, 163n
National Guard (French), 32, 40, 41, 45, 47, 89, 173, 182, 199n177
Nieuwpoort, 50, 55, 80
Nivelles, 19, 20, 21, 25, 27, 28, 51, 58, 68, 72, 80, 81, 120, 121, 176, 181; table of marches, 188
Nive River, 5, 127n120
Northern France, 40, 41, 42, 171, 210
Northern Germany, 11, 37, 71n
North German Federal troops, 54, 61, 187
Noyelles-sur-Sambre, 182

O'Etzel, Franz August, 13
Ohain, 130

Paget, Henry William. *See* Uxbridge
Pajol, Claude-Pierre Count, 116–18, 120, 133, 134, 138, 148, 149; order of battle, 236
Papelotte, 121, 122n, 126
Payot, 132, 159
Peninsular War, 37, 51n42, 53n49
Perponcher(-Sedlnitsky), Hendrik George de, 51, 55, 78, 80, 109, 110, 112, 115, 126, 161; order of battle, 224
Pfuel, Ernst Heinrich Adolf von, 10
Philippeville, 69, 75, 142, 172, 177, 180, 181, 182, 208; table of marches, 188
Picton, Sir Thomas, 23, 25, 28, 52, 80, 110, 111; order of battle, 222
Pierremont, 111, 112
Pirch (I), Georg Dubislav Ludwig von, 53, 54, 77, 98, 141–43, 179, 191; order of battle, 212
Pirch (II), Otto Karl Lorenz von, 53, 77, 95; order of battle, 211
Piré, Hippolyte-Marie-Guilliame de Rosnyvinen, Count, 111, 112; order of battle, 231

Plessis-Piquet, 193, 194, 204; table of marches, 189
Point du Jour, 84, 86, 103, 108, 117
Ponsonby, Sir William, 126; order of battle, 218
Pont-Ste-Maxence, 182, 186, 190, 192; table of marches, 188–89
Prussian General Staff (the general staff), 9, 10, 13, 72, 83, 86, 129, 209, 243

Quatre Bras, 19, 20, 23, 25–29, 53n50, 53n52, 58, 67, 68, 70, 72, 78–81, 84–86, 88, 90–93, 102, 106, 109–12, 114, 115, 120, 121, 149, 151, 177, 242

Reille, Honoré-Charles-Michel-Joseph, Count, 49, 78, 90, 109, 124, 125, 200; order of battle, 230
Reserves, the (Wellington's Army), 20, 24, 25, 26, 52, 57, 58, 60, 67, 71, 72, 81, 85, 120
Revolutionary Wars, 3, 8, 34, 36, 37, 49, 50, 51, 53, 54, 78, 89, 116, 120, 124, 128, 134, 140, 170, 196, 198, 200, 203, 207
Rixensart Woods, 138, 139
Royal Guard (French), 203n186
Royal Navy, 5
Russo-German Legion, 10, 11

Sambre River, 19, 56, 64, 66, 74, 76, 86, 142, 143, 167, 170, 177, 179, 180, 187
Sart-à-Walhain, 118, 134, 146, 164
Scharnhorst, Gerhard Johann David von, 9, 11, 12
Sèvres, 194; table of marches, 189
Smohain, 121, 126, 132
Soignes Woods, 20, 25, 26, 71, 72, 110, 120, 122, 130, 146, 147, 154, 161
Solre-sur-Sambre, 69, 75
Sombreffe, 18, 20, 58, 64–66, 70, 72, 77, 80–84, 86, 88, 90, 98, 99, 101, 102, 107

St. Agatha-Rode, 140, 141, 181; table of marches, 188
St. Amand, 76, 82–84, 86, 87, 91, 93–98, 100, 101, 103–105, 107, 108, 117, 120, 148
(St. Amand) la Haye, 94, 95, 97, 104, 105, 107, 121, 122, 126
St. Balâtre, 99, 101, 102
Stedman, Jena-André, 51, 80; order of battle, 224
St. German, 192, 193, 200; table of marches, 189
St. Lambert, 130–32, 135, 140, 147, 152, 153, 157, 158, 165
Stülpnagel, Wolf Wilhelm Ferdinand von, 139; order of battle, 214
Subervie, Jacques-Gervais Baron, 125, 126, 131; order of battle, 236
Suchet (Count of Albufera), Louis-Gabriel, 36, 41, 207

Teste, François-Antoine Baron, 116, 118, 133, 138; order of battle, 235
Thielemann, Johann Adolph von, 12, 54, 87, 98, 99, 102, 103, 108, 118, 135–41, 164, 165, 179, 192; order of battle, 214
Thuin, 21, 22, 75, 76, 180, 181
Tirlemont: meeting at, 18, 56, 58
Tongrenelle, 84, 86, 89
Tongrinne, 84
Tournai, 56, 65

Uxbridge, Henry William Paget, (2nd) Earl of, 28, 53, 80; order of battle, 218

Valenciennes, 49, 57, 58, 65, 69, 157, 181, 207
Vandamme (Count d'Unsebourg), Dominique-Joseph-René, 49, 77, 86, 108, 112, 116, 117, 149, 164, 169, 185, 191, 194; order of battle, 232
Vandeleur, Sir John Ormsby, 126, 127; order of battle, 218

Vendée, 36, 37, 39, 41, 111, 124
Villiers-Cotterêts, 190, 191, 199; table of marches, 189

Wagram, Battle of, 4, 49, 110, 111, 116, 120, 124, 128, 155, 184, 196, 198, 203
Wagnelée, 82, 86, 95, 101, 104, 105, 107, 108
Wallmoden, Ludwig Georg Thedel Count von, 11
War Ministry (Pr), 9
Wars of Liberation (1813–15), 6, 11, 13
Waterloo, Battle of, 3–6, 12–18, 22, 23, 26–28, 37n15, 43, 49–53, 55, 60, 68, 71n, 78n82, 83, 89nn94–95, 110–12, 116nn110–11, 120n, 121, 124, 128n, 129n124, 134n, 135, 136, 138–41, 144n138, 146, 152, 159, 161–63, 165, 168, 170, 171, 173, 175, 176, 179, 209, 210, 241–43
"Waterloo Despatch," 22, 23, 60n, 72n73, 79n, 241, 242
Wavre, 12, 83n86, 115, 117–19, 123, 130, 131, 133–40, 146, 147, 150–52, 162, 164, 168, 179–81, 187, 210; table of marches, 188
Wellesley (Wesley), Arthur; (1st) Duke of Wellington; the duke, 3–6, 14–29, 31n4, 32, 37, 40, 42, 43, 46, 47, 50, 52–58, 60–65, 67, 68, 70–74, 78–82, 84, 85, 87, 88, 93, 103, 106, 108, 110–14, 117–23, 125, 127–30, 133, 136, 142, 144, 150–52, 154–63, 166–70, 174, 176, 180–82, 186, 187, 192, 197, 198, 202, 209, 210, 241, 242; order of battle, 218; table of marches, 188
White Terror, 37, 207n194

Ziethen, Wieprecht Hans Karl Friedrich Ernst Heinrich Count von, 20–22, 53, 66, 69–73, 75–78, 82, 84, 126, 129, 130, 133, 160, 182, 191, 194; order of battle, 211

www.ingramcontent.com/pod-product-compliance
Lightning Source LLC
Chambersburg PA
CBHW020834160426
43192CB00007B/650